Real Business Cycle Models in Economics

Real Business Cycle (RBC) Theory holds that random fluctuations in productivity are what cause the business cycle. Over the years, economists have developed different models which attempt to explain patterns in real business cycles, though the two which dominate proceedings are Kydland and Prescott's and Long and Plosser's models.

The purpose of this book is to describe the intellectual process by which RBC models were developed. The approach taken focuses on the core elements in the development of RBC models: (i) building blocks, (ii) catalysts, and (iii) meta-syntheses. This is done by detailed examination of all available unpublished variorum drafts of the key papers in the RBC story, so as to determine the origins of the ideas. The analysis of the process of their discovery is then set out, followed by explanations of the evolution and dissemination of the models, from first generation papers through to full blown research programs. This is supplemented by interviews and correspondence with the individuals who were at the center of the development of RBC models, such as Kydland, Prescott, Long, Plosser, King, Lucas, and Barro, among others.

This book gets straight to the heart of the debates surrounding RBC models, and as such it contributes to a real assessment of their impact upon modern macroeconomics. This volume, therefore, will interest all scholars looking at macroeconomics, as well as historians of economic thought more generally.

Warren Young is Associate Professor of Economics at Bar-Ilan University, Israel.

Routledge studies in the history of economics

1 **Economics as Literature**
Willie Henderson

2 **Socialism and Marginalism in Economics 1870–1930**
Edited by Ian Steedman

3 **Hayek's Political Economy**
The socio-economics of order
Steve Fleetwood

4 **On the Origins of Classical Economics**
Distribution and value from William Petty to Adam Smith
Tony Aspromourgos

5 **The Economics of Joan Robinson**
Edited by Maria Cristina Marcuzzo, Luigi Pasinetti and Alesandro Roncaglia

6 **The Evolutionist Economics of Léon Walras**
Albert Jolink

7 **Keynes and the 'Classics'**
A study in language, epistemology and mistaken identities
Michel Verdon

8 **The History of Game Theory, Vol 1**
From the beginnings to 1945
Robert W. Dimand and Mary Ann Dimand

9 **The Economics of W. S. Jevons**
Sandra Peart

10 **Gandhi's Economic Thought**
Ajit K. Dasgupta

11 **Equilibrium and Economic Theory**
Edited by Giovanni Caravale

12 **Austrian Economics in Debate**
Edited by Willem Keizer, Bert Tieben and Rudy van Zijp

13 **Ancient Economic Thought**
Edited by B. B. Price

14 **The Political Economy of Social Credit and Guild Socialism**
Frances Hutchinson and Brian Burkitt

15 **Economic Careers**
Economics and economists in Britain 1930–1970
Keith Tribe

16 **Understanding 'Classical' Economics**
Studies in the long-period theory
Heinz Kurz and Neri Salvadori

17 **History of Environmental Economic Thought**
E. Kula

18 **Economic Thought in Communist and Post-Communist Europe**
Edited by Hans-Jürgen Wagener

19 **Studies in the History of French Political Economy**
From Bodin to Walras
Edited by Gilbert Faccarello

20 **The Economics of John Rae**
Edited by O. F. Hamouda, C. Lee and D. Mair

21 **Keynes and the Neoclassical Synthesis**
Einsteinian versus Newtonian macroeconomics
Teodoro Dario Togati

22 **Historical Perspectives on Macroeconomics**
Sixty years after the 'General Theory'
Edited by Philippe Fontaine and Albert Jolink

23 **The Founding of Institutional Economics**
The leisure class and sovereignty
Edited by Warren J. Samuels

24 **Evolution of Austrian Economics**
From Menger to Lachmann
Sandye Gloria

25 **Marx's Concept of Money**
The God of Commodities
Anitra Nelson

26 **The Economics of James Steuart**
Edited by Ramón Tortajada

27 **The Development of Economics in Europe since 1945**
Edited by A. W. Bob Coats

28 **The Canon in the History of Economics**
Critical essays
Edited by Michalis Psalidopoulos

29 **Money and Growth**
Selected papers of Allyn Abbott Young
Edited by Perry G. Mehrling and Roger J. Sandilands

30 **The Social Economics of Jean-Baptiste Say**
Markets and virtue
Evelyn L. Forget

31 **The Foundations of Laissez-Faire**
The economics of Pierre de Boisguilbert
Gilbert Faccarello

32 **John Ruskin's Political Economy**
Willie Henderson

33 **Contributions to the History of Economic Thought**
Essays in honour of R. D. C. Black
Edited by Antoin E. Murphy and Renee Prendergast

34 **Towards an Unknown Marx**
A commentary on the manuscripts of 1861–63
Enrique Dussel

35 Economics and Interdisciplinary Exchange
Edited by Guido Erreygers

36 Economics as the Art of Thought
Essays in memory of G. L. S. Shackle
Edited by Stephen F. Frowen and Peter Earl

37 The Decline of Ricardian Economics
Politics and economics in post-Ricardian theory
Susan Pashkoff

38 Piero Sraffa
His life, thought and cultural heritage
Alessandro Roncaglia

39 Equilibrium and Disequilibrium in Economic Theory
The Marshall-Walras divide
Michel de Vroey

40 The German Historical School
The historical and ethical approach to economics
Edited by Yuichi Shionoya

41 Reflections on the Classical Canon in Economics
Essays in honour of Samuel Hollander
Edited by Sandra Peart and Evelyn Forget

42 Piero Sraffa's Political Economy
A centenary estimate
Edited by Terenzio Cozzi and Roberto Marchionatti

43 The Contribution of Joseph Schumpeter to Economics
Economic development and institutional change
Richard Arena and Cecile Dangel

44 On the Development of Long-run Neo-Classical Theory
Tom Kompas

45 F. A. Hayek as a Political Economist
Economic analysis and values
Edited by Jack Birner, Pierre Garrouste and Thierry Aimar

46 Pareto, Economics and Society
The mechanical analogy
Michael McLure

47 The Cambridge Controversies in Capital Theory
A study in the logic of theory development
Jack Birner

48 Economics Broadly Considered
Essays in honour of Warren J. Samuels
Edited by Steven G. Medema, Jeff Biddle and John B. Davis

49 Physicians and Political Economy
Six studies of the work of doctor-economists
Edited by Peter Groenewegen

50 The Spread of Political Economy and the Professionalisation of Economists
Economic societies in Europe, America and Japan in the nineteenth century
Massimo Augello and Marco Guidi

51 **Historians of Economics and Economic Thought**
The construction of disciplinary memory
Steven G. Medema and Warren J. Samuels

52 **Competing Economic Theories**
Essays in memory of Giovanni Caravale
Sergio Nisticò and Domenico Tosato

53 **Economic Thought and Policy in Less Developed Europe**
The nineteenth century
Edited by Michalis Psalidopoulos and Maria-Eugenia Almedia Mata

54 **Family Fictions and Family Facts**
Harriet Martineau, Adolphe Quetelet and the population question in England 1798–1859
Brian Cooper

55 **Eighteenth-Century Economics**
Peter Groenewegen

56 **The Rise of Political Economy in the Scottish Enlightenment**
Edited by Tatsuya Sakamoto and Hideo Tanaka

57 **Classics and Moderns in Economics, Volume I**
Essays on nineteenth and twentieth century economic thought
Peter Groenewegen

58 **Classics and Moderns in Economics, Volume II**
Essays on nineteenth and twentieth century economic thought
Peter Groenewegen

59 **Marshall's Evolutionary Economics**
Tiziano Raffaelli

60 **Money, Time and Rationality in Max Weber**
Austrian connections
Stephen D. Parsons

61 **Classical Macroeconomics**
Some modern variations and distortions
James C. W. Ahiakpor

62 **The Historical School of Economics in England and Japan**
Tamotsu Nishizawa

63 **Classical Economics and Modern Theory**
Studies in long-period analysis
Heinz D. Kurz and Neri Salvadori

64 **A Bibliography of Female Economic Thought to 1940**
Kirsten K. Madden, Janet A. Sietz and Michele Pujol

65 **Economics, Economists and Expectations**
From microfoundations to macroeconomics
Warren Young, Robert Leeson and William Darity Jnr.

66 **The Political Economy of Public Finance in Britain, 1767–1873**
Takuo Dome

67 **Essays in the History of Economics**
Warren J. Samuels, Willie Henderson, Kirk D. Johnson and Marianne Johnson

68 **History and Political Economy**
Essays in honour of
P. D. Groenewegen
Edited by Tony Aspromourgos and John Lodewijks

69 **The Tradition of Free Trade**
Lars Magnusson

70 **Evolution of the Market Process**
Austrian and Swedish economics
Edited by Michel Bellet, Sandye Gloria-Palermo and Abdallah Zouache

71 **Consumption as an Investment**
The fear of goods from Hesiod to Adam Smith
Cosimo Perrotta

72 **Jean-Baptiste Say and the Classical Canon in Economics**
The British connection in French classicism
Samuel Hollander

73 **Knut Wicksell on Poverty**
No place is too exalted
Knut Wicksell

74 **Economists in Cambridge**
A study through their correspondence 1907–1946
Edited by M. C. Marcuzzo and A. Rosselli

75 **The Experiment in the History of Economics**
Edited by Philippe Fontaine and Robert Leonard

76 **At the Origins of Mathematical Economics**
The Economics of A. N. Isnard (1748–1803)
Richard van den Berg

77 **Money and Exchange**
Folktales and reality
Sasan Fayazmanesh

78 **Economic Development and Social Change**
Historical roots and modern perspectives
George Stathakis and Gianni Vaggi

79 **Ethical Codes and Income Distribution**
A study of John Bates Clark and Thorstein Veblen
Guglielmo Forges Davanzati

80 **Evaluating Adam Smith**
Creating the wealth of nations
Willie Henderson

81 **Civil Happiness**
Economics and human flourishing in historical perspective
Luigino Bruni

82 **New Voices on Adam Smith**
Edited by Leonidas Montes and Eric Schliesser

83 **Making Chicago Price Theory**
Milton Friedman–George Stigler correspondence, 1945–1957
Edited by J. Daniel Hammond and Claire H. Hammond

84 **William Stanley Jevons and the Cutting Edge of Economics**
Bert Mosselmans

85 **A History of Econometrics in France**
From nature to models
Philippe Le Gall

86 **Money and Markets**
A doctrinal approach
Edited by Alberto Giacomin and Maria Cristina Marcuzzo

87 **Considerations on the Fundamental Principles of Pure Political Economy**
Vilfredo Pareto
Edited by Roberto Marchionatti and Fiorenzo Mornati

88 **The Years of High Econometrics**
A short history of the generation that reinvented economics
Francisco Louçã

89 **David Hume's Political Economy**
Edited by Carl Wennerlind and Margaret Schabas

90 **Interpreting Classical Economics**
Studies in long-period analysis
Heinz D. Kurz and Neri Salvadori

91 **Keynes's Vision**
Why the great depression did not return
John Philip Jones

92 **Monetary Theory in Retrospect**
The selected essays of Filippo Cesarano
Filippo Cesarano

93 **Keynes's Theoretical Development**
From the tract to the general theory
Toshiaki Hirai

94 **Leading Contemporary Economists**
Economics at the cutting edge
Edited by Steven Pressman

95 **The Science of Wealth**
Adam Smith and the framing of political economy
Tony Aspromourgos

96 **Capital, Time and Transitional Dynamics**
Edited by Harald Hagemann and Roberto Scazzieri

97 **New Essays on Pareto's Economic Theory**
Edited by Luigino Bruni and Aldo Montesano

98 **Frank Knight and the Chicago School in American Economics**
Ross B. Emmett

99 **A History of Economic Theory**
Essays in honour of Takashi Negishi
Edited by Aiko Ikeo and Heinz D. Kurz

100 **Open Economics**
Economics in relation to other disciplines
Edited by Richard Arena, Sheila Dow and Matthias Klaes

101 **Rosa Luxemburg and the Critique of Political Economy**
Edited by Riccardo Bellofiore

102 **Problems and Methods of Econometrics**
The Poincaré lectures of Ragnar Frisch 1933
Edited by Olav Bjerkholt and Ariane Dupont-Keiffer

103 **Criticisms of Classical Political Economy**
Menger, Austrian economics and the German historical school
Gilles Campagnolo

104 **A History of Entrepreneurship**
Robert F. Hébert and Albert N. Link

105 **Keynes on Monetary Policy, Finance and Uncertainty**
Liquidity preference theory and the global financial crisis
Jorg Bibow

106 **Kalecki's Principle of Increasing Risk and Keynesian Economics**
Tracy Mott

107 **Economic Theory and Economic Thought**
Essays in honour of Ian Steedman
John Vint, J Stanley Metcalfe, Heinz D. Kurz, Neri Salvadori and Paul Samuelson

108 **Political Economy, Public Policy and Monetary Economics**
Ludwig von Mises and the Austrian tradition
Richard M. Ebeling

109 **Keynes and the British Humanist Tradition**
The moral purpose of the market
David R. Andrews

110 **Political Economy and Industrialism**
Banks in Saint-Simonian economic thought
Gilles Jacoud

111 **Studies in Social Economics**
Leon Walras
Translated by Jan van Daal and Donald Walker

112 **The Making of the Classical Theory of Economic Growth**
Anthony Brewer

113 **The Origins of David Hume's Economics**
Willie Henderson

114 **Production, Distribution and Trade**
Edited by Adriano Birolo, Duncan Foley, Heinz D. Kurz, Bertram Schefold and Ian Steedman

115 **The Essential Writings of Thorstein Veblen**
Edited by Charles Camic and Geoffrey Hodgson

116 **Adam Smith and the Economy of the Passions**
Jan Horst Keppler

117 **The Analysis of Linear Economic Systems**
Father Maurice Potron's pioneering works
Translated by Christian Bidard and Guido Erreygers

118 **A Dynamic Approach to Economic Theory: Frisch**
Edited by Olav Bjerkholt and Duo Qin

119 **Henry A. Abbati: Keynes' Forgotten Precursor**
Serena Di Gaspare

120 **Generations of Economists**
David Collard

121 **Hayek, Mill and the Liberal Tradition**
Edited by Andrew Farrant

122 **Marshall, Marshallians and Industrial Economics**
Edited by Tiziano Raffaelli

123 **Austrian and German Economic Thought**
Kiichiro Yagi

124 **The Evolution of Economic Theory**
Edited by Volker Caspari

125 **Thomas Tooke and the Monetary Thought of Classical Economics**
Matthew Smith

126 **Political Economy and Liberalism in France**
The contributions of Frédéric Bastiat
Robert Leroux

127 **Stalin's Economist**
The economic contributions of Jenö Varga
André Mommen

128 **E.E. Slutsky as Economist and Mathematician**
Crossing the limits of knowledge
Vincent Barnett

129 **Keynes, Sraffa, and the Criticism of Neoclassical Theory**
Essays in honour of Heinz Kurz
Neri Salvadori and Christian Gehrke

130 **Crises and Cycles in Economic Dictionaries and Encyclopaedias**
Edited by Daniele Bensomi

131 **General Equilibrium Analysis: A Century After Walras**
Edited by Pascal Bridel

132 **Sraffa and Modern Economics, Volume I**
Edited by Roberto Ciccone, Christian Gehrke and Gary Mongiovi

133 **Sraffa and Modern Economics, Volume II**
Edited by Roberto Ciccone, Christian Gehrke and Gary Mongiovi

134 **The Minor Marshallians and Alfred Marshall: An Evaluation**
Peter Groenewegen

135 **Fighting Market Failure**
Collected essays in the Cambridge tradition of economics
Maria Cristina Marcuzzo

136 **The Economic Reader**
Edited by Massimo M. Augello and Marco E. L. Guido

137 **Classical Political Economy and Modern Theory**
Essays in honour of Heinz Kurz
Neri Salvadori and Christian Gehrke

138 **The Ideas of Ronald H. Coase**
Lawrence W.C. Lai

139 **Anticipating the Wealth of Nations**
Edited by Maren Jonasson and Petri Hyttinen, with an Introduction by Lars Magnusson

140 **Innovation, Knowledge and Growth**
Edited by Heinz D. Kurz

141 **A History of *Homo Economicus***
The nature of the moral in economic theory
William Dixon and David Wilson

142 **The Division of Labour in Economics**
A history
Guang-Zhen Sun

143 **Keynes and Modern Economics**
Edited by Ryuzo Kuroki

144 **Macroeconomics and the History of Economic Thought**
Festschrift in honour of Harald Hagemann
Edited by Hagen M. Krämer, Heinz D. Kurz and Hans-Michael Trautwein

145 **French Liberalism in the 19th Century**
An anthology
Edited by Robert Leroux

146 **Subjectivisim and Objectivism in the History of Economic Thought**
Edited by Yukihiro Ikeda and Kiichiro Yagi

147 **The Rhetoric of the Right**
Language change and the spread of the market
David George

148 **The Theory of Value and Distribution in Economics**
Discussions between Pierangelo Garegnani and Paul Samuelson
Edited by Heinz Kurz

149 **An Economic History of Ireland Since Independence**
Andy Bielenberg

150 **Reinterpreting the Keynesian Revolution**
Robert Cord

151 **Money and Banking in Jean-Baptiste Say's Economic Thought**
Gilles Jacoud

152 **Jean-Baptiste Say**
Revolutionary, entrepreneur, economist
Evert Schoorl

153 **Essays on Classical and Marxian Political Economy**
Samuel Hollander

154 **Marxist Political Economy**
Essays in retrieval: selected works of Geoff Pilling
Edited by Doria Pilling

155 **Interdisciplinary Economics**
Kenneth E. Boulding's engagement in the sciences
Edited by Wilfred Dolfsma and Stefan Kesting

156 **Keynes and Friedman on Laissez-Faire and Planning**
'Where to draw the line?'
Sylvie Rivot

157 **Economic Justice and Liberty**
The social philosophy in John Stuart Mill's utilitarianism
Huei-chun Su

158 **German Utility Theory**
Analysis and Translations
John Chipman

159 **A Re-Assessment of Aristotle's Economic Thought**
Ricardo Crespo

160 **Real Business Cycle Models in Economics**
Warren Young

Real Business Cycle Models in Economics

Warren Young

Routledge
Taylor & Francis Group
LONDON AND NEW YORK

First published 2014
by Routledge
2 Park Square, Milton Park, Abingdon, Oxon OX14 4RN

and by Routledge
711 Third Avenue, New York, NY 10017

Routledge is an imprint of the Taylor & Francis Group, an informa business

British Library Cataloguing in Publication Data
A catalogue record for this book is available from the British Library

Library of Congress Cataloging in Publication Data
Young, Warren, 1949–
Real business cycle models in economics / Warren Young.
pages cm. – (Routledge studies in the history of economics)
1. Business cycles. 2. Business cycles–Mathematical models. I. Title.
HB3711.Y68 2013
338.5'42015195–dc23
2013022956

ISBN: 978-0-415-47569-3 (hbk)
ISBN: 978-1-315-85754-1 (ebk)

Typeset in Times New Roman
by Wearset Ltd, Boldon, Tyne and Wear

Contents

Preface and acknowledgments

Some three decades ago, in a number of papers which linked growth and business cycle theory, the Kydland–Prescott and Long–Plosser research programmes were set out. Over the period 1977–1983, these papers underwent revisions that eventually brought about a new paradigm in economics: the Real Business Cycle approach (RBC) or quantitative macroeconomics. The history of these developments—based on primary sources, such as variorum drafts of the papers, and the analysis of the cross-fertilization between the authors—has not been recounted up to now. This book is the product of a decade-long effort to collect material, and to get the RBC "history straight," as Ed Prescott put it in the *Journal of Political Economy* version of his Nobel lecture (2006e, 203).

In January 2013, on behalf of the History of Economics Society Sumru Altug and I organized a panel at the ASSA on "The RBC after three decades." The panelists were Edward Prescott, Finn Kydland, Charles Plosser, John Long, Thomas Cooley, and Gary Hansen. The objective was to record for posterity their recollections of, and reflections on, the development of the Kydland–Prescott and Long–Plosser approaches in a context similar to the cross-fertilization of ideas that had occurred three decades earlier, between, for example, Prescott and Plosser, as will be shown in this volume. We were fortunate to have in the audience other central figures in the story we tell in this book, such as Charles Nelson and Charles Upton. The story of Nelson–Plosser, crucial to an understanding of the development of quantitative macroeconomics, is not told in this volume; it will appear elsewhere. The reason for this is the application of the Tinbergen–Mundell maxim "one paper-one idea" to writing a book on such a multi-layered topic as RBC: that is to say, "one book-one multifaceted story."

As such, heartfelt thanks are due to Finn Kydland and Ed Prescott, for providing their recollections, unpublished papers, and correspondence; John Long and Charles Plosser, for providing recollections and materials used here; Sumru Altug, Thomas Cooley, and Gary Hansen for their recollections, drafts of their papers, and moral support for the project; Robert King, Robert Barro, and John Taylor, for providing recollections, drafts of their papers, and referee reports; Charles Nelson, for his recollections and ongoing personal support of my work; Robert Lucas, Charles Upton, Robert Hodrick, Rajnish Mehra, Michael Lovell, William Brock, Leonard Mirman, John Whalley, Alan

Blinder, Olivier Blanchard, Gregory Chow, and David Kendrick, for their recollections and drafts of their papers.

Some of the material in this book has appeared, in abridged form, in my paper "The Evolution of the Kydland–Prescott Research Program" in R. Leeson (ed.) *The Anti-Keynesian Tradition* (2004; Palgrave Macmillan), and is used here with permission.

I also want to thank the editors at Routledge for their understanding of my persistent personal difficulties that delayed finishing this project. As many of those mentioned above know, it was not an easy task for me to juggle teaching, research, and especially family responsibilities over the past decade. And thus my greatest debt is to my daughters, Shani and Natalie, their families, my ninety-year-young mother, Florence, and especially my long-suffering wife, Sara, without whose strength in adversity this volume would have never been completed.

Introduction and analytical method

The history of economics is replete with examples of how seminal books evolved and were disseminated, such as the editions of Ricardo, Mill, Walras, or the drafts of Keynes's *General Theory*, and the reactions to them. Almost no effort has been expended on the evolution of papers from draft through publication stages, as most historians of economics focus only on the final published version. Indeed, the fact that drafts of papers may be difficult to find is one reason why most historians of economics usually focus on their published versions. This, however, can mean a significant loss of information regarding the papers, as changes in—and cross-fertilization of—ideas may be overlooked. What little has been done in this area has related to the presentation of papers at conferences, such as the case of IS-LM and Rational Expectations (see Young, 1987; Young, *et al.*, 2004), and their subsequent impact in published form, or the process of evolution from the lecture notes stage and seminar presentation, through to publication, such as in the case of the relationship between the IS-LM model and its optimizing form (McCallum and Nelson, 2000; Nelson, 2004). Moreover, there has, in my view, been a misplaced focus upon precursors and priority of ideas and papers by historians of economics. Instead, I think that the focus should be upon variorum drafts of papers, the cross-fertilization of ideas, and their meta-synthesis.

What has been overlooked then, until now, is the historical efficacy involved in the analysis of: (i) the evolution of variorum drafts of seminal papers; (ii) the interaction between authors and referees, and authors of parallel papers, in the evolutionary process by which seminal papers finally "see the light"; (iii) the evolutionary and symbiotic relationship between seminal papers that demarcate research programs; and (iv) the process of "meta-synthesis" as it applies to the building blocks of seminal papers.

There are a number of retrospective narratives regarding the development of the path-breaking works of Kydland and Prescott (1977, 1982) for which they received the Nobel Prize in Economics. These include the personal recollections of Prescott (1998, 2004, 2006e), Kydland (2005a, autobiography), and Lucas (2001, 2005), and the survey of the Royal Swedish Academy (2004). While important in their own right, the history of the Kydland–Prescott research program is even more intriguing than that recounted in these narratives, especially when the development of their ideas is dealt with in detail by combining the recollections and documents that characterize their evolution. The approach taken here both complements and supplements these narratives. The published accounts of Prescott, Kydland, and Lucas mentioned above are supplemented via additional recollections collected—by means of correspondence and in-depth background interviews—from them and others who influenced and were influenced by the Kydland–Prescott research program, while detailed textual analyses of drafts of papers involved in its evolution complement the narrative recollections.

Moreover, as Hicks put it, since "memory is treacherous" (1973, 2), utilization of these drafts can clear up minor anomalies in the narratives themselves. Some examples should suffice to illustrate the efficacy of the approach taken here. In his insightful Prize lecture, Prescott mentioned that he and Kydland "had read the Lucas critique," and searched for the "best rule to follow"—from the context of the paragraph where the account appears—as early as 1973 (2004, 374; 2006e). But in the references, only the 1976 version of the Lucas critique is cited (1976a), although in additional recollections, both Prescott and Kydland recalled reading and being influenced by the 1973 drafts of Lucas.

Indeed, just how and to what extent they were influenced will be recounted below. According to Prescott, a "key" element in the evolution of the Kydland–Prescott approach was the development by Lucas and Prescott of "recursive competitive equilibrium theory" in their seminal 1971 paper "Investment under Uncertainty" and in Lucas (1973a, b), and its further development "in Prescott and Mehra (1980)" (2004, 392; 2006e). But while the difference between the published and draft versions of Lucas and Prescott *is* mentioned by Prescott in a note (2004, 392 note 15; 2006e), the December 1977 draft of Prescott and Mehra is not, leaving the impression of a long gap in the evolution of the theory. Moreover, the cardinal role of the 1971 Lucas–Prescott paper (written in 1969) and how it changed Prescott's approach to macroeconomics will be shown by using the information he provided in correspondence; while other key episodes in the evolution of the Kydland–Prescott approach will also be enriched by utilizing correspondence and interview material as supplementary narrative. Finally, in his retrospective "recollections" (2005) Lucas posed the crucial—albeit up to now unanswered—question regarding the 1982 Kydland–Prescott paper: "How did they ever think to put all these pieces together in just this way?" (2005, 777).

Our first objective is to show how Kydland and Prescott put all the "pieces" together; that is to say, how their overall approach—which, as will be shown, encompasses both their 1977 and 1982 papers—evolved, and brought about what Prescott, in his Nobel lecture, called "a transformation" in modern macroeconomic analysis. This is done by:

1. surveying their early work on optimal policy rules and stabilization, and dynamic equilibrium models of the business cycle;
2. analyzing the impact of those "pieces" which catalyzed their approach, such as the early drafts of the Lucas Critique (1973) and Hodrick–Prescott (1978);

3. integrating this with the evolution of their approach based upon the variorum drafts of their 1977 "Rules" and 1982 "Time to Build" papers and the relationship between these papers;
4. unifying the accounts and narratives, by means of in-depth questioning as to the intellectual process involved in their path-breaking work.

In his Prize lecture, Prescott wrote that "all stories about transformation have three essential parts: the time prior to the key change, the transformative era, and the new period that has been impacted by the change" (2004, 370; 2006e). But what is the "transformation" that Kydland and Prescott brought about?

The "essential parts" are as follows. We first deal with the "pre-dynamic general equilibrium" phase of the early work of Prescott and Kydland, over the period 1967–1973. We go on to describe the "transitional" phase in their approach, over the period 1973–1978. We then examine in detail the evolution of their work on business cycles, covering the period from 1978–1982 onwards.

The second object is to show how the "cross-fertilization" of ideas in the work of Kydland–Prescott and Long–Plosser occurred. This is done by surveying the reactions of informal and formal commentators regarding the respective contributions in the form of: (1) comments from colleagues on drafts; (2) editors' and referees' reports on versions submitted to journals, and the resultant amendments to these drafts and submitted versions; and (3) cross-citation and presentation patterns of the respective papers themselves. We focus on the development of Kydland and Prescott's 1982 paper from its initial form onwards, and cross-fertilization in terms of the written comments of colleagues and correspondence relating to these comments. We then deal with the cross-fertilization between Kydland–Prescott and Long–Plosser via a "clearinghouse" for ideas in the form of Fischer Black. We also utilize referees' comments and the authors' correspondence with editors to show how Kydland–Prescott (1982) and Long–Plosser (1983) came to be published in the form that they took. In addition, patterns in cross-citation and presentation of the respective papers, including the almost parallel development of King–Plosser, will also be dealt with in this context.

Dotsey and King presented a survey of "rational expectations business cycle models" which discussed what they termed "the basic real business cycle models" of Kydland–Prescott and Long–Plosser vintages (1988, 3). A decade later, McGrattan also dealt with "real business cycles" (2006), and noted that the term first appeared in Long and Plosser (1983); however, it is nowhere to be found in Kydland–Prescott (1982), nor in the variorum drafts of that paper. She went on to say that "the term … was often associated with a methodology," and not necessarily with the "original findings" of Kydland–Prescott (1982), continuing that "the methods of their 1982 paper" have been applied "to study many different sources of business cycles, including monetary shocks" (2006, 1). And, as will be seen below, what can be considered to be the earliest draft of "Time to build" (1978a), according to Kydland himself, dealt with both real shocks and the possibility of monetary shocks. Indeed, the published version contained a "sting in its tail" (1982, 1369), which pointed towards analysis of the role of money in "a real model of aggregate fluctuations" (Kydland, 1980; 1981; 1987, 3–10; 1989b).

The Long–Plosser paper, for its part, it is based solely on a real business cycle foundation. It should also be recalled here that there is no "*precedence issue*" involved when dealing with the Kydland–Prescott and Long–Plosser, as they are not competitors, but "alternative"—that is to say, *complementary*—models for dealing with business cycles (Long and Plosser, 1983, 45 note 8).

Chapter 1 focuses on the building blocks of the Kydland–Prescott and Long–Plosser approaches, and the catalysts for their development. In this context, Frisch's approach to the cycle between 1931 and 1933, presented at the University of Minnesota and Econometric Society meetings, and which constituted the core of his research program, is discussed as it constituted one of the "building blocks," according to Kydland and Prescott. Following this, the history of the Optimal Stochastic Growth Models of Radner and Brock–Mirman vintage will be outlined and their impact upon the RBC models assessed, based upon technical reports and discussion papers, their final published form, and correspondence with Radner, Brock and Mirman. In addition, the development of the Recursive Competitive Equilibrium (RCE) approach and its application will be surveyed, based upon the Lucas–Prescott approach, the Lucas *JET* paper, and unpublished drafts of Prescott–Mehra. The story will be supplemented by correspondence with Kydland and Prescott regarding the impact of these works upon them.

The early "calibration" approaches of Shoven and Whalley and Miller and Upton will also be presented, and the impact of these on the RBC story assessed. Finally, the development of the Hodrick–Prescott filter will be surveyed, based upon the variorum drafts of their paper from its August 1978 version onwards, the reaction to it—in the form of Friedman's referee report and Prescott's reply—and its impact upon the Kydland–Prescott approach.

In Chapter 2, the origins and development of the Kydland–Prescott research program are dealt with. This is based upon textual analysis of the variorum unpublished drafts of the papers that characterized and impacted upon its development, provided by Finn Kydland and Ed Prescott, and the recollections of those involved. The chapter will deal with the impact of critiques of econometrics and control theory of Lucas and Kydland–Prescott, based upon early unpublished drafts of the Lucas Critique and Kydland–Prescott critiques of control theory and the debate surrounding this. This chapter also presents, for the first time, textual analysis of both their "Time Inconsistency" and earliest versions of their "Time to Build" approaches, which is placed in the perspective of their correspondence surrounding the development of the papers, and highlights the linkage between them. Indeed, as will be shown, the "Time to build" research program is not only inherent, but is also set out in detail, in their "Time Inconsistency" paper. The final section of the chapter deals with the 1977 debate between Prescott and Modigliani over the question of whether control theory should be utilized for the purpose of economic stabilization.

Chapter 3 surveys the development of and cross-fertilization between the Kydland–Prescott and Long–Plosser RBC models. The impact of Lucas's

"Understanding Business Cycles" on the development of the Kydland–Prescott approach from 1978 onwards will be discussed, and the important differences between the 1976 draft of Lucas and its 1977 published version highlighted. In this context, the significant change in the introduction of the Kydland–Prescott "Time to build" papers will be discussed.

The previously unknown role of Fischer Black as "clearinghouse" in the interaction between Kydland–Prescott and Long–Plosser, and the referees' reports—especially that of John Taylor, who refereed the Kydland–Prescott paper for *Econometrica*—and their impact upon the development of the respective papers, is also presented for the first time in Chapter 3.

Chapter 4 deals with initial extensions to and variations on the respective approaches. In the first section of this chapter, the King–Plosser (1982, 1984) and King–Plosser–Rebelo (1988) approaches will be discussed, and the differences between King and Plosser's 1982 NBER Working Paper and 1984 *AER* paper presented. The second part of the chapter deals with extensions, variations, and the initial critique of "Time to build." This includes extensions by Sumru Altug, Gary Hansen, Thomas Cooley, and Kydland and Prescott themselves, the critique of Heckman, and Kydland's reply. The focus here is on Altug's econometric estimation of Kydland–Prescott and its utilization in Heckman's critique of Kydland and Kydland–Prescott, Hansen's extension in the form of "indivisible labor," Kydland and Prescott's "workweek of capital" and "cyclical movements of labor input," and the contributions of Cooley to the story in the form of the dissemination of the Kydland–Prescott approach via the volume he edited (1995).

Chapter 5 deals with further extensions of Kydland–Prescott, the debate surrounding their approach, and the work of others, in the context of the equilibrium approach to the business cycle and the synthesis with New Keynesian Economics to generate the DSGE approach. The first section focuses on Prescott's "Theory Ahead of Business Cycle Measurement" (1986a, b) and the comments on it made by Rogoff. The Prescott–Summers exchange is put into the context of Prescott's initial presentation of his paper at the NBER Summer Workshop in 1986. Moreover, McCallum's two critiques of the RBC approach are dealt with in the context of Prescott's unpublished response to the latter. In addition, Mankiw's critique of RBC from a New Keynesian perspective is also dealt with. The importance of these critiques will be seen in the subsequent synthesis between RBC and New Keynesian approaches as seen in DSGE modeling. The exchange between Kydland–Prescott and Hansen–Heckman regarding the methodological basis of the "computational experiment" and "calibration" is then briefly discussed. The second section discusses the extension of Kydland–Prescott into the Backus–Kehoe–Kydland international model. The third section focuses on the contributions of Barro over the period 1979–1993. This includes the evolution of his survey paper "Equilibrium approach to business cycles," and how he came to recognize the "Time to build" in Kydland–Prescott (1978). It also includes his account of how the RBC was introduced into his textbook *Macroeconomics*. The final section "sums up" the origins and evolution of the

Kydland–Prescott approach, based upon Prescott's retrospective 1998 "Business Cycle Research" paper.

The conclusion first sums up the origins and evolution of the Kydland–Prescott approach, based upon Prescott's "Business Cycle Research" paper. We then deal with convergence and synthesis. The synthesis of RBC with New Keynesian Economics—the basis for the DSGE policy models utilized by Central Banks—is dealt with in the context of what has been called the "New Neoclassical Synthesis." We utilize an account provided by Taylor to assess the developments in macroeconomics, including the "convergence" hypothesis. The evolution of DSGE is dealt with, as are views on its applicability and future applications. Finally, the issue of terminology—RBC, DGE, DSGE—raised by Backus and Zimmerman is presented.

1 Building blocks

Cycle and growth theory: evolution and integration

Since the early decades of the twentieth century, business cycle theories have been the focus of much economic research and analysis, while concepts of economic growth are manifest from Smith onwards. The assumption of a dichotomy between fluctuations and growth was prevalent to the end of the 1960s (Aghion and Howitt, 1998, 223), and their integration is a product of breakthroughs made in the 1970s and 1980s, as seen, for example, in the works of Kydland–Prescott, Long–Plosser, and others. The mathematical and empirical approaches to cycles and growth that characterized these developments immediately give rise to the following questions: (1) how should the mathematical and empirical approaches be described—as formal models per-se, or as modeling methodologies?; and (2) how did the approaches to cycles and growth evolve, and how were they integrated? Below, I will attempt to deal with the issues raised by these questions, which are, as will be shown, fundamentally connected.

In a somewhat overlooked survey, Kydland (2004) made the distinction between "traditional" and "recent" approaches to business cycle theory. Over the past century, since the earliest works of Aftalion (1913, 1927), Mitchell (1913, 1923, 1927), Frisch (1927,1931,1933), Robertson (1915), Pigou (1927), Slutzky (1937), Tinbergen (1935, 1939), Burns and Mitchell (1946), the compilations and critiques of Haberler (1937), and up to the work of Lucas (1972, 1973a, b), Barro (1979a, b, 1980a, b, c), Kydland–Prescott (1982, 1989), Long–Plosser (1983), and their extensions in King–Plosser (1982; 1984a, b) and King–Plosser–Rebelo (1988a,b), approaches to the business cycle have ranged from empirical and econometric, through to monetary, equilibrium, real, and dynamic general equilibrium, the "recent" approaches being based upon "rational expectations business cycle models" (Dotsey and King, 1988).

Indeed, while Mitchell's 1913 volume, *Business Cycles* exhibited an endogenous empirical approach (Kydland, 2004), the approach of Aftalion is closer to the Kydland–Prescott "Time to build" approach (e.g. Aftalion, 1927, 165). Robertson's 1915 volume on "industrial fluctuations" has also been seen as a precursor to the "real" approach—that is to say, based on productivity and technology shocks (Goodhart and Presley, 1994). Interestingly enough, Mitchell somewhat negatively reviewed Robertson's 1915 volume in the *American Economic Review* (Mitchell, 1916); the second "general" part of which he described as "a study of industrial fluctuations without the businessman" (1916, 639). Pigou's 1927 volume, *Industrial Fluctuations*, for its part, has been described as an example of an "equilibrium" approach, encompassing both monetary and real "impulses" (Collard, 1996, 913). The work of Slutzky (1937) and Frisch (1927, 1931, 1933) also deserve attention here, as the former's contribution went somewhat unrecognized, at least according to Friedman (1997, 209–210), while the latter greatly influenced the "first generation" of those who, as Kydland (2004) put it, developed "recent" business cycle theory. Let me first deal with Frisch's contributions, and the subsequent work of Tinbergen.

The impact of Frisch's 1933 essay on "propagation" and "impulse"—being a macroeconomic approach to the cycle—is oft-cited as having had a significant impact upon the thought processes of business cycle theorists of "recent" vintage. What should be recalled here, however, is that the 1933 essay was only one in the series of papers comprising Frisch's business cycle research program, which essentially started with his 1927 paper (in Swedish) on "primary investment" and "reinvestment." In his 1927 paper, he presented a theoretical analysis of "cyclical movements in the economic system" in terms of "fluctuations" and their "damping" (1927, Chipman edition, 1–3).

Frisch visited the University of Minnesota twice, invited by Hansen; the first during the Summer of 1930, and then in Spring 1931. While at Minnesota he lectured and wrote a number of papers that not only became the basis for some of his seminal contributions, but also for his legacy in the areas of empirical macroeconomics and econometrics. In July 1930, he spent a week there and gave a series of lectures. These were entitled: "General considerations on static and dynamic economics"; "Dynamic formulation of some parts of economic theory"; "The significance of economic theory in modern life"; and "Statistical verification of the laws of dynamic economics." He returned to Minnesota's School of Business Administration at the beginning of April, leaving at the end of May 1931. While there, he gave courses under the joint rubric "Modern economic theory from a quantitative viewpoint," on productivity theory, and on statistical verification. During his stay in 1931, he also wrote three papers. One was entitled "The optimum regression." Another was the first draft of what was to eventually become a part of his famous "propagation" and "impulse" paper (1933), which was originally entitled "Business cycles as a statistical and theoretical problem." He wrote this draft of the paper for a meeting in Stockholm which was to take place in June 1931. The first presentation was at an invited talk given by him at the University Campus Club on 15 May 1931, hosted by Hansen. The third paper written while at Minnesota was his critique of Clark's approach to production and the "acceleration principle" (*JPE*, 1931), which brought on an exchange between Frisch and Clark that extended into 1932. Before publishing it, however, he convinced Hansen that his argument was correct. His draft manuscript on the business cycle and his critique of Clark formed the basis for his now classic 1933 paper that eventually stimulated the modern or "recent" approach to the business cycle as manifest in the works of Kydland and Prescott, among others.

Frisch wrote theoretically and mathematically based papers on the business cycle, which were presented at professional meetings and published, up to his 1933 seminal piece (for a complete bibliography of his works, see Edvardson, 2001). Parallel to this was Tinbergen's "econometric business cycle research program," comprised of work presented and published up to his classic 1939 work sponsored by the League of Nations (1933, 1935, 1938, 1939). Indeed, business cycles was one of the main topics discussed at the 3rd European meeting of the Econometric Society, held over the period 30 September–2 October 1933 in Leyden, Holland. Both Tinbergen and Frisch made presentations. In his paper, Tinbergen dealt with the question of the usefulness of the theory of oscillations for the study of cycles, distinguishing between "exogenous … endogenous movements of a system." Frisch, for his part, presented a paper entitled "Some problems in economic macrodynamics"; his concept of dynamic being parallel to Tinbergen's notion of "exogenous movements." In addition, he distinguished between "micro" and "macro" areas of concern in dynamics, the latter relating "to the economic system as a whole." Frisch's mathematical approach followed from his 1932 *JPE* debate with Clark and Mitchell mentioned above. According to the Report of the meeting, Kalecki also presented a paper on the theory of cyclical movements, albeit with different assumptions and results from those of Frisch (Report of 1933 Meeting, *Econometrica*, 1934, 187–194).

Three years later, at the September 1936 Econometric Society meeting held in Oxford, at the session on "Dynamic systems and cycles" held on the Saturday afternoon (26 September), Frisch gave a paper entitled "Macro-dynamic systems leading to a permanent unemployment." He presented a simple equation system based upon his 1933–1934 Oslo lectures. He showed how such a simple system "might be modified and developed in a more realistic direction," concluding that "the task was not so much to develop new systems as to test different systems against the facts" (Report of 1936 meeting, *Econometrica* 1937, 363–364).

In another paper given at this session, Tinbergen discussed "Dynamic equations underlying modern trade cycle theories." In it, he surveyed the "different attempts" that had "been made to describe the endogenous movements of an economic system by a complete system of equations, i.e. by a system showing as many equations as variables." Because of its importance—albeit overlooked until now—regarding the development of his "systems of equations" approach, which was subsequently displaced at the core of modern quantitative macroeconomic analysis by the Kydland–Prescott and Long–Plosser approaches, Tinbergen's presentation and his "defense" of it will be cited at length here.

According to the Report on the content of Tinbergen's presentation (Report of 1936 meeting, *Econometrica*, 1937, 364–365):

> By choosing suitable units and zero points for his variables, which were measured as deviations from a moving equilibrium … Tinbergen succeeded

> in obtaining a system of linear homogenous equations. The aim of these equations was to indicate the "direct causal relationships" existing between the variables as long as no exterior forces are acting ... The constants used are 'reaction coefficients', whose values depend largely on institutional, technical, and natural factors, and as a rule, change only slowly. As a solution of the system of equations shows, they determine the nature of the endogenous movements through which the system can go. In many cases their values can be determined by multiple or simple correlation analysis, so far as exterior forces can be considered to be accidental. The question can then be put, what changes in these coefficients are necessary in order to obtain a system that will not show heavy fluctuations: this is the problem of business-cycle policy.

The Report went on to say (1937, 365):

> In replying to discussion, Dr. Tinbergen put forward a number of considerations to justify the taking of a single system to fit the course of a sequence of cycles: (1) It was insufficiently realized that the mechanism which yields a cumulative process may also yield an explanation of the whole cycle: there is then no need to introduce special causes of turning points, for these are implicit in the single mechanism. (2) Though it is true that the system is disturbed by shocks, the shock is none the less transmitted *through* the system ... (3) It was suggested that a fuller account might be obtained if different systems were fitted to different phases or cycles; but it was difficult to get sufficient data for the short period, and when he had tested the fit in different periods, he had not found any systematic difference according to the phase of the cycle. In general, it is better to include more variables than to resort to more complicated functions.

After the papers were discussed, there was a "subsequent colloquium" led by Frisch, who presented what was described as "an ideal program for Macrodynamics studies." He divided this into "theoretical" and "statistical inquiry." Regarding the former, the Report cited Frisch as saying that the steps involved in such an inquiry would be as follows (Report of 1936 meeting, *Econometrica* 1937, 365–366):

> (1) Define your variables. (2) State the structural relations which you suppose to exist between the variables. (3) Derive a number of confluent [reduced form] relations, which lead to confluent elasticities, showing the response of one variable in a certain sub-group to another when all the rest are held constant. (3a) Use these relations for reasoning about variations compatible with the subsystem. (3b) Consider the response of the system to exogenous shocks: a dynamic analysis leading to criteria of stability. (3c) consider how the whole system will evolve in time.

As for the latter, he stated that "when we have found ... how the system *would* proceed through time [italics in original], we do not expect actual history to move like that, for this history is affected by a stream of erratic shocks."

In 1946, Burns and Mitchell's NBER volume *Measuring Business Cycles* was published, some three decades after the appearance of Mitchell's initial study on the cycle (1913), and two decades after the first of Mitchell's NBER sponsored works on it (1927). A number of reviews of the volume appeared. Among them, those of Shaw (1947), Hurwicz (1947), and especially Koopmans (1947) stand out. Shaw noted the relationship between Burns–Mitchell and Mitchell's 1913 work, stating that the 1946 volume was "the first installment in the revision" of the second part of the 1913 volume, Mitchell's earlier 1927 volume having been the revision of its first part. Moreover, he wrote that in 1941 Mitchell had consented to the publication of its third part. As he put it, the Burns–Mitchell volume "survived an agonizing gestation," and went on to say that the title was not "apt" as it suggested "macroanalysis" while "the contents were microanalytic" and that they "neither construct nor prove a model of business instability" (1947, 281–284). In his review, Hurwicz (1947), later a Nobel laureate, took issue with their overall methodological approach, which, in his view, scorned the work of both economic theorist and econometrician alike. He noted that they hardly used "tools, terminology and notation of modern statistical inference" and that "further work along entirely different lines" was necessary (1947, 463–467).

Koopmans review essay (1947) on Burns–Mitchell entitled "Measurement without theory" is well known, especially as it argued for what he called a "system of equations" approach to fluctuations, something which dominated the Keynesian macroeconomic approach to the business cycle, as will be seen below. What the Burns–Mitchell volume did provide, however, was an alternative to the Keynesian theorizing and "thinking" that was in the process of coming to dominate post-war approaches to the business cycle, including the econometric approach. Indeed, there was a debate between Hansen and Burns in the NBER annual report for 1946, which counter-pointed "economic research" as against "the Keynesian thinking of our times"; a theme that was also addressed in the Burns–Mitchell volume itself (Hansen, 1947; Burns, 1947). However, as a result of the shortcomings in Burns–Mitchell, the following decade saw Keynesian thinking coming to dominate *both* business cycle modeling and growth, as exemplified by Harrod–Domar.

In his 2004 survey (cited above), Kydland focused on the development of "quantitative theory," and delineated "endogenous" as against "exogenous" approaches to cycles—fluctuations in Mitchell (1913, 1923, 1927) and Burns–Mitchell (1946) being endogenously generated, while those in Frisch (1933) were exogenously generated. He noted that while Frisch's work "received considerable attention" at the time, "no one built upon it." He said that, given this, it is not surprising that Keynesian approaches dominated. In his view this could be explained by the fact that the neoclassical growth model and the "necessary tools to do quantitative dynamic general equilibrium analysis" were not yet developed (2004, 3). Interestingly enough, a decade prior to Kydland's survey, Kehoe and Prescott wrote that the term "real business cycle model" was "unfortunate" as it did not cover the case where money and rigid nominal contracts were built into "a GE business cycle model" (1995, 8). Indeed, in an interview, Kydland said that he preferred the term "dynamic equilibrium" and, even more, "dynamic general equilibrium" business cycle "model," adding that the Kydland–Prescott approach was not a model per se, but a "modeling methodology" (Kydland, 2005). How was the neoclassical growth model needed for quantitative theory forged? And what, then, were the necessary tools needed for the quantitative GE analysis that would enable the displacement of the "system of equations" approach? It is to this that I now turn.

Optimum and stochastic growth: Ramsey to Brock–Mirman

From optimal savings and maximal growth to optimum stochastic growth

In the early part of the twentieth century, economists started to adopt the theory that people are "shortsighted" and tend not to properly assess their future needs, and may therefore "reduce" their future utilities. Pigou (1920) posed an interesting conundrum: if people tend to underestimate their future utility, they will probably not make proper stipulation for their future needs, and therefore save less than they would have wished, had they made the calculation correctly. Pigou suggested that the outcome of this probably meant that the rate of saving, as a whole, was less than the "optimum." Pigou surmised that there was thus a "market failure" in the market for savings. However, in order to verify that the rate of savings generated by a market system with myopic agents is indeed sub-optimal, one must first determine what the optimal savings rate might be. It was at this point that Ramsey (1928) picked up on Pigou's suggestion. Ramsey offered a practical calculus to determine the "optimal rate of savings" for a society. He proposed an inter-temporal social welfare function, and then tried to obtain the "optimal" rate of savings as the rate which maximized "social utility," subject to some basic economic constraints. He intentionally negated discounting of future utility from this social welfare function. He proposed that just because people are individually myopic, it did not mean that society, as a whole, would be correspondingly "myopic." Ramsey's conclusion was to confirm Pigou's suggestion that the optimal rate of savings is higher than the rate that myopic agents in a market economy would choose.

After the impact of the Harrod–Domar approach (1939–1948), during the 1950s and 1960s growth theory moved into the neoclassical framework of the Meade–Solow–Swan model (Young, 1989), and questions about "effective" programs of accumulation were being asked. The Solow–Swan growth model is a term used to encompass the contributions of several authors to the model of long-run economic growth into the framework of neoclassical economics. In the Harrod–Domar model, the capital-output ratio was exogenous. Solow (1956), Swan (1956), and Meade (1936, 1961) contested this. They asserted that the capital-output ratio should not be considered exogenous, suggesting a model where the capital-output ratio (v) was exactly the adjustment variable that would bring an economy back to its steady-state growth path, i.e. that v would move the relation between the savings ratio (s) and the capital-output ratio (v), i.e. s/v, into equality with the natural rate of growth (n). This model has become known as the "Solow-Swan" or simply the "Neoclassical" growth model. Tobin (1955) presented a growth model comparable to Solow–Swan which also included money; However, Tobin did not deal with the stability of the steady-state. In addition, Tinbergen (1942) in effect outlined the same model as Solow–Swan, including empirical estimates of the growth coefficients. Meade, in correspondence with Harrod in 1936, also developed an early version of the non-classical growth accounting framework (see Young, 1989).

In the early 1960s, many researchers (independently) dealt with the question of optimal savings for the neoclassical model. The answer appeared simple: a "Golden Rule" or optimal rate of savings which made the rate of return on capital equal to the natural rate of population growth. Phelps (1961) posed the question as to what was the "best savings rate" for an economy. He called the solution to this problem the "Golden Rule" of growth. The "Golden Rule" was developed more or less concurrently by Phelps (1961), Desrousseaux (1961), Allais (1962), Robinson (1962), von Weizsäcker (1962), and Swan (1963). Koopmans then considered maximal growth (1963, 1964). Cass (1963, 1965a, 1965b), Koopmans (1964, 1965), Malinvaud (1965), Mirrlees (1967), Shell (1967) and others focused on developing a one-sector optimum growth model. This is sometimes called the "Ramsey," the "Cass–Koopmans," or the "Ramsey–Koopmans–Cass" optimum growth model, while Cass (1964a, b, 1966) and Radner (1960, 1961), among others, also developed a "turnpike approach" to optimum growth, based upon von Neumann's classic paper, "A model of general economic equilibrium," first read in 1932, published in 1937 in German, and only translated in 1945 (von Neumann, 1945 [1937/8]; Champernowne, 1945).

During the 1960s there was also the question of how to extend Solow's approach (1956, 1957) to two sectors. Starting with Solow's model, a number of papers describing two-sector competitive growth models and specialized technology were published. They described a competitive equilibrium and its efficiency properties. Among those who developed such models were Shinkai (1960), Uzawa (1961), and Srinivasan (1962). For his part, Uzawa focused on the development of a neoclassical two-sector version of Shinkai's model (1961, 40 note 1). Uzawa then decided to go into optimal growth theory and produced a series of papers which was basically a two-sector optimal growth model with a linear objective function. Essentially, he recreated the calculus of variations himself, and discovered the maximum principle that became associated with it. Ramsey (1928) had no discounting, and made a point of talking about the justness of the social welfare function from a moral viewpoint. It had, however, become much harder to solve the problem with no discounting.

Koopmans was working on this problem, and Uzawa may have talked to him about it, possibly at the Boston meeting of the Econometric Society, in

December 1963, which he attended, and where Koopmans gave a paper on "maximal" growth (Econometrica, 1964). For, when Koopman's described what he was doing, Uzawa said, "Well, I have a graduate student who did that problem" (Spear and Wright, interview with David Cass, 1998). In a series of recent papers, the origins, development, and evolution of optimal and two-sector growth models, and the contributions of Uzawa, Koopmans, Malinvaud, and Cass, among others, have been dealt with in detail (Spear and Young, 2013a, b).

The optimal stochastic growth model (classic analysis of optimal economic growth with stochastic shocks) is also known as the Brock–Mirman model (Brock and Mirman, 1972). The optimal stochastic growth model is the point of departure for much empirical macroeconomics. The real business cycle model is a variation of it. If the economy admits a representative household, it turns out that, notwithstanding the stochastic shocks, the First and Second Welfare Theorems still hold, so equilibrium growth is the same as optimal growth. Now, according to Lucas, the Brock–Mirman model is one of the starting points of Kydland–Prescott (1982). Indeed, as he put it, "Technically, the immediate ancestor of Kydland and Prescott" was Brock and Mirman's 1972 *JET* paper (Lucas, 1987, 32 note 1). Thus, the impact of Brock–Mirman on the Kydland–Prescott approach, in both its 1977 and 1982 vintages, is now discussed.

The impact of Brock, Mirman, and Brock–Mirman: from competitive equilibrium, RCE, and Prescott–Mehra to RBC

Mirman's thesis and Brock–Mirman

In what is now considered their most important *JET* paper—that is to say, "Optimal Growth and Uncertainty: the Discounted Case"—Brock and Mirman wrote that "The basic framework for the paper was developed by Mirman in [9, 10], for discrete time one-sector stochastic growth models" (1972, 482). Reference 9 was to Mirman's 1970 PhD thesis, entitled "Two Essays on Uncertainty and Economics" (Mirman, 1970a); reference 10 was to Mirman's (then) "unpublished" 1970 paper, entitled "The Steady State Behavior of a Class of One Sector Growth Models with Uncertain Technology," which emanated from his thesis and was later published, as will be seen below.

With regard to his thesis and early interaction with Brock, Mirman recalled (9 February 2007):

> Brock and I overlapped at Rochester … he as an assistant professor and I as a graduate student—for one semester … as he told me he had no idea what I was doing—but we were friends—I turned in my thesis the next spring—I was at Cornell—and he was assigned to read it—from what he told me he was very excited by what I did and he called me and told me he thought we could do the optimal case and we did! My advisor was McKenzie—Brock and Zable were on my committee from economics—but the biggest help I got was from a mathematician (a probabilist) named Kemperman—who was

> also on my committee—a statistician—who taught me stochastic processes was also on the committee—Keilson … I was really lucky to be surrounded by a group of great scholars.

Another paper that Mirman wrote at the time was his 1971 *Econometrica* paper entitled "Uncertainty and Optimal Consumption Decisions," received in March 1969; the final revision was dated November 1969. In the first note to the paper, Mirman acknowledged "the encouragement and advice of Prof. J.H.B. Kemperman" (1971, 179).

Now, what Mirman called the "optimal case"—that is to say, the 1972 B-M paper—was received at *JET* in June 1971. Six months earlier, in January of that year, Mirman had sent a paper entitled "On the existence of steady state measures for one sector growth models with uncertain technology" for publication to *IER* and, after revision in September 1971, it was published in June 1972. Now, in his *IER* paper, Mirman cited his "unpublished" 1970 paper as having introduced "a stochastic generalization of the concept of a steady state equilibrium for a model of economic growth" (1972, 271). However, in his *IER* paper, Mirman did not cite his own 1970 thesis [as against its citation in Brock–Mirman (1972)], and in the *IER* paper, Mirman cited his paper with Brock as "forthcoming" (1972, 286). Mirman's 1970 paper finally appeared in the June 1973 issue of *JET*. When asked about the differential citations, Mirman replied (8 February 2007):

> This is easy to answer—I think my thesis paper and the … *IER* paper are almost exactly the same so there was no need to quote the thesis—but then I needed to quote *the not yet forthcoming JET paper* [my emphasis, as Mirman is talking here about the June 1973 version of his 1970 paper published in *JET*]—but the 73 *JET* paper and the thesis paper are different—the referee insisted that I change the proof.

And indeed, in the introductory note to the June 1973 version of his 1970 paper, Mirman wrote: "This paper contains results reported in my Ph.D thesis … However, the organization of the paper and the proofs of the main theorem have undergone considerable change." Interestingly enough, in the references to his 1973 *JET* paper—which, as Mirman wrote (1973, 219), was based on his 1970 Ph.D thesis (1970a)—both Cass (1965) and Koopmans (1965a, b) are cited, as is Radner (1971). Brock and Mirman (1972), however, only cite Cass and Koopmans, and a paper by Brock entitled "Sensitivity of Optimal Growth Paths with Respect to a Change in Final Stocks" [actually published as (Brock, 1971) in the same conference volume as Radner (1971)].

Radner's contributions

From 1960 onwards, Radner wrote about growth—including optimal growth—and linked it to turnpike theory in his 1961 *RES* paper. This is not the place for detailed analysis of his seminal contributions, but by looking at his 1960 and 1961 papers we can gain insight into the impetus for his subsequent research. In April 1960, Radner put out a working paper entitled "Paths of economic growth that are optimal with regard only to final states: 'two turnpike theorems'." This was circulated by the Bureau of Business and Economic Research Committee on econometrics and mathematical economics at Berkeley. The February 1961 issue of *RES* contained a section entitled "Prices and the turnpike," comprised of three papers by Hicks, Morishima, and Radner respectively. The title of Radner's paper was similar to that of his April 1960 working paper, with the exception of a new subtitle: "a turnpike theorem."

Examination of Radner's April 1960 working paper and his *RES* paper of a similar title reflects the impetus for his approach—that is, his aim at revealing the "intimate connection between optimal growth and von Neuman equilibrium" (1961, 101), a phrase added in the 1961 *RES* version of the paper. But perhaps more interesting, for our purpose, is his statement that "the problem and results" he dealt with in his papers emanated from "certain problems of efficient capital accumulation" (1960, 2; 1961, 98), evident in the volume of Dorfman, *et al.*, (1958). These problems also impacted upon Uzawa, bringing about his focus on optimal economic growth and turnpikes

Brock, Brock–Mirman, and Radner: uncertainty, stochastic growth, and competitive equilibrium

As shown above, from 1960 onwards Radner had dealt with the issue of optimal and stochastic growth. In December 1972, at the Toronto Winter Meeting of the Econometric Society, Radner presented a "review paper" entitled "Market Equilibria and Uncertainty: concepts and problems," which was later published, in amended form (1974, 43), in Intriligator and Kendrick (1974). As Radner noted (1974, 45 note 1), sections of this paper were based upon, and adapted from, his papers on "Competitive Equilibrium" (1968), and "Problems in the Theory of Markets under Uncertainty" (1970). Brock was a discussant of the original paper, and an adapted version of his comments was also published in the Intriligator and Kendrick volume (1974, 91–93). In an interview with Woodford (2000), Brock recalled:

> I wrote a little thing as a discussion of a paper by Roy Radner. I think this was at the Toronto Winter Meeting of the Econometric Society, in 1972. It was early in the morning and the audience seemed kind of drowsy, so I decided to do something crazy. And so I took the neoclassical stochastic growth model that I was working on with Mirman, and said, let's think of this as a competitive equilibrium for an economy. What would it look like? You would see random movements in capital and consumption, et cetera. And maybe that would look like something bad; but it's a competitive equilibrium, so it's Pareto optimal, you can't beat it. And I didn't think that was exciting enough to wake up the audience, so I proceeded to

> show how Marx's labor theory of value breaks down in a world like this. I said, recall the nonsubstitution theorem, for multi-factor setups with one primary factor of production, no joint production, and so on. In that equilibrium the relative price of goods would be the relative congealed labor contents. I showed that the analog of that in the deterministic growth model is that the capital-labor ratio in steady state depends only on the subjective rate of time discount on the future utility. It doesn't depend on any parameters of the period utility function. But that's all for the case of certainty. In the stochastic growth model, parameters of the utility function all get wadded up into the stochastic steady state. So there is the end of the labor theory of value. And, I think I made some smart-aleck remark about Marx not having thought about that, and its striking a gaping hole in his theory. But I still don't think I was successful in waking up the audience at that time in the day. I thought that was fascinating. There were a bunch of other people, too, of course—Lucas, Prescott and the rational expectations literature, and so on. But I was too naïve to understand what I was doing, and that these things were all related.

In the published version of his comments on Radner, Brock mentioned the "labor theory of value," but elided any specific mention of Marx (1974, 92) What is important, however, is that in his comments he provided what he saw as the central message of his 1972 *JET* paper with Mirman. As he wrote (1974, 91):

> First look at the simplest possible general equilibrium model over time with uncertainty—viz. a one-sector optimal growth model with random production function, and objective the expected value of the discounted sum of utilities. This is an equilibrium model. To see it, let the representative consumer consume and accumulate capital subject to his budget constraint ... The consumer forecasts prices, rental rates, and wages. He lays out a plan based on these expectations by maximizing the expectation of the discounted sum of utilities. Firms maximize expected profits conditional on previous information. A perfect foresight equilibrium over time is when planned supply equals planned demand for all times. As is shown in the 1972 *JET* paper of Brock and Mirman, an equilibrium over time is a stochastic process and that stochastic process converges to a steady state distribution independent of initial wealth. Unlike the certainty case, however, in general the steady state will depend on the utility function.

In correspondence with this author (2004), Brock put the comments above into the perspective of three decades. He wrote about what he called "this standard result of abstract general equilibrium theory" as follows:

> I want to emphasize that it was standard in abstract general equilibrium theory at that time to think of optimal planning problems with concave

> objectives and convex constraint sets as "Robinson Crusoe" economies where the equilibrium process were generated by applying a separating hyperplane theorem to the planner's optimum. For example, the great general equilibrium theorists, Arrow, Debreu, McKenzie, and Radner wrote not only on special cases like Robinson Crusoe economies in abstract spaces but also on general equilibrium economies with heterogeneous consumers and heterogeneous firms in abstract spaces. So I didn't say anything new in the above paragraph. Our contribution (Brock and Mirman, 1972) was in developing the model, and proving key assumptions about it such as the convergence theorem using only assumptions on the "primitives" of the model (e.g. the utility and the technology).

Now, in his 2000 interview with Brock, Woodford also posed the following question: "Your model with Mirman was subsequently invoked as providing the foundations for the kind of stochastic growth model used in real business cycle theory. Was that the sort of application you had in mind at the time?" To this, Brock replied:

> I hadn't really thought of that at the time. You know, I wish I had thought of that. I had thought of it terms of decentralization of an optimal allocation—that you could manufacture a competitive equilibrium, kind of like in the classical papers of Debreu, where you maximize a weighted sum of utilities subject to a bunch of constraints including, and then under the right kinds of assumptions, you could manufacture competitive equilibria corresponding to the optimization problems. I thought, well, you could do that in infinite-dimensional spaces, too; isn't that neat. But those guys were really clever in recognizing that you could actually do business cycle theory using that kind of model as the base. Maybe Mirman might have thought of it, but I was still muddling around in pure mathematics.

In the 2004 correspondence with Brock cited above, he went further when he wrote that the Brock–Mirman (1972) result, as a "standard result of abstract general equilibrium theory," did not take

> anything away from Kydland and Prescott's splendid work on real business cycle theory. As I see it, they aimed the apparatus of abstract general equilibrium theory at the business cycle problem and showed how powerful it is in organizing data and explaining patterns in this area.

In any event, before assessing the impact of Brock–Mirman on Kydland–Prescott, the connection between Brock's work and the RCE approach developed by Prescott and Mehra must be dealt with, as the RCE approach is another building block in the RBC story.

Brock and Prescott–Mehra: optimal and stochastic growth theory, finance, and asset pricing

Spinoffs of Brock–Mirman

A number of papers can be considered as spinoffs of the original set of Brock–Mirman papers (1972, 1973). These include Mirman and Zilcha (1975, 1977), Brock and Majumdar (1978), and an important component in the development of the Prescott–Mehra RCE approach (1977, 1980) in the form of a working paper by Brock (1978a, b).

Brock and Prescott–Mehra

The link between Brock's 1978 [1979] paper on stochastic growth and asset prices, and Prescott–Mehra RCE (1977, 1980) is an interesting example of conceptual cross-fertilization, as can be seen by examination of the drafts of Brock's paper (1978a, b), which refer to the 1977 working paper version of Prescott–Mehra, "Recursive Competitive Equilibrium and Capital Asset Pricing," and the use of Brock's 1978 working paper "An Integration of Stochastic Growth Theory and the Theory of Finance." The earliest version of Brock's 1978 working paper is dated 17 January, while its first revision is from 9 February 1978. The published version of the paper appeared in the *festschrift* for Lionel McKenzie, edited by Green and Scheinkman (1979a). In it, Brock referred to the "optimal growth model" he presented in his February 1978 draft (1979a, 167), but elided reference to Prescott–Mehra (1977) in this paper. However, Brock split his February 1978 draft into two parts. What he called "Part I: the Growth Model" was issued as a joint Working Paper of the Department of Economics and GSB at Chicago in April 1978 (1978c), and published in Green and Scheinkman's *festschrift* for McKenzie (1979a). The second part of the February 1978 draft initially appeared in April 1978 as "Asset Prices in a Production Economy" at the University of Chicago (1978d), and then with the same title as Cal Tech Working Paper Number 275 in June 1978 (1978e) [revised July 1979 (1979b)]. It is *this* paper that cited Prescott–Mehra (1977) [1978e (1979b), 81]. As Brock wrote [1978e (1979b), 73–74]: "This paper is half of my 'An Integration of Stochastic Growth Theory and the Theory of Finance,' February 9, 1978. The other half of the Feb. 9, 1978 paper is ... 'Part I: the growth model'... April 1978." Brock's paper "Asset Prices in a Production Economy" was published in 1982, in a volume edited by McCall (1982, 1–44). Cross-fertilization of ideas is readily seen in the fact that Brock's 1978 working paper "An Integration of Stochastic Growth and the Theory of Finance" is not only cited in Prescott–Mehra (1980), but the recursive structure of Brock's model with regard to preferences and technology is "mapped" onto the Prescott–Mehra RCE approach and discussed in detail (1980, 1376–1377). In the acknowledgements to Prescott–Mehra (1980), Brock is cited as having made "helpful comments."

RCE and the development of Prescott–Mehra

Prescott described the development of RCE theory presented by Lucas and Prescott (1971) and Lucas (1973a, b) as being "crucial to the revolution in macroeconomics." Comprehensive treatments can be found in a number of texts (Harris, 1987; Stokey, *et al.*, 1989; Lundquist and Sargent, 2000, 2004). Indeed, Harris's 1987 text is based upon his early lectures at Carnegie-Mellon on the topic [Harris (1978), as cited by Donaldson and Mehra (1983, 288, 311)].

However, the relationship between the RCE approach utilized by Lucas and Prescott (1971) and Lucas (1972b) on the one hand, and that "further developed" in Prescott and Mehra, on the other hand, requires both explanation and accurate historical underpinnings. First of all, as Prescott relates (2006e, 231 note 18), there was more than one version of his paper with Lucas, "Investment under uncertainty," that was originally submitted to *Econometrica* in June 1969 and eventually published in September 1971, and the difference between the versions, which Prescott noted, must be recalled here. Second, there were also a number of versions of the Prescott–Mehra paper itself, which appeared in the form of a thesis chapter (Mehra, 1977) and, later, working papers that were presented at seminars and widely circulated and cited (Prescott and Mehra, 1977; 1978).

With regard to the difference between the original and published versions of Lucas and Prescott (1971), as Prescott recalls (2006e, 231 note 18): "The published version of 'Investment under Uncertainty' did not include the section formally defining the recursive equilibrium with policy and value functions depending on both an individual firm's capacity and the industry capacity and was an industry equilibrium analysis."

Now, while RCE theory originated and was first applied in the works of Lucas and Prescott (Lucas and Prescott, 1971; Lucas, 1972b; Lucas 1978), the development of the Prescott–Mehra RCE approach must also be dealt with historically. This is because, as Rogerson wrote (1988, 419), "although recursive methods were used in many prior instances," the Prescott–Mehra paper was "the first to prove welfare theorems for economics defined recursively." Suffice it to say, at this point, that the Prescott–Mehra paper also impacted significantly upon the RBC research program, and thus its history must also be gotten "straight."

The Prescott–Mehra paper was circulated in draft form in December 1977, with the title "Recursive competitive equilibria and capital asset pricing" (Prescott and Mehra, 1977). This was Chapter 3 of Mehra's Carnegie-Mellon PhD thesis, supervised by Prescott, which had been approved in December (Mehra, 1977). In their 1977 draft, Prescott and Mehra further developed the recursive competitive equilibrium framework originally presented in Lucas and Prescott (1971). Moreover, they extended it to the analysis of the cases of "many consumers" and "small fluctuations in aggregate output." In the former case, their analysis was of "an economy with many consumer classes, where each class has different preferences, but the same discount factor" (1977, 21). The latter was an analysis of the case where "fluctuations in aggregate output are but a few percent" (1977, 22). They concluded that "These difficult and important extensions and applications will be the subject of future inquiry within our recursive competitive equilibrium framework" (1977, 23).

The former case is an important one, since—based upon the 1977 draft, as cited above—if all agents have the same discount rate, and if conditions satisfy that a competitive equilibrium Pareto Optimum is ensured, then, as Prescott and Mehra later wrote (1980, 1365), "equilibrium processes for economic aggregates and prices [for some heterogeneous consumer economy] will be observationally equivalent to those for some homogeneous consumer economy."

In 1978, this paper was revised and given the title "Recursive competitive equilibrium: the case of homogenous households," and circulated as a Columbia University Graduate School of Business Working Paper. The paper was eventually published in the September 1980 issue of *Econometrica*; this, after acceptance, was announced in the journal in November 1979, and the paper was listed as a "forthcoming selected" article in the January 1980 issue (1979a, 1579; 1980a, 279). According to the information that appeared at the end of the published version of the paper, it was initially received in December 1978, and the "final revision received" in December 1979 (1980a, 1378).

However, correspondence between the co-editor of *Econometrica* [Sheshinski] and Prescott shows that as early as March 1979 the Prescott–Mehra paper had been provisionally accepted for publication, contingent upon revision according to the referee's comments, which the co-editor agreed with, and condensing it. The co-editor wrote: "I think your paper contains some interesting applications based on two previous papers [Lucas and Prescott (1971); Lucas (1978)] and we shall be happy to publish it" (Sheshinski to Prescott, 5 March 1979). According to the referee's report on the paper, their consideration of many identical consumers was problematic, and "It would be much better to stick to one consumer as Lucas does" [referring to Lucas (1978), which had already been published, albeit cited in Prescott and Mehra (1977) as "forthcoming"] (Referee's Report on Prescott and Mehra, 1979). Prescott and Mehra eliminated the "many (identical consumers) case," according to the suggestions of both the referee and the co-editor (Sheshinski to Prescott, 5 March 1979), and focused upon the "representative individual"—that is to say, the "one consumer case." Their assumption of the "homogeneity of consumers" enabled them to write "since all individuals are alike ... the density of the representative individual's demand just equals aggregate consumer demand" (1980, 1367). And it was this, according to the referee of their paper, which enabled "the authors to find equilibria via simple decision rules" (Referee's Report on Prescott and Mehra, 1979).

In early June 1979, Prescott sent the revised version of the paper to the co-editor, thanking him for its "rapid turnaround" (Prescott to Sheshinski, 4 June 1979). Two weeks later, the co-editor wrote that he had read the revised version, and that "it is publishable as it is." He asked Prescott to "send a copy directly to the production editor" (Sheshinski to Prescott, 18 June 1979). The 22 month turnaround—from submission to publication in *Econometrica*—was indeed "rapid" when compared to 28 months for Lucas and Prescott (1971), and some three years for Lucas (1978)—that is to say, the two papers on which the Prescott–Mehra paper was "based," according to the co-editor of *Econometrica* (Sheshinski to Prescott, 5 March 1979).

Calibration and computational experiment: Shoven–Whalley, Miller–Upton, and Kydland–Prescott

In his December 2004 Nobel Lecture "Quantitative Aggregate Theory" Kydland wrote (2004, 341):

> The key tool macroeconomists use is the *computational experiment*. Using it, the researcher … performs precisely what I just described—places the model's people in the desired environment and records their behavior. But the purpose of the computational experiment is broader than simply to evaluate policy rules. The computational experiment is useful for answering a host of questions, in particular quantitative ones, that is, those for which we seek numerical answers.

He went on to say (2004, 342–343):

> I've described two elements of typical models used for computational experiments: the millions of model inhabitants and the thousands of businesses. An essential aspect, however, is the calibration of the model environment. In a sense, models are measuring devices: they need to be calibrated, or otherwise we would have little faith in the answers they provide. In this sense, they are like thermometers. We know what a thermometer is supposed to register if we dip it into water with of chunks of ice, or into a pot of boiling water. In the same sense, the model should give approximately correct answers to questions whose answers we already know. Usually, there are many such questions. In the context of business-cycle analysis, we know a lot about the long run of the economy, or we may use the Panel Study of Income Dynamics, say for the United States or similar panel studies from other nations to collect the data to calibrate the model. Thus, the calibration is part of the action of making a quantitative answer as reliable as possible.

A computational experiment yields time series of aggregate decisions of the model economy's people. Through the model formulation and its calibration, we have determined what the economic environment should look like. Then, the millions of people and the thousands of businesses in the economy make the decisions over time, and the computer records their decisions. We obtain time series as if we were confronted with an actual economy. These time series may be described statistically and compared with analogous statistics from the data for the nation under study. In a business-cycle study, the statistics may include standard deviations of detrended aggregates describing the amplitudes of their business-cycle movements, as well as correlation coefficients as measures of the co-movements.

And, interestingly enough, at the end of this lecture, Kydland added (2004, 355):

> It may be amazing to you, however, that I've continued to use for so long (supplemented by my own notes) a textbook first published in 1974 by Merton Miller and Charles Upton. It presents a dynamic framework with many of the features I have talked about, even life-cycle behavior. These two authors were simply great economists, and included in the text the key elements they thought ought to be present in basic dynamic models of microeconomics.

Shoven and Whalley, Mansur and Whalley, and the origins of "calibration"

Now, many observers, such as Hansen and Heckman (1996) attribute "calibration"—as utilized by Kydland and Prescott—to the approach developed and applied by Shoven and Whalley (1972, 1973, 1975, 1977). In late 2004, Whalley was asked the following with regard to this (Young to Whalley, 15 December 2004):

> I am writing you to ask your help in clearing up a point made in the treatment of the Kydland–Prescott approach in the 1996 *Journal of Economic Perspectives* paper by Hansen and Heckman. In their 1996 paper, Hansen and Heckman (1996, 89) wrote: "Kydland and Prescott ought to be praised for taking the general equilibrium analysis of Shoven and Whalley [1972, 1992] one step further by using stochastic general equilibrium as a framework for understanding macroeconomics". My question is, in your view, is your work between 1972 and 1977 a precursor to Kydland and Prescott? And if so, can you explain to me why you think it may be a precursor? [I refer to your papers between 1972 and 1977, i.e. Jnl.Pub.Eco., 1972; RES, 1973,1977; Rev. Eco. Stat. (1975); Man.Sch. (1975)]. I ask because while Kydland and Prescott acknowledge Brock and Mirman, e.g., in their respective pieces in the volume edited by Cooley *Frontiers of business cycle research* (1995) [Cooley and Prescott, 4; Hansen and Prescott, 40; Kydland, 134], there is no mention in the volume of Shoven and Whalley. Moreover in the Nobel citation of Kydland–Prescott, while Brock and Mirman (1972) *are* mentioned, there is no mention of Shoven and Whalley (1972) and yet, in their piece in the *Journal of Economic Perspectives*, Hansen and Heckman mention your work, not that of Brock and Mirman!

Whalley replied (24 December 2004) as follows:

> The precursors are I think way back but I need to explain a little more. Micro calibrators used data preadjustments to produce a benchmark

> equilibrium data set and use exact calibration to reverse the roles of endogenous and exogenous variables in solving models for parameterization that support the benchmark equilibrium. This is a procedure set out in the appendix (as I recall) of the 1972 Jnl.Pub.Eco. piece with John Shoven, which in turn was in both of our theses. It is implicitly in Harberger's 1962 JPE Paper.
>
> You will find this discussion of micro calibration (which I think differs from what is in Kydland and Prescott, as I understand what they do), in a paper in the Handbook of Econometrics in 2001 (I think) by Dawkins, Srinivasan and myself and also in Mansur and Whalley in the 1984 Scarf and Shoven ed. CUP volume on Applied General Equilibrium.
>
> I don't think any of the earlier pieces by me you mention uses the term calibration. It was in the 1984 piece with Mansur written in ignorance of Kydland and Prescott, but the earlier pieces you mention and others set up procedures of calibration as reverse solutions (as I recall).
>
> As I recall (maybe I'm wrong) Kydland and Prescott in their 1982 Econometrica piece only use the term calibration once as a section heading and (again as I recall) do not define the term. Modern literature now has many senses of calibration (exact/inexact, multiple).

When later asked about Mansur and Whalley and the possible origins of the *term* "calibration," Whalley replied (26 February 2007):

> 1 The Mansur–Whalley piece was presented at a San Diego conference in late summer 1982 (as I recall), and so would have been written spring 1982…
> 2 The paper discusses micro consistent data sets and GE estimation as well as calibration.
> 3 At those times in micro modeling circles the term "calibration" was used interchangeably with several others, including "benchmarking", "supporting parameterizations", and "reverse solution".
> 4 Basically the approach to calibration was quite mechanical; namely to change the designation of endogenous and exogenous variables in a Walrasian (or any other) system and treat, say, prices and quantities as observed and then to solve for preferences and technology which would regenerate the same prices and quantities as an equilibrium solution. For Cobb–Douglas parameters are uniquely determined. For CES you need to pre-specify elasticities (literature based). We highlighted how poor the literature on elasticities is, as empirical work in economics focused on hypothesis testing more so than parameter generation. We called for an elasticity bank to archive and grade estimates.
> 5 As such calibration was viewed as an exact procedure with no explanatory power. Many models could exactly be calibrated to the same data set; and nowadays micro people also use the terms in exact multiple calibrations to refer to variants on this.

6 I think calibration as a term may have come to us from the kinds of things going on in the Energy Modeling Forum on early GHG models and from a sense of what was going on in other disciplines (global circulation models and in life sciences). But it is implicit in the reverse solution in Shoven and Whalley 1972, even though not labeled as such. It could be in a 1977 WP with John Piggot of which I no longer have a copy which I remember submitting to REStat and them saying it was too obvious.

7 I also remember looking at KP when it was first published and the macro people here [Western Ontario] being very impressed. I recall noticing (maybe I am wrong) the term calibration only appeared as a header to a later section in the paper and seemed not be defined. The approach seemed to be one of trying to restrict oneself to parsimonious models, draw on literature estimates of key parameters, and then try to get as close in solution as one could to raw data. My reaction was that if you gave me enough freedom with structure and parameters I could probably exactly calibrate anything to anything else. This raised the issue of what explanatory power there was or is in calibration.

In a supplemental reply, Whalley added (27 February 2007):

> The 1982 WP was put out as a working paper by the Center for the Study of International Relations (CSIER) at Western ... my recollection is that it was much the same as the published version as we didn't get that many comments. Larry Lau was the commentator and he characterized calibration as estimation with zero degrees of freedom. At the time he probably got more cites for this than we did!

As Whalley noted, there is a difference between his approach to calibration and that used by RBC theorists. His approach is based upon exact model calibration to a model admissible unadjusted data set generated by, or constructed from, a range of statistical sources, as presented in Mansur and Whalley (1984). In the unique Kydland–Prescott approach, as will be seen in Chapters 2 and 3 below, the data was not readjusted, and the values of the model parameters they chose were by reference to the economics literature, with the crucial object of making the model solution as close as possible to actual data.

What then, were the headwaters from which the Kydland–Prescott approach to calibration and the computational experiment flowed? Perhaps the answer lies in Kydland's Nobel lecture, when he mentions Miller and Upton (1974). Now, while there is a semantic issue involved regarding whether Miller and Upton "simply calibrated" their model, as will be seen below, there is no doubt that their book—while cited by those moving away from Keynesianism at the time—did not have an immediate impact. Indeed, it was reviewed in only two places—the *Journal of Finance* (1975) and *Kyklos* (1977)—with only the former being positive (Smith, 1975; Banks, 1977).

Miller and Upton's Macroeconomics: experiments and calibration

In the preface to their 1974 book, Miller and Upton wrote (1986 [1974], xiv–xv):

> Instead of merely listing the system of simultaneous equations and relying on implicit differentiation for tracing out the interactions, we have developed a computer model of an imaginary economy built up from the underlying micro components described in the text. Simulation experiments based on the model are described in some detail ... Insofar as possible, we have tried to set the basic parameters of the experimental models to produce numbers for the capital-labor ratio, the capital-output ratio, the savings investment ratio, the real rate of interest, the share of wages in the national income and so on, that are of the same order of magnitude and yield the same "stylized facts" as those found in modern economies.

When asked how the book came about, Upton wrote (Upton to Young, 18 February 2013):

> I was an assistant professor at the University of Chicago from 1968–76. I met Merton Miller shortly after arriving there. Mert was, as you know, formerly at Carnegie-Mellon (or Carnegie Tech when he was there) and we soon struck up a friendship. We began working on the macro book around 1970. At this time, I do not remember who wrote what. Mert probably wrote first drafts of more chapters than I did, and I supervised the computer work: the simulation model was important to the book. We had a programmer Gary Curtis who worked with us (actually a Chicago undergrad). We would make runs and then debate what we had learned from them.

Over the period November 2006–January 2007, Upton and Prescott were contacted regarding their views as to whether calibration was present in Miller and Upton's 1974 book, and the book's impact upon the Kydland–Prescott approach. Upton replied in a letter (Upton to Young 15 November 2006) as follows:

> I leave to you the choice of words to describe how Miller and I calibrated our model; let me simply tell you what we did. The key determinant, again and again, was the desire to have something that could be easily explained to students. In some cases we sacrificed accuracy to get ease of exposition.
> Our basic production function is the simple Cobb-Douglas: $Y=AK^{a}L^{(1-a)}$, where L is in inelastic supply, consisting of all persons between ages 20 and 65. K is aged by a simple depreciation function $Kt=K_{t-1}\,(1-d)+I_{t-1}$. We set $d=0.04$ because that made total depreciation as a percentage of GDP seem "about right". Similarly, we chose our starting value of A so that the implicit wage rate looked "about right" for 1974. A, of course, grew at a rate of 2% a year. The data support a long-term historical rate somewhat lower than that,

but we rounded off for ease of exposition. The coefficient a, was set equal to 0.3, again because that seemed about right. I remember a discussion of a paper by Modigliani where he used a value of something like 0.32145; I am sure I have the digits wrong, but it was about five digits of accuracy. Franco had computed—to five digits—the historical average of capital share of output over some time period. No doubt this made for more accuracy, but, so we reasoned, this was only an example and the precision seemed unnecessary [...] Similar conversations drove our money demand function, which is derived by including money (more formally the services derived from real money balances) ... There was a long argument with Fisher Black who argued we should put real money balances in the production function or have a household production function where money was included. We played with these options briefly, but we could see them becoming the expositional madness and stuck with a simplistic formulation.

Upton's letter was forwarded to Prescott for his comments. Prescott replied (2 January 2007):

I found Charlie's letter very interesting. The capital share parameter (he uses a to denote it) is the same as the one used for the basic RBC model. It is larger than the one that Solow came up with. I am curious as to how they defined the capital stock. Charlie thinks there is more curvature than the log. I think log is reasonable. When there is leisure and the leisure share parameter is reasonable, say two-thirds, the effective curvature is moved two-thirds of the way to the log (see Kydland and Prescott 1991).

The business cycle facts as statistical properties of the aggregate time-series were not defined and reported until Hodrick and I did it in 1978. The final version of that paper (1981) was not published until 1996.

I note that the labor is supplied inelastically in the Miller–Upton model. Without the time allocation decision between market and non-market activities, the model can not be used to address business cycle questions and public finance questions. Lucas–Rapping (1969) were the ones that brought the labor-leisure decision into macro. Lucas's classic (1972) has that key decision and the equilibrium is a stochastic process. However, there is no capital accumulation and it is not truly a dynamic-stochastic equilibrium.

To do what Finn and I did we had to have expertise in the growth model, recursive competitive equilibrium theory, stochastic processes, national accounts, Kalman filtering, and computer programming.

Prescott's reply was sent to Upton for his comments. Upton replied (2 January 2007):

Thanks for sending me Ed's comments. Two points worth following upon. First, the choice of a log utility function; and second the lack of labor supply.

We were driven by a desire to put things in a life-cycle context, and the desire to have something that was relatively easy to manipulate (that is, something that MBA's could handle) drove a lot of decisions. That includes the log utility function. There is some research about consumption over the life cycle, and my guess is that the function is not well behaved. At an aggregate level this does not matter, the micro properties of a simple log utility function are not good: we had consumption growing over an individual's life cycle at the rate of interest.

Second, labor supply. We did play with labor supply function, but we wanted to keep it simple, so we made labor supply exogenous. That always concerned us. We generated business cycles through imperfect information and an assumption of sticky wages (Ed is kind not to mention chapter 17, which introduces business cycles through a short run Phillips curve). Were I redoing this today, I would do something different.

Interestingly enough, Joines (2006) maintained that Miller and Upton "simply calibrated" their life cycle model. When asked about this, Upton replied (19 February 2013):

It depends on what you mean by calibration. We used a simple Cobb Douglas production where we set the coefficient on capital to 0.3. Most studies suggest a slightly different coefficient, but we stuck with 0.3 because it was simpler to use a rounded number in class.

The real issue which arises is the consumption function. We used a function of the form: $U = \log(c_1) + \log(c_2) + \log(c_3) + \ldots$

The optimal consumption rate is then $c(t) = z/$(remaining years of life).

By using this function, we get a key property that, in equilibrium, $c(t) = (1+r)c_{(t-1)}$ where r is the rate of interest. Sticking with the simple log linear function, a far better function is $U = \log(c_1) + g\log(c_2) + g^2\log(c_3) + \ldots$ where g is a coefficient, empirically clearly less than one. If you use this, you get the property that $c(t) = g(1+r)c_{(t-1)}$. [I hope my notation is clear]. This way you get a consumption function where $c(t)$ is proportional to wealth, with the constant depending on g. And consumption is a much higher percentage of wealth. And, consumption does not necessarily rise as an exponential rate over one's lifetime.

We did it that way to make the model simple to manipulate, knowing that it also made it less accurate.

So, to Joines comments, I would plead guilty but offer a defense of justification: we often made assumptions which we knew were heroic but which in our opinion made the model much easier for students to understand.

Kydland and Prescott on calibration and computational experiment

In an interview, Kydland (2005) acknowledged that at the time of the development of the notion of "calibration" as utilized in "Time to build," he had not read the work of Shoven and Whalley, but was aware of that of Scarf (1967). He recalled "looking for data sources to quantify parameters." He did not "have the word calibration in mind"; he "simply did it." It may be said that Kydland and Prescott "did a Lucas," for, just as Lucas brought Muth's rational expectations from micro to macroeconomic utilization (see Young, *et al.*, 2004), Kydland and Prescott brought the "calibration" approach from micro to macroeconomics, and also developed what Kydland called a "dynamic macrocalibration" method—that is to say, at what stage parameters are to be introduced into a macromodel.

About a decade after their "Time to build" paper, Kydland and Prescott published a paper in *Scandinavian Journal of Economics* entitled "The econometrics of the general equilibrium approach to business cycles" (1991a). In this, they took issue with the Scarf–Shoven–Whalley approach, as according to Kydland and Prescott (1991a, 168–169) it was "ill-suited for the general equilibrium modeling of business fluctuations." The reason, as they put it, was that

> Perhaps these researchers were still under the influence of the systems of equations approach and thought a model had to be a system of supply and demand functions. These researchers lacked the time series needed to estimate these equations. Given the fact they could not estimate the equations, they calibrated their model economy so that its static equilibrium reproduced the sectoral national income and product accounts for a base year. In their calibration, they used testaments of the elasticity parameters obtained in other studies.

Kydland and Prescott (1991a, 170–171) went on to outline their "model economy" approach and their approach to "calibration," "computational experiments," and reporting of "findings." With regard to the "model economy" they wrote (1991a, 170):

> To address a specific question one typically needs a suitable model economy ... tractability and computability are essential in determining whether the model is suitable ... Unlike the system-of-equations approach, no attempt is made to determine the true model. All model economies are abstractions and are by definition false.

As for calibration, they stated (1991a, 170):

> The model has to be calibrated. The necessary information can sometimes be obtained from data on individuals or households ... Because the language used in the these business cycle models is the same as that used in other areas of applied economics, the values of common parameters should be identical across these areas and typically have been measured by researchers working in these other areas.... In fact it is in the stage of calibration where the power of the general equilibrium approach shows up more forcefully. The insistence upon internal consistency implies that parsimoniously

> parameterized models of the household and business sector display rich dynamic behavior through the intertemporal substitution arising from capital accumulations and from other sources.

They went on to deal with "computational experiments" and "findings," stating that: "Once the model is calibrated, the next step is to carry out a set of computational experiments. If all the parameters can be calibrated with a great deal of accuracy, then only a few experiments are needed" (1991a, 171). Regarding "findings" they wrote that

> the final step is to report the findings ... The numerical answer to the research question, of course, is model dependent ... The degree of confidence in the answer depends on the confidence that is placed in the economic theory being used.

Five years later, Kydland and Prescott (1996) repeated these points in their debate with Hansen and Heckman (1996) on the nature of calibration and the computational experiment—there is more about this in Chapter 4.

The Hodrick–Prescott filter

Variorum drafts of Hodrick–Prescott

The importance of the Hodrick–Prescott filter in the evolution of the Kydland–Prescott approach to aggregate fluctuations cannot be overstressed. Indeed, it was cited as early as the April 1978 draft of the Kydland–Prescott NBER "Time to build" conference paper, and also in its 1980 version, as will be seen in Chapter 3.

The first draft of the Hodrick–Prescott paper was originally entitled "Money and business cycles in dynamic competitive equilibrium." This was the title that appeared in the published program of the Econometric Society meeting (1978, 245).

The first version of the paper was presented on Wednesday afternoon, 30 August 1978, at the Econometric Society meeting in Chicago. The Chair of the session—"Macroeconomic implications of rational expectations"—was McCallum; the discussant was Kmenta. Other papers in the session were by Evans and Sargent. But the title of the paper actually presented at the session was "Postwar U.S. business cycles: a descriptive empirical investigation" (Hodrick–Prescott, 1978).

As the Hodrick–Prescott paper is a central component of the "Time to build" approach, its origins and development are important elements in the Kydland–Prescott research program overall. In correspondence, Hodrick provided his detailed recollections. He wrote (2005a, b):

> The genesis of the Hodrick–Prescott paper occurred when [Ed] asked me what were the stylized facts regarding the velocity of circulation of money over the business cycle. We started thinking about this issue and submitted

a preliminary idea for a paper to the Econometric Society meetings. What we realized when we started working on the project was that the only way people had to describe the cyclical properties of any data series was the NBER's specific cycle and reference cycle terminology, which was not amenable to time series analysis. We needed to develop something new. We decided that we needed a way to decompose any time series into a trend and cyclical component, and we wanted the trend component to be able to change over time, but not too much. All that we were able to accomplish by the time of the Econometric Society meetings was the HP filter and some descriptive statistics ... The "Money and Business Cycles title was what we hoped to deliver, and the "Post-War..." was a descriptive title of what we actually delivered...

I presented the paper, and Jan Kmenta was the discussant. I remember him being not particularly positive about the paper, and I was at a loss for how to respond. Tom Sargent came to my defense with an eloquent speech about the importance of this type of work. There is another interesting story about the paper. We first submitted the paper to the *AER*, and it was rejected because the referee wanted us to use formal Bayesian smoothness priors. Around the time of the rejection, Ed was talking at the Carnegie-Rochester Conference to Bill Dewald, who was the editor of the *Journal of Money, Credit and Banking*. Bill said that he would like to have the paper reviewed for the *JMCB*, and promised to get a good referee. We submitted the paper and received a rejection, because Dewald's referee didn't like to paper, at all. The referee was Milton Friedman! He indicated this in his report stating "I have no reason the authors should not know my opinion of their paper." He didn't like the idea that we were doing "measurement without theory." He thought that this issue had been settled by the Cowles Commission in the 1950s–1960s. I wish I had that report, but I don't think I do. It always seemed ironic to me that Friedman had made part of his reputation on the Monetary History of the US, and later developed theory to support the measurements done in that book.

By this time, Ed had left CMU for Minnesota, and I was on my way to Kellogg's Finance department at Northwestern. We planned to revise the paper and resubmit it, and I spent a week one summer at Minnesota in the mid-1980s doing some revisions. But, we never resubmitted it.

Hodrick continued (2005b):

In early 1996, I got a call from Steve Cecchetti, who was editing the *JMCB*. He asked if he could publish the HP filter paper, and after talking with Ed, we said yes. We agreed that Ed and I would update the descriptive statistics, but we would not modify the paper with lots of references to the intervening

> literature. Steve did not know the history of the paper and was shocked by the Friedman story.

Below, we will discuss in detail Friedman's reaction and Prescott's written reply from October 1981. Suffice it to say at this point, however, that there were actually three referees, and their reports will also be cited.

This is not the place for a detailed discussion of the differences between the August 1978 and November 1980 versions of Hodrick–Prescott. However, it should be noted that the title itself was changed by elision of the word "descriptive."

In the 1978 version, the April 1978 Kydland–Prescott "Persistence" paper is cited, while mention of this paper is elided in the November 1980 version of Hodrick–Prescott. In the introduction to the 1978 version, both stochastic monetary and real shocks *are* mentioned, and "correlation between deviations from trend rate of inflation and deviations from trend real output" are analyzed (1978, 2–3). A "two shock theory of the business cycle is also presented" (1978, 3; section 4). According to the 1978 version (1978, 3):

> it appears reasonable to conclude that an econometric analysis using dynamic equilibrium theory which is structured around real supply side and monetary or inflation shocks will one day explain a large part of the aggregate economic fluctuations including the persistence of deviations from trend experience by the U.S.

In the 1980 version, the emphasis is upon the interaction of growth and cycle in investigating "aggregate economic fluctuations." According to this introduction (1980, 2) "At a substantive level our primary objective … is to examine the magnitudes and stability of covariances between various economic time series and real output and the autocovariances of real output." The 1980 version concludes by saying (1980, 23)

> In this article no explanation of the cyclical regularities is offered. We think such an explanation can be provided only within the context of a well specified economic model. We do think it appropriate, however, to study the observations prior to theorizing.

In June 1980, Nelson wrote Hodrick regarding the Hodrick–Prescott paper (Nelson to Hodrick, 10 June), referring to the August 1978 version, and asked for information as to its revision or publication status, so as to be able to cite the paper in the "Two Charlie's paper" he was putting together with Plosser (Nelson and Posser, 1980, 1981, 1982). In November 1980, Prescott sent Nelson a copy of the November 1980 revision, and in a covering letter wrote (Prescott 1980b):

> Enclosed is the revised version … subsequent to our telephone conversation I learned that our method has a long history of use. We do agree that the

method of decomposing high and low frequency variation matters. The question is whether first differencing is a good procedure for studying cyclical fluctuations or Bob's and my procedure or some other procedure. My view is that there are many ways to look at the data, and theory is needed in the selection of the way.

Reactions to Hodrick–Prescott: Friedman and Prescott, August–October 1981

The Hodrick–Prescott paper entitled "Post-War U.S. Business Cycles: an Empirical Investigation" was sent to the *Journal of Money, Credit, and Banking* for publication. The editor of the journal, Dewald, sent the paper to Milton Friedman and two other referees for their comments. On 25 August 1981 Friedman sent Dewald a letter in which he was very critical of the form, substance, and statistical procedure of the Hodrick–Prescott Paper. The second referee was also critical:

> The paper has its purpose "to document some features of aggregate economic fluctuations sometimes referred to as business cycles". The paper does this, after first justifying its method of approach.
>
> However, the authors never explain what is important about the results that they do document. They do not adequately explain why the result they display in tables 2 through 7 are of any interest (although on page 3 they state they have found some interesting regularities). In their short discussion of these results, the authors make no mention of any other study and thus they do not tell the reader whether their findings support or contradict results that have be found or suggested before. This is the major shortcoming of the paper.

After describing some "minor problems," the second referee went on to say:

> Finally, I do not see why the authors limit themselves to comparisons of all series to the GNP series. There may be more important and interesting cyclical patterns elsewhere, such as velocity or money or interest rates to price indices. (I expect the velocity and money are positively correlated, despite a great many assertions that they are negatively related, and interest rate should move closely with rate of inflation.)

The third referee was somewhat more positive, and wrote, in comments received on 31 August 1981 by the editor of the journal:

> The general thesis of seeking new dimensions to business cycle analysis is certainly worthy of professional and policy-making attention. The professional receives some useful technical insights and refinements from the article but the policy-maker is unlikely to derive much assistance.

> In my judgment, basic longer run changes or structural developments, e.g. inflation, energy, slower growth, regional shifts, U.S. competitiveness, environmentalism, chronic lack of long-term funds, etc., have dominated the 1970s and now account for a substantial amount of the disturbances in what earlier were deemed cyclical rhythms.
>
> Certainly the diminishing size of the U.S. in the total global economy, dramatic shifts in resource ownership, and rapid monetary expansion across the world have had new and lasting repercussions upon the U.S. domestic scene.
>
> The new volatility in economic measures, so widely observed, must be rooted in basic not transitory changes. Moreover, this added volatility itself constitutes a new structural force in national and international financial markets.
>
> These are examples of profound changes which must be recognized in any analysis of the Post War Business Cycles.
>
> The authors can be commended for their professional skills in refining the available data for some new insights and interpretations, but also asked to clarify what specific goals they have in mind to help public and private decision-makers.
>
> A mathematical approach almost invariably leads to abstractions from the policy world, but in this case provides some guidance to move analysts away from traditional cyclical thinking which has become steadily less useful in evaluating and projecting the economy.

On 6 October 1981, Prescott wrote Friedman and said:

> I received a copy of your comments on Bob Hodrick's and my paper "Post-War U.S. Business Cycles: An Empirical Investigation". Thank you for authorizing that a copy of your letter be sent to me.
>
> My response is as follows:
>
> We proposed neither an alternative to the National Bureau specific cycle/reference cycle method of analyzing business cycles nor an alternative technique for decomposing a time series into trend, cyclical and seasonal. We reported statistics that are inconsistent with standard growth theory. The motivation for reporting this particular set of statistics is that there are now methods for constructing aggregate competitive equilibrium models that place restrictions upon standard deviations and correlations. Possibly the use of the expression "business cycle" in the title was a mistake, but, following Lucas, we wanted to emphasize the recurrent nature of the fluctuations and the similar comovements as the observations to be explained rather than the Keynesian approach that was dominant from the mid-forties to mid-seventies.
>
> Studies documenting deviations from existing theory play an important role in science as do replications of the studies using a different data set. Do you reject such studies as being nonsubstantive?

I was puzzled by your reference to "spurious correlations". Neither means nor correlations are spurious. What are sometimes spurious are the interpretations of correlations, but we offered no interpretations. As we state in the paper, the method we employed has been used by other sciences well before the advent of the electronic computer. This is inconsistent with your assertion that the novel feature of the paper is the use of more sophisticated computer techniques. The novel feature of the paper is that we employed a highly-respected scientific methodology that, unfortunately, is out of vogue in economics.

I know of no other place where these correlations and standard deviations for the U.S. post-war economy are reported. Others have found this summary of business cycle facts for the period useful. The paper is being used in the Ph.D programs at a number of universities including Chicago, Harvard, and MIT.

Under separate cover is a copy of a paper in which Finn Kydland and I develop and test an integrated competitive model of growth and fluctuations. The statistics reported in Hodrick's and my paper play a major role in the test of the theory. Statistics reported by other scientists as well.

Interestingly enough, as Prescott mentioned, he sent a copy of "Time to Build" to Friedman. And, while this was published in 1982, the Hodrick–Prescott paper—although widely circulated and cited—was only actually published in the *Journal of Money, Credit, and Banking* in 1997, as recounted by Hodrick above.

2 The Kydland–Prescott research program

From "optimal stabilization" and "time inconsistency" to "time to build"

The objective of this chapter is to show how Kydland and Prescott put all the "pieces" together—that is to say, how their overall approach, which encompasses both their 1977 and 1982 papers, evolved and brought about what Prescott, in his Nobel lecture, called "a transformation" in modern economic analysis (2004, 370). In his Prize lecture, Prescott wrote (2004, 370, 2006e) "all stories about transformation have three essential parts: the time prior to the key change, the transformative era, and the new period that has been impacted by the change."

But what is the "transformation" that Kydland and Prescott brought about?

It is not simply the synthetic combination of the work of Frisch, Solow, Lucas, and others. It is a totally new approach, one that extends the work of these giants, in conjunction with a new economic *weltanschuung* and empirical methodology that brought about a sea-change in macroeconomic research and policy analysis.

The "essential parts" in the context of this chapter are as follows. In the first part, the "pre-dynamic general equilibrium" phase of the early work of Prescott and Kydland, over the period 1967–1973, is surveyed. The second part of the chapter deals with the "transitional" phase in the Kydland–Prescott approach, encompassing dynamic equilibrium models, their "search" for rules, and their work on stabilization policy and time inconsistency, over the period 1973–1977. The third part deals with their early "Time to build" approaches between 1977 and 1979.

Prescott's early contributions

In his Nobel lecture, Prescott described the nature of macroeconomic models and policy discussion prior to what he called the "transformation," saying that he had "worked in this tradition," and went on to outline the approach to policy selection taken in his dissertation (2004, 372–373). Prescott's early published contributions (1971, 1972), along with his collaboration with others (Lovell and Prescott, 1968, 1970; Lucas and Prescott, 1971) are important to an understanding of how his thought evolved. Prescott's 1967 Carnegie Tech dissertation was entitled "Adaptive decision rules for macroeconomic planning" and was supervised by Lovell. It dealt with the optimization problem, with special emphasis on the issue of how uncertain parameters affect decisions. Prescott considers that his dissertation "was in the old tradition" (2005a). According to Lovell (2005a), the thesis

> was concerned with a problem of optimal learning while doing. Theil was using macro econometric models he had estimated in a control theory framework to determine optimal fiscal policy for the next period. As each new observation became available with the passage of time Theil would re-estimate the model, and then work out the optimal policy under the assumption that the policy parameters had been estimated with precision. Among other results, Ed showed that one could do better than successive one-period optimizations, in terms of minimizing loss, if one sacrificed a little of next-period optimization of the control problem in order to design a better experiment which would yield more precise parameter estimates that would more accurately guide future policy decisions.

There are two important points in Lovell's description of Prescott's 1967 thesis: control theory and experimentation. These aspects are key issues in the work that emanated from his thesis and the collaborative work between them during the period. The first of these was a joint paper with Lovell published in *Southern Economic Journal* (1968), originally presented at the December 1964 meeting of the Econometric Society (1968, 60).

Almost four decades later, Lovell and Prescott provided recollections of the central message of their 1968 paper. According to Prescott (2005a), in the paper, they

> broke from treating the equations governing the evolution of the national account statistics as data tradition … we had rational expectations with regard to "desired capital stock" and examine the mapping from policy rules to statistical properties of the time series.

In his retrospective assessment of the paper, Lovell wrote (2005a):

> I would put a rather different spin on it. Our paper challenged the assertion that the Fed's actions were necessarily destabilizing if it allowed the money supply to move procyclically. To show this in as simple a framework as possible we introduced money into the multiplier-accelerator model of the business cycle. We made the money supply endogenous, the Fed adjusting the money supply in response to movements in GNP. The interest rate was influenced by M, and investment depended in part on the rate of interest. We then showed that one could not say without knowing the parameters of the system what value of the policy parameter would best smooth the cycle (i.e., yield the smallest characteristic root). We then added stochastic shocks to the system and found that the value of the policy parameter minimizing

> the variance of output could not be specified *a priori*. Obviously, this is not RBC Prescott. He had not yet liberated himself from my influence.

To this, Prescott added (2005b):

> I am in basic agreement with Mike on the SEJ paper. But there the idea of evaluating a policy rule by looking at operating characteristics of the model (the model was not an economy so I do not say model economy) was a different way to think about things. Also in the investment equation, there was a future value of a variable. This means that expectations as to this variable had to be formed. One expectation scheme we considered was rational expectations. Except for this the model was in the pre dynamic general equilibrium tradition.

In his recollections, Lovell also described the impact of his 1970 paper with Prescott on his own view of econometric results (2005a):

> Ed and I wrote a second paper, "Multiple Regressions with Inequality Constraints: Pretesting Bias, Hypothesis Testing and Efficiency," (Lovell and Prescott, 1970). We found that dropping variables with incorrect sign from a multiple regression would lead to biased estimates of the parameters of the variables remaining in the model; although the estimates would be efficient *if the* stochastic disturbance was normally distributed. Worse, the statistics could be grossly exaggerated. Partly as a result of this paper, I became more and more disillusioned about the validity of econometric results.

It is not surprising, then, that Prescott would also turn away from empirical econometrics when this outcome was combined with the early impact of the Lucas critique (1973a, b) upon him, as will be seen below.

At this point, a caveat is necessary. Due to its importance as the turning point in the evolution of his thought—on his own account, as will be seen below—Prescott's 1971 paper with Lucas "Investment under uncertainty" will be dealt with after the papers emanating directly from his 1967 dissertation.

Prescott published a paper with the same title as his thesis in the December 1971 issue of *Western Economic Journal*. This paper cites both the unpublished thesis and his forthcoming paper "The multi-period control problem under uncertainty." Both papers indicate that Prescott was starting to think about alternative methods of analysis, albeit still in "the old tradition." In his 1971 paper, Prescott introduced the "concept of experimentation" as an "additional element" (1971, 369–370) and "backward inductions and numerical methods" for two-period analysis (1971, 370–372). He noted that "a more complete analysis of the multi-period control problem" could be found in his forthcoming *Econometrica* paper (1971, 372 note 9; 1972). In the final part of his 1971 paper, Prescott utilized, as a baseline, the small-scale Keynesian econometric model formulated by Chow (1967) to simulate the US economy and assess the outcome of linear as against adaptive—and both against perfect information—decision rules. He found that the outcome of the testing procedure he used clearly demonstrated that the adaptive approach gave superior results in the context of the economies simulated. Prescott concluded that additional research was required, including "how best to approximate policy makers' preference ordering using a quadratic function" (1971, 374–378). The importance of this will be seen below.

Prescott's paper "The multi-period control problem under uncertainty" appeared in the November 1972 issue of *Econometrica.* It was also presented in May 1972 at the first Optimal Control Conference (Chow, 2005). The manuscript was received in December 1970 and its revised version in June 1971 (1972, 1057). This paper constitutes perhaps the earliest application of multi-period control theory to economics (Prescott, 1972, 1043 note 2; Kendrick, 2005a, 18). In this paper, he analyzed the control problem by applying numerical methods and showed, among other points, that "the more periods remaining in the planning horizon, the more important is experimentation" (1972, 1056). Indeed, as Kendrick recently wrote in correspondence (2005b) "Prescott's 1972 paper was one of his most important contributions and one that has not received the attention it deserves."

Lucas and Prescott published their paper "Investment under Uncertainty" in the September 1971 issue of *Econometrica,* although the work had been completed in 1969. This paper, according to Prescott, was also in the pre-transformation tradition. In his words (2004, 373, 2006e) "the macroeconometric models organized the field. Success in macroeconomics was to have your equation incorporated into the macroeconometric models. Indeed, Lucas and I were searching for a better investment equation when in 1969 we wrote our paper..." But more is involved here than simply the search for a "better investment equation." And indeed, in subsequent correspondence, Prescott stated just how his paper with Lucas changed the direction of his thought. He wrote that (2005d):

> Investment under Uncertainty was the paper that led me to work on dynamic equilibrium models of business cycles. After writing that paper in 1969 (it appeared in 1971 after a very long delay subsequent to acceptance), I stopped teaching macro. Another approach was needed. Finn and I developed the needed approach.

The Lucas Critique and its impact upon Prescott and Kydland

At this point, the role of the Lucas Critique has to be taken into account. However, before assessing its impact upon Prescott and Kydland, the evolution of this watershed paper itself must be dealt with. In his Nobel lecture, Prescott indicates that he and Kydland had read the Lucas Critique paper as early as 1973 (2004, 373–374, 2006e). There are, in fact, two drafts of "Econometric Policy Evaluation: A Critique." The first is dated April 1973, and was prepared for the Phillips curve conference, University of Rochester, 20–21 April; the second is the May 1973 revision of the April 1973 paper, which was the version eventually published in 1976. There are differences between the April and May drafts of the Critique, such as changes in the model in the section entitled "Taxation and investment demand," inclusion of responses to discussion at the Rochester Conference, and a specific point made by Prescott. In the April 1973 draft, the section on taxation and investment contains an approach based upon a "standard accelerator model of investment behavior with a cash flow expression incorporating the tax structure, following Jorgenson [1963]," and aggregated from the firm to industry level (Lucas 1973a, 17). The May 1973 revision, which was eventually published in 1976, also has a section entitled "Taxation and investment demand," but the approach is that of a standard accelerator model of investment behavior, based, in part, on Hall and Jorgenson (1967). In recent correspondence, Lucas recalled (2006) that "the later model is an improvement ... the problem here was exposition: How to explain what the point was simply." In the acknowledgements on the title page of the May draft, Lucas thanked Prescott, among others, for "helpful reactions to an earlier draft of his paper." Lucas recalled (2006) that

> It is hard to isolate Ed's influence. He and I had working [*sic.*] out the theory of investment together long before this, so all my thinking on investment was influenced by him. Note 16 in the May version is certainly a response to Ed: He had kidded me about being careless about time units earlier: "If you want a big effect, why not measure time in seconds?"

Moreover, as Lucas also recalled (2006), the concluding paragraphs in the section on Phillips curves in the May draft were "probably added on in response" to the Rochester discussions. In the April 1973 draft, Lucas concluded this section by writing "Evidently, the *actual* [his emphasis] consequences of an increase in π (that is an increase in the average inflation rate...) will have no relation to the long-run prediction based on [equation] (22)" (1973a, 25). In the May 1973 revision, Lucas added two paragraphs to the end of this section. In these he stated the central message of his Critique regarding empirical Phillips curves: first, that the "long run ... relationship as calculated or simulated in the conventional way has *no* bearing on the actual consequences of pursuing a policy of inflation"; second, that "empirical Phillips curves will appear subject to 'parameter drift' ... unpredictable for all but the very near future" (1973b, 29).

Interestingly enough, the importance of detailed textual analysis can also be seen in the January 1976 *Econometrica* paper of Cooley and Prescott, "Estimation in the presence of stochastic parameter variation." A close inspection of this paper shows that the manuscript was originally received in August 1972, before the presentation of the April 1973 draft of the Lucas Critique. The "last revision" was received in November 1974 (1976, 180). This explains the inclusion in the text of the central message of the Lucas Critique (1976a, 167). The reference, however, is not to the published version of the Lucas Critique, but to a "Carnegie-Mellon working paper, 1973" (1976a, 183).

The Lucas Critique impacted upon Prescott even before the April 1973 draft, on Prescott's own account, for, as he recalled (2006a):

> When Bob discussed with me the theme of Econometric Policy Evaluation, (which was when he was orchestrating the theme in his paper) the importance of his insight did not hit me. That was in1972. As soon as I saw the paper, it hit me and hit me hard.

In further correspondence, he wrote (2006c):

> When in 1972 he pointed out to me that the equations of the macro econometric models were not policy invariant, I did not realize the importance of the point. After hearing the Critique presented and reading one of the versions, I realized the importance of the point. We had to do something different to evaluate policy. I did see how to evaluate policy rules in theory at least after hearing the Critique. I did not consider the details of the examples important. The Critique led me to conclude that econometrically, something had to change. Eventually I came to the conclusion that we had to organize our empirical knowledge around preferences and technology, that is people's willingness and ability to substitute and not around equations. Given the policy rule and preferences and technology, economists should compute the equilibrium law of motion for that policy rule.

Moreover, in his Nobel lecture, he wrote (2004, 373, 2006e):

> A key assumption in the system-of-equations approach is that the equations are policy invariant. As Lucas points out in his critique ... this assumption is inconsistent with dynamic economic theory. His insight made it clear that there was no hope for the neo-classical synthesis—that is, the development of neo-classical underpinnings of the system-of-equations macro models. Fortunately, with advances in dynamic economic theory an alternative set of tractable macro models was developed for drawing scientific inference. The key development was recursive competitive equilibrium theory in Lucas and Prescott (1971) and Lucas (1972). Equilibrium being represented as a set of stochastic processes with stationary transition probabilities was crucial to the revolution in macroeconomics.

In an interview (2005), Kydland said that the contribution of Lucas that impacted upon him was Lucas (1973), while for Prescott, it was Lucas (1972). Kydland also maintained that it was "inevitable" that macroeconomics would move away from IS-LM type Keynesian approaches to models based on consumers' and firms' decision making. In this context, he mentioned the textbook by Miller and Upton (1974), which was discussed in Chapter 1, as an example of a macroeconomics textbook *without* IS-LM, and that it represented "macroeconomics at as it *should* be taught" [his emphasis], and consistent with how Lucas, and Miller, "were teaching it at Carnegie." He also said that the "departure from Lucas" manifest in his work with Prescott was the "focus on *quantitative* questions" [his emphasis], and that their modeling method could be used for both short and long run analysis.

The evolutionary story of the overall Kydland–Prescott approach, however, does not end with Lucas and Prescott (1971), Lucas (1973a, b), and the Lucas Critique (1973); rather, *it starts there*. In correspondence, Prescott recalled (2001):

> Kydland in his dissertation (1973) ... extends recursive methods to ... class symmetric dynamic games. This formulation is exploited in Kydland and my paper "Rules rather than discretion: the time inconsistency of optimum plans" (1977a), written 1975 while I was visiting the Norwegian School of Business and Economics and in my and Rajnish Mehra's paper "Recursive competitive equilibrium" (1980).

Kydland, for his part, described his 1973 Carnegie-Mellon thesis entitled "Decentralized macroeconomic planning," which was supervised by Prescott, as placing emphasis on Stackelberg dynamic games, the time inconsistency issue, and player dominance, with the fiscal policy maker dominant, and the monetary policy maker the follower (2005, interview).

However, in order to fully comprehend the evolution of the Kydland–Prescott approach, we must now turn to the phase of transition and transformation—that is, from 1973 to 1978—which encompasses their "search" for dynamic models and rules in order to evaluate policy. For as Prescott said in correspondence (2005d) "Lucas's Critique did influence Finn and me to search for optimal policy rules. This is discussed in my Nobel address." And indeed, in it he wrote (2004, 374; 2006e):

> Finn and I had read the Lucas critique and knew that for dynamic equilibrium models, only policy rules could be evaluated. This led us to search for a best rule to follow, where a rule specifies policy actions as a function of the state or position of the economy. We had worked on this problem before Finn left Carnegie-Mellon to join the faculty of the Norwegian School of Business and Economics in 1973. In academic year 1974–1975 I visited the Norwegian School of Business and Economics, and in the spring of 1975 Finn and I returned to this problem. This is when we wrote our paper "Rules rather than discretion: the inconsistency of optimal plans..."

Kydland and Prescott, then, had read the Lucas Critique in 1973, and by 1975 had written a first draft of their "Rules vs. Discretion" paper, as will be discussed below. But before this, they had to throw off what they considered to be the intellectual blinder of optimal control.

From "optimal stabilization" to "optimal plans"

In late 1973, Ed Prescott compiled a plan of research for his application for a Guggenheim fellowship, entitled "A general equilibrium approach to macroeconomic policy evaluation." In this proposal Prescott stated that he hoped to "develop an *operational* [Prescott's emphasis] procedure for correctly evaluating alternative policies" (1973, 2). He then outlined three steps to accomplish this. The first was based on characterization of preferences and technology via a small number of estimated parameters, utilizing quadratic functions for approximation, so as to ensure optimal linear decision rules for agents. The second step assumed the policy rule—based upon linear state variables—and subsequently quantitatively determining equilibrium decision rules. The final step was to apply the decision and policy rules "to determine the operational characteristics of the economy under that policy" (1973, 2).

Prescott then outlined the "assumed structure of the economy" he intended to set out. In this section, he "emphasized the importance of money" as he had "a price level variable" in his proposed approach (letter to Kydland, 2 January 1974). Prescott went on to describe the work he and his student, Finn Kydland, had done on computational aspects of the analysis he proposed, as manifest in their joint paper entitled "Optimal stabilization: a new approach," which was presented at the June 1973 University of Chicago-NBER conference on "stochastic control." Finally, Prescott described the methods he proposed for analyzing the "stability of equilibrium" and "dynamic stochastic equilibrium," and their relationship to expectations, rules, and plans. The proposal was accepted for a Guggenheim, and formed the basis of his joint proposal with Kydland, which was approved by the Central Bank of Norway. Indeed, Prescott's visit to work with Kydland at the Norwegian School of Economics and Business Administration (NHH) in 1975 resulted in the initial versions of what was later to become their "rules vs. discretion" paper and, eventually, their "Time to build" paper.

The first of the joint Kydland–Prescott papers influenced by the April 1973 Lucas Critique was their paper "Optimal Stabilization: A New Approach," which was presented at the Second NBER-Chicago Stochastic Control conference on 9 June 1973 (Chow and Athans, 1974, 8). As Kydland recalled (2005c):

> Ed and I … [were] influenced by a paper by Lucas in writing our paper for the June 1973 conference in Chicago at which we presented the first draft of the paper, which we started to work on in April 1973 (I remember mainly because we started just before I defended my dissertation).

As Chow recalled (2005):

> There were a number of papers presented in that conference by (at least by now) well-known economists, including Ed Burmeister, J. Philip Cooper, Richard Cyert, Richard Day, Morris DeGroot, Ray Fair, Stan Fischer, David

> Kendrick, Robert Holbrook, Michael Intriligator, Morton Kamien, Robert Pindyck, Gordon Rausser, Steve Ross, Michael Rothschild, Nancy Schwartz, Chris Sims, and John Taylor, among others. The paper by Kydland and Prescott did not seem to stand out among some of these other good papers.

In the 1973 paper, as Kydland later wrote (1975, 334)

> the problem of finding optimal stabilization policies for a competitive economy was formulated as a dominant player stochastic game. The policy-maker is the dominant player, taking into account the reaction functions of economic agents. The results were found to have important implications for econometric policy evaluation.

Kydland also recalled the expositional impact of Lucas's April 1973 draft, writing (2005a): "that paper by Bob already included an investment-tax-credit example, and Ed's and my key example, in both our 1973 paper and later in the rules vs. discretion paper, involved investment tax credit."

Prescott sent the paper to Neil Wallace for comments, and, in a letter dated 3 July 1973, agreed with Wallace's suggestion regarding the nature of the specified tax policy and investment rule, also introducing increasing costs of adjustments, and thereby obtaining a "well behaved equilibrium." The result was that "the rule works poorly relatively to a passive policy when costs of adjustment are small and well when they are large." Prescott went on to write:

> We also plan to illustrate clearly that the industry is in equilibrium if and only if that consumer surplus problem is maximized. In addition, we shall attempt to come to grips with the stability of rational expectations questions. We also plan to change the title to "Optimal stabilization of a competitive economy."

In fact, a revised version of the paper with the title "Optimal Stabilization Policy: a New Formulation" was presented by Prescott at the NBER Rational Expectations Conference, in Cambridge, Massachusetts, 21–22 March 1974, and a month later, at the Fifth Annual Conference on Modeling and Simulation, held in Pittsburgh, 24–26 April 1974 (Prescott to Kydland, 26 April 1974).

The abstract of their March 1974 NBER conference paper consisted of the following paragraphs (NBER Conference Report, 1974, 9–20):

> Current econometric practice is to estimate a set of behavioral equations that constitute a macroeconomic model and then to use these relationships to evaluate alternative policies. Lucas argues that this is inconsistent with economic theory for the following reason: the structure of an econometric model represents the optimal decision rules of economic agents. From dynamic economic theory these optimal decision rules vary systematically with changes in the structure of the series relevant to the decision makers.

> Since changes in policy will systematically alter the structure of the series been forecasted by the agents, they will alter the behavioral relationships as well. If one accepts this argument, which we do, the concept of optimal policy is not at all clear.
>
> We found that attempts at Keynesian stabilization using current policy theory are likely not to have anywhere near the anticipated effect. It is indeed possible that stabilization effects will have the perverse effect of contributing to economic instability. This occurs because the parameters of the decision rules or behavioral relationships vary systematically with the policy rule. Ignoring this fact will result in incorrect evaluation of alternative policy as we illustrated via the investment tax credit example. It was also illustrated how to correctly predict the effect of a policy rule and this problem turns out to be non-trivial. The determination of the optimal policy rule becomes a dynamic stochastic gaming problem between the policymaker maximizing some social objective function and the private competitive sector which behaves as if it were maximizing a particular discounted consumer surplus problem.

Interestingly enough, in this abstract, they cited Lucas's unpublished GSIA Working Paper "Econometric policy evaluation: a critique," which he had presented a year earlier, in April 1973, at the Phillips curve conference held at University of Rochester.

The abstract of the May 1974 version of the Kydland–Prescott paper presented at the Pittsburgh conference was changed to:

> In evaluating alternative investment tax policies, we first determine the unique dynamic stochastic competitive equilibrium associated with a given policy. This analysis is simplified once we observe that the competitive economy behaves as if it were maximizing a particular "consumer surplus" function given the policy rule. This permits us to formulate the problem of optimal policy as a game. The economy maximizes this consumer surplus problem given policy, while the policymaker maximizes some social objective function. Numerical examples are included and it is shown that current approaches to optimal stabilization are inferior and can even contribute to economic instability.
>
> (Pittsburgh Conference, 1974, 217)

In addition, the first paragraph of the March 1974 abstract now became the opening paragraph of the introduction to the May 1974 version of the paper.

According to Shiller's report, Sims and Solow commented on the Kydland–Prescott paper at the March 1974 conference. As he reported (NBER Conference Report, 1974, 10):

> Sims asked what would happen in the case in which the government assumed incorrectly that individuals believed the tax policy was permanent

> if the government repeatedly revised its optimal policy as the investment function changed. Sims said this iterative procedure might converge on the true optimal policy. Solow discussed the estimation of models taking explicit account of the dependence of certain parameters on government policy rules.

But more is involved here than Prescott presenting an early version of his paper with Kydland on optimal stabilization at the March 1974 NBER conference. For this conference—albeit somewhat overlooked—was perhaps one of the most significant meetings of the decade, as it brought together those who would also bring the new classical and real business cycle paradigms into the mainstream of macroeconomics. The conference was organized by Brainard and Modigliani, and the report on it was compiled by Shiller. Among those who attended, gave a paper, commented, and actively participated were: Juster, Hart, Sargent, Wallace, Lucas, Prescott, Ben Friedman, Muth, Barro, Brock, Eisner, Fischer, Iwai, Mussa, Merton, Nelson, Poole, Sims, Solow, and Taylor. Indeed, of the 26 economists who attended, seven went on to become Noble Laureates, and two of the papers, by Sargent and Wallace, and Kydland and Prescott, formed the basis of the path-breaking Sargent–Wallace (1976) and Kydland–Prescott (1977, 1982) papers, respectively.

Some six months earlier, Prescott had actually sent the first version of the paper to *RES* (Prescott to Kydland, 12 October 1973). The reaction of the *RES* referee was not positive, to say the least. This is manifest in a letter to Kydland dated 18 July 1974 in which Prescott wrote: "Enclosed is a copy of the referee's comments, Sims letter and my letter to Sims. People sure get emotional in this macro policy area." In retrospect, however, the comments of the *RES* referee may have actually been instrumental in bringing about a synthesis between this paper and earlier work by Prescott, culminating in both "rules vs. discretion" and "Time to build." For, as Prescott continued in his letter to Kydland of 18 July 1974:

> My first thoughts are that we should (1) pull out some of the material in my "money, etc." paper, really laying out the problem of computing the equilibrium given policy; (2) layout the gaming policy in excruciating detail with computational detail specified; and (3) develop a general equilibrium example with lots of state variables but *no* money [Prescott's emphasis]. The paper will be a longer but better one.

Prescott's April 1974 paper was entitled "Money, expectations and the business cycle." This paper, "written for discussion only" (Prescott,1974) was presented by Prescott "in the fall of 1974" at the Norwegian School of Business and Economics, which, as noted above, he visited in 1974–1975 (2005e). On the title page, Prescott said that the paper represented "work in progress." In the introduction, he outlined the "*operational* framework" [his emphasis] he wanted to develop. This involved the utilization of "a dynamic general equilibrium framework, in its true sense"

(1974, 1). Prescott went on, in a note, to refer to both the 1973 version of Lucas's Critique, and also his 1973 paper with Kydland, cited above (1974, 2). As he wrote "Kydland and Prescott [1973] used this approach [i.e. the analysis and evaluation of "policy *rules*" (his emphasis) which specify, as he put it "a vector of policy variables ... as a function of state variables (and possibly lagged variables)] to evaluate investment tax credit policies . ." (1974, 2).

Following from his Guggenheim Plan of Research, Prescott's April 1974 paper can be said to have set out a dual purpose research agenda. This is seen in his statement of "goals" and again in his summary and conclusions. As he put it, these goals were "(1) to develop a theory of the business cycle which is a competitive equilibrium ... and (2) to develop operational procedures to evaluate alternative stabilization policy rules" (1974, 19). He also talked about the relationship between the "business cycle application" and a "full employment path, which can be determined using optimal growth theory" (1974, 18) and the need for "methods ... to compute the competitive equilibrium" (1974, 19). He then presented as an example of the proposed approach a model including a production function with a technology shift parameter, capital stock equations, a utility function for preferences, policy functions, and an objective function; the model also included state and decision variables (1974, 20–21). He went on to say "there is a need for developments which permit the direct calculation of the competitive equilibrium for structures of reasonable complexity" (1974, 24). Finally, Prescott concluded (1974, 25) "In summary, this is but a first step towards the development of a theory of the business cycle and an operational framework for correctly evaluating stabilization policy. Much research remains to be done."

Kydland's early contributions

In a series of conference presentations and published papers over the period 1974–1977, and based upon his own 1973 dissertation "Decentralized macroeconomic planning," Kydland dealt with, among other issues, the question of whether "decentralized policy-making" could be considered "as a dynamic game": for example, in his June 1975 *IER* paper (1975, 334) (received March 1974, revised August 1974).

The same year, 1975, according to his own recollections, Kydland submitted his "assignment problem paper ["Decentralized stabilization policies: optimization and the assignment problem"] to a stochastic control conference to take place in Boston in May" (Kydland, Nobel autobiography, 2005). According to the conference program, as reported in the Spring 1976 issue *Annals of Social and Economic Measurement*, this was the paper that was listed in the May 1975 conference program (Chow, 2005). And indeed, the "assignment problem" paper was published in 1976 in the *Annals*. However, as Kydland recalled:

> At some point early in the conference, Gregory Chow announced a session for work in progress. I signed up to talk about Ed's and my paper, and was told I could go first. All hell broke loose. Everyone was trying to locate the

> error [time inconsistency]. Admittedly, we had chosen a rather provocative title for our first draft: "On the inapplicability of optimal control for policy-making". I was certain nothing was wrong. With all my experience in dynamic dominant-player games, I knew time inconsistency had to be an issue. I suppose at that point, after what happened at that presentation, I realized our findings could generate considerable attention. Moreover, as a consequence of the difficulty people had in understanding the time inconsistency, we decided to add, for expository reasons, a Phillips-curve example to our investment-tax-credit example before we submitted our revised version of the paper to the *Journal of Political Economy*. As I recall, it was motivated by a model in a recent paper by Phelps and Taylor. Of course, that example has turned out to be used a lot by subsequent writers.
>
> (Kydland, Nobel Autobiography, 2005)

Kendrick, for his part (2005a, 15) recalled that Kydland's "talk at the meeting was well attended and listened to carefully." According to Kendrick, this talk, in conjunction with the Lucas Critique, brought about a situation in which

> work on control theory models in general and stochastic control models in particular went into rapid decline and remained that way for a substantial time … the work on uncertainty (other than additive noise terms) in macroeconomic policy mostly stopped and then slowly was replaced with methods of solving models with rational expectations and with game theory approaches.
>
> (2005a, 15)

Kendrick qualified this (2005a, 15 note 6), however, by referring to exceptions in papers by Turnovsky and Brock (1980, 1981).

In March 1975, while at the Norwegian School of Economics and Business Administration, Kydland circulated a discussion paper entitled "Equilibrium solutions in dynamic dominant-player models," which was eventually published in *JET* in August 1977. Kydland referred to this paper in his 1976 paper "Decentralized stabilization policies: optimization and the assignment problem," published in *Annals of Social and Economic Measurement*, as noted above, and this discussion paper was also referred to by Kydland and Prescott in their June 1977 *JPE* "Rules vs. Discretion" paper.

From "inconsistency of optimal policy" to "time inconsistency"

Preliminary versions of Kydland and Prescott's paper "The inconsistency of optimal policy" were presented at the Chicago Money Workshop, the Mathematical Economics Seminar at Cambridge, at Rotterdam, Oslo, Copenhagen, and the Stockholm School of Economics prior to June 1975 (1975a). It was then issued as a discussion paper by the Norwegian School of Economics and Business Administration in June 1975 (1975b). These versions were based upon a synthesis of Prescott's "money etc." and the Kydland–Prescott "optimal stabilization" papers, following from Prescott's letter to Kydland of 18 July 1974. A comparison of these with the 1975 drafts of the "inconsistency of optimal policy" (1975a, b) and the subsequent "Rules vs. Discretion" (1975c, 1977) papers is presented below, in the framework of the correspondence between Prescott and Kydland regarding the drafts and changes in them. This will enable us to understand how their watershed 1977 *JPE* paper evolved.

Variorum drafts of "inconsistency of optimal policy," "rules vs. discretion," and correspondence between Prescott and Kydland, 1975

In a letter to Kydland, then at the Norwegian School of Economics in Bergen, dated 2 June 1975, Prescott wrote "Our paper went over very well in both Oslo and Rotterdam and OK in Copenhagen." He then made a number of points regarding possible revisions. Among them was adding references to Eisner and Strotz (1963) and Lucas (1967a, b). Interestingly enough, foreshadowing the link between "Time Inconsistency" and "Time to build," Prescott said that "Leif Johansson mentioned that our lag assumptions is related to ones made by Frisch in analyzing business cycle phenomena." But more was involved in the process of revising the paper from its preliminary version to that circulated in June 1975. They significantly amended the introduction to their "inconsistency of optimal policy" paper. The introduction to the "preliminary draft" was as follows:

> Many have proposed the application of "control theory" to dynamic economic systems. The plan selected is the one which yields the best path of outcomes, or distribution of paths if there is uncertainty, relative to some agreed upon fixed objective function, *given the current situation* [their emphasis]. If agents' current decisions depend upon their expectations of future events and these expectations are not invariant to the plan selected, the optimal plan, typically, will be inconsistent in the sense that it will not be optimal to continue with the original plan in subsequent periods. Only if there is an appropriate set of public ethics or institutional arrangements to ensure that policy plans will be followed can the objective function be maximized.
>
> In this paper we explain why the optimal plans are inconsistent for both finite and infinite period planning problems, and then consider in detail the implications of this result for stabilization policy. We also mention briefly the implications for such issues as flood control and patent policy. It should be clear that the results of this paper are applicable to a host of problems of economic planning. We demonstrate that if at each stage the best decision is selected *given future policies* [their emphasis], plans will be consistent but suboptimal.
>
> The major point of this paper is that optimal control theory is not the appropriate tool for dynamic economic planning. It is inappropriate because

> current decisions of economic agents depend directly or indirectly upon future policy decisions. Control theory, which takes as given past decisions, ignores the effect of future policies upon current agents' decisions. An alternative to control theory is to rely on policy rules which have good operating characteristics. In effect, this is an argument for rules rather than discretion, but unlike Friedman's [1948] argument, it does not rely on policy makers being ignorant of the structure.

The introduction to the June 1975 version of "the inconsistency of optimal policy" was changed and read as follows:

> Optimal control theory is a powerful and useful technique for analyzing dynamic systems. At each point in time the decision selected is best given the current situation and given that decisions will be similarly selected in the future. Many have proposed its application to dynamic economic planning. The thesis of this essay is that it is not the appropriate tool for economic planning even when there is a well defined and agreed upon fixed social objective function.
>
> We find that a discretionary policy for which policymakers select the best action given the current situation will not typically result in the social objective function being maximized. Rather, by relying on some policy rules, economic performance can be improved. In effect this is an argument for rules rather than discretion but, unlike Friedman's [1948] argument, it does not depend upon ignorance of the timing and magnitude of the effects of policy.
>
> The reasons for this nonintuitive result are as follows: Optimal control theory is an appropriate planning device for situations in which current outcomes and the movement of the system's state depends only on current and past policy decisions and upon the current state. But, we argue, this is unlikely to be the case for dynamic economic systems. Current decisions of economic agents depend in part upon their expectations of future policy actions. Only if these expectations were invariant to the future policy plan selected would optimal control theory be appropriate. In situations where the structure is well understood, agents will surely surmise the way policy will be selected in the future. Changes in the social objective function reflected in, say, a change of administration, do have an immediate effect upon agents' expectations of future policies and affect their current decisions. This is inconsistent with the assumptions of optimal control theory. This is not to say that agents can forecast future policies perfectly. All that is needed for our argument is that agents have *some* [their emphasis] knowledge of how policy makers' decisions will change as a result of changing economic conditions. For example, agents may expect tax rates to be lowered in recessions and increased in booms.
>
> The problem also arises in situations where the underlying economic structure is not well understood, which is surely now the case for aggregate

economic analysis. Standard practice is to estimate an econometric model and then, at least informally, to use optimal control theory techniques to determine policy. But as Lucas [1975] has argued, since econometric models consist of economic agents' optimal decision rules, changes in policy will systematically alter the structure of econometric models. Thus changes in policy induce changes in structure which in turn necessitate reestimation and future changes in policy, and so on. We found for some not implausible structures that this iterative procedure does not converge and instead stabilization efforts have the perverse effect of contributing to economic instability. For most examples, however, it did converge and the resulting policy was consistent, but sub-optimal. It was consistent in the sense that at each point in time the policy selected was best given the current situation. In effect the policy maker is failing to take into account the effect of his policy rule upon the optimal decision rules of the economic agents.

In this paper, we first defined consistent policy and explain for the two-period problem why the consistent policy is suboptimal. The implications of the analysis are then considered for patent policy and flood-control problems for which consistent policy procedures are not ever seriously considered. Consistency for infinite period recursive economic structures is then considered. In equilibrium optimizing agents follow rules which specify current decisions as a function of the current state [new note 1, discussed below, added here by Kydland and Prescott]. Methods are developed for computing these equilibrium decision rules for certain specialized structures. The methods are used to evaluate alternative investment tax credit policies designed both to stabilize and to yield optimal taxation. Among the policies evaluated is the suboptimal consistent policy. Within the class of feedback policy rules we found that the optimal one depended upon the initial conditions. Thus it was not optimal to continue with the initial policy in subsequent periods, or, in other words, policy was inconsistent.

As mentioned above, an additional footnote was added to the final paragraph of the June 1975 introduction (1975b, 24 note 1):

> The ex-ante motivation for this paper was to apply optimal control theory methods to structures with rational expectations to find the consistent policy. We knew it was not optimal but felt consistency was essential and assumed that the consistent policy would be nearly optimal. Future analyses, motivated in part by Chris Sims' criticisms of our first approach, led us to the conclusion that the inconsistency of optimal policy is a serious dilemma.

Other changes were made in the June 1975 version of the paper. A formal definition of consistent policy was added, and following from this, the first order condition for the optimal decision rule was also redefined (1975b, 3–4).

The revision of the June 1975 version was issued as Carnegie-Mellon GSIA Working Paper 27–75–76 in October 1975, entitled "Rules Rather than

Discretion: The Inconsistency of Optimal Plans." Below, we detail the evolution of the October 1975 version of the paper which was that submitted for publication in the *Journal of Political Economy*, and published in 1977.

From "optimal policy" to "rules vs. discretion": Prescott–Kydland correspondence, June–October 1975

Over the period June–October 1975, Prescott and Kydland exchanged ideas on how to revise and improve their paper. Prescott was traveling in Europe, and returned to Carnegie-Mellon University, while Kydland, at the time, was at the Norwegian School of Economics and Business Administration. In his letter to Kydland of 2 June 1975, Prescott suggested:

> Let's give stability another try *once you have this paper out of the way* [his emphasis] and let's focus on convergence in the decision rule space. *Given* the aggregate investment function one finds the optimal firm. That is given
>
> $X = D_n(Y, Z)$
>
> One finds best d
>
> $X = d_n(y, Y, Z)$
>
> given that $Y' = F(X, Y)$ and $Z' = \Omega(Z, \xi)$. Now
>
> $D_{n+1}(Y, Z) = D_n(Y, Z) + \lambda\{d_n(y, Y, Z) - D_n(Y, Z)\}$
>
> By making λ sufficiently small I assume (given equilibrium exists) that D_n will converge.

Prescott's suggestion appeared, in modified form, in the appendix to the October 1975 revision in the section "Stability of competitive equilibrium."

In his replies to Prescott's letter of 2 June, dated 11 and 13 June, sent from Bergen, Kydland acknowledged that he was starting to revise the draft. Prescott replied on 3 July, writing from Carnegie-Mellon: "I agree with your general comments and there are some other revisions I think should be made.... Let's wait until you get here before we make the final set of revisions." On 22 August, Prescott again wrote Kydland: "Enclosed is a rough draft of the first three sections. Please revise, polish, extend, etc., and get the material back to me as soon as possible." On 4 September 1975, Kydland replied to Prescott:

> Enclosed is rewritten draft of the first two sections. The main correction I've suggested is in section 2 after the definition. I also enclose a copy of section 3 with some suggested corrections. The example is very nice. Possibly the exposition is not as clear as it might have been, but I'm not sure how to improve on it. I'll think some more about it.

A week later, on 12 September, Kydland sent a letter to Prescott, from Bergen, detailing what he had done up to that point:

> I thought I'd give you a little progress report. Progress has been slower than hoped for due to slowness of the computer after the semester start, along with the fact that I had to prepare lectures in monetary economics ... I have run quite a few examples by now, and guess I could have used a couple of them, although they always seem to have one feature or other that I don't like.
>
> I did make the necessary modifications in our original example to make it correct ... The same conclusions can be drawn as before. In fact, the example is now nicer ... I thought about making the necessary changes so that we had reasonably correct version to send to people before we get the next one ready. By the way, I wish I had your comments on this section in the original version. The section will be substantially reordered and rewritten, but the comments could still be of help.
>
> I got a letter from Leif Johansen (in Norwegian) commenting on our paper. A quick translation: "I will mention the reaction that I thought the problem is posed in a way which is too 'provocative'. Wouldn't it be worth investigating how the problem would be formulated and solved if one introduced a variable representing expectations of future decisions? One would then, of course, have to introduce functions telling how these expectations depend on previous and current decisions. When the future decision is made it does not, of course, have to be equal to the expected, but a decision maker could have a term and preference function which depends on the possible deviation. Such variables are, of course, not very hard and fast compared to the other components of the model, but as far as I understand they are implicit in the reasoning of the manuscript, and as long as the primary point is to make the principles clear, then why not include these variables and functions explicitly? What is gained by this is that one does not have to include functions telling how the decisions of decision makers today depend on future decisions of other decision makers, which may look a little artificial. Furthermore, I think that in this case, there would not be such a paradoxical difference between what is called the consistent plan and optimal decisions. Also, the main question may then no longer be whether control theory is or is not an appropriate tool for the analysis". Well, I can see many people making comments of this sort, but I think that the new introduction, and in particular the section on the Phillips curve, are very clarifying on this point.

Prescott replied a week later, on 18 September and asked:

> Where are the revised section 5 (the investment-tax-credit example) and the appendix? I will be presenting this paper at Colombia in late October and want the working paper out by then.

> Enclosed are further revisions of the first four sections. I think it is close to being a final draft. Please proof it carefully being particularly certain that tenses are used consistently.

He ended his letter by asking:

> What is your reaction to the title "Rules rather than discretion: The inconsistency of Optimal Plans"?

On 25 September, Kydland responded:

> I can understand that you're anxiously waiting for section 5. However I've had certain problems coming up with what he wanted, in addition to having to contend with slowness getting jobs through…
>
> I have run quite a few examples by now but they always seem to have one feature or other that I don't like.

Kydland gave some computational results and then said:

> Given the time constraint, I'll use what I have now and get it typed as soon as possible so that you can comment. However, since I'll keep on working after that, I'd be interested in any comments you might have based on this letter.
>
> Actually I was kind of waiting for the new section 4 because you had talked about rewriting it and moving some of the stuff from later sections into it. I see now that it is essentially unchanged.

Prescott replied on 2 October:

> I feel little guilty about pressuring you … The more I talk to people about our analysis the better it sounds. In the conclusion I am thinking of summarizing things by arguing if policymakers use utility functions to rationalize private agents' choice and to predict how they will behave in alternative situations, then isn't it reasonable for agents to use utility functions to rationalize policy selections and to predict what policy or policy rule will be followed in the future? If so, our radical conclusions that the current theory of optimal economic policy is invalid follows. Gaming theory not control theory constitutes the appropriate conceptual framework for policy selection. This gets around Johansen's criticism.
>
> The examples you have worked out sound very good … We … have an excellent paper which I think should attract considerable attention.
>
> If you want to rewrite section 4 by moving stuff into it, go ahead.

Kydland's initial reply to Prescott's letter of 2 October was dated 6 October. In this he wrote:

> I wanted to get the stuff off before the weekend ... I have made a copy of the first four sections so that my own comments are easily distinguishable from yours...
>
> I think the title is fine. It will probably cause some people to get interested in the paper, which is a good reason to change the title.
>
> I did not have time to polish the presentation of section 5 ... I was quite happy with Example 1, although you may disagree with the presentation, of course. Also please be critical of the presentation of the model as well.
>
> I realized I had forgotten the footnotes, so I'll send them along too.

Four days later, on 10 October, Kydland, still in Bergen, wrote Prescott again:

> I agree with your suggested comments for the conclusion to get around Leif Johansen's criticism.
>
> I haven't experimented any with the theoretical model of Section 5. There were a couple of alternative ways of formulating it that would lead to the same numerical results, and you may prefer a different one than the one I've chosen. Maybe you'd like to make the point about the separability in the value function of the influence of depreciation for tax purposes, for example in footnote 9. Anyway, I'll think some more about whether the model can be improved while keeping within our framework...
>
> Gary Becker visited us last week and gave a talk in our staff seminar. He told me he had looked at our paper, and my impression was that one of the reasons was that you're among the people they might try to get to Chicago. Maybe you should send him a copy of the revised version, and if you need an excuse, you can tell them I asked you to.

Two weeks later, on 23 October, Prescott replied:

> Here is an almost final draft. Before submitting I will await your corrections and revisions. I would like to submit the paper to the JPE because that journal has a large audience and should not be hostile to the views presented. In reading through the paper, I think we make a strong case.

On 4 November, Kydland replied:

> Enclosed are my corrections. You should check them to see if you agree. Some of them are not all that essential. For instance, to be consistent I've omitted all the equation numbers that are never referenced elsewhere in the paper.
>
> I have to inform you that the reference to me on page 22 is not entirely accurate. I do not take up the problem particularly for an oligopoly model in that paper. The results I had showing a big increase of profits for the closed vs. the feedback solution were obtained after I wrote the paper and were

> really meant for a different paper specifically on oligopoly theory which so far exists only as a preliminary draft. On the other hand, it would be natural to mention the results in reference [9] too, which is due for a revision now. If you think this is a sufficient basis on which to refer to the paper in that context, that's OK with me.

Some six weeks later, on 17 December Kydland wrote Prescott:

> I got the final version of the paper, and it looks fine. The additional references were quite appropriate. Unfortunately, I have not yet received the paper by Phelps and Taylor that I wrote for in September. I guess I'll try Taylor instead.
>
> Have you sent a copy to David Kendrick? I sent one to Leif Johansen, whose name is still misspelled in the footnote on the first page.

Kydland also listed a number of additional minor corrections.

Two weeks later, on 29 December, Prescott replied: "A copy of our paper has been sent to Kendrick and I will make the corrections you listed in your recent letter ... Our paper was well received at both Columbia and Rochester."

On 21 May 1976, Prescott wrote Kydland: "I heard from the JPE that they had trouble with the first referee who felt he was not qualified to referee it. We should hear soon." Two weeks later, on 4 June, Prescott again wrote Kydland to report: "Good news (see enclosures). Please have your input to me by the end of June (I will be away until June 26). I will then make my revisions and will forward them to you for final approval." On 22 June, Kydland replied to Prescott regarding the referee's reports:

> Just a few comments on the referee's reports before I leave [for the University of Minnesota]. So far I haven't had time to think about other changes than what concerns the numerical examples. It seems to me, that there are basically three alternative routes to follow (in order of decreasing drasticness):
>
> 1 Omit the examples entirely. This would cut the paper in half, as the Appendix would have to go as well. I still think the examples add enough to make this route undesirable.
> 2 Keep the first example, and just say a few words about the other two. The description of the model and Example 1 could also be shortened, like omitting the variance component business and possibly other things, keeping the essentials.
> 3 Keep all the examples, but shorten the exposition. Because the variance component is essential for Example 3, this also means that Example 1 could not be shortened by as much as under alternative two.
>
> It seems to me that something like alternative 2 above is the way to go. At least until I hear from you, I'll work on that basis. I'll also see if the

> Appendix can be shortened. By the way, it seems difficult to take account of comment 4 of the second referee while at the same time keeping the paper short. We still need the behavioral relations and identities laid out. Besides, I don't see what paradoxes there are to eliminate. I think our exposition is at about the appropriate level to make it available to a wide audience (which is what we want, right?).
>
> I'll leave section 3 to you. By the way, I still haven't got the paper from Phelps and Taylor (even though I asked for it last fall).

A fortnight later, on 2 July, Kydland again wrote Prescott in answer to the latter's phone call: "Enclosed is a revised version of pages 16–22 and the last page of the footnotes. I've tried to cut as much as I could (perhaps too much). Please read carefully and make whatever changes you think are appropriate." About a month later, on 11 August, Prescott wrote Kydland, who was by then at the University of Minnesota: "Enclosed is a revised version. We are not locked into the presentation—it is just a try." Two months later, in a letter dated 19 October 1976, Prescott wrote Kydland: "Enclosed is a copy of a letter from the JPE. Our paper appears January 1977."

"Time inconsistency": the June and October 1975 drafts and *JPE* 1977 version

The Kydland–Prescott paper actually appeared in the June 1977 issue of *Journal of Political Economy*. A comparison between the June and October 1975 drafts and the 1977 published version reflects the results of the intensive revision process described in the Prescott–Kydland correspondence cited above. There were major changes in and elisions of wording, text, tables, and examples in the body of the paper, the appendix, the notes, and the references.

For example, the term "problem" was replaced by "paradox" between the June and October versions (1975a, b, 2; 1977, 474). There was a significant change in text between the June and October 1975 drafts in the last paragraph of the introduction that also appeared in the published version. The June 1975 version read (1975a, 2):

> In this paper we first define consistent policy and explain for the two-period problem why the consistent policy is suboptimal. The implications of the analysis are then considered for patent policy and flood control problems for which consistent policy procedures are not ever seriously considered. Consistency for infinite period recursive economic structures is then considered. In equilibrium, optimizing agents follow rules which specify current decisions as a function of the current state. Methods are developed for computing these equilibrium decision rules for certain specialized structures. The methods are used to evaluate alternative investment tax credit policies designed both to stabilize and to yield optimal taxation. Among the policies evaluated is the suboptimal consistent policy. Within the class of feedback

> policy rules we found that the optimal one depended upon the initial conditions. Thus it was not optimal to continue with the initial policy in subsequent periods, or, in other words, policy was inconsistent.

In the October 1975 version the following sentences were added between "the implications of the analysis..." and "Consistency for infinite period..." (1975b, 3):

> Then for the aggregate demand management problem it is shown that the application of optimal control theory is equally absurd, at least if expectations are rational. Doing what is best given the current situation results in an excessive level of inflation but unemployment is no lower than it would be if inflation (possibly deflation or price stability) was at the socially optimal rate.

This reflected the addition of "The Inflation-Unemployment Example" (1975b, 8–10). The 1977 version included the additional text accordingly (1977a, 475).

Other significant changes were the inclusion of new subsections entitled "Uncertainty" and "The Inflation-Unemployment Example" in the October 1975 version, as noted—although the "Uncertainty" subsection was actually elided in the 1977 published version (1975b, 7–11; 1977, 477–480). Other additions to the 1977 published text included the statement (1977, 477): "In other words, economic theory is used to predict the effects of alternative policy rules, and one with good operating characteristics is selected." A long footnote was added in the October 1975 version and also appeared in the published version (1975b, 31 note 4; 1977, 481 note 5):

> Optimal policy refers to the best policy, assuming that exists, within a certain class of policies. Within the class of linear feedback rules $\Pi\,(y_t)$, we found that the best policy rule depended upon the initial condition. The most general class of decision policies are characterized by a sequence of probability measures indexed by the history $\{\Pi_t\,(x^t, \pi^t, y^t)\}$, with the superscripted variables denoting all previously observed values of the variables. It was necessary to consider probability distributions because for some games randomized strategy will be optimal and not dominated by a deterministic one. For games against nature, only deterministic strategies need be considered.

Text was elided and replaced between the June and October 1975 versions, and then became footnotes in the published version (1975a, 10–13; 1975b, 16–18; 1977, 483 note 7), and some equations were changed between the June and October versions (1975a, 12; 1975b, 17). Moreover, Tables 1, 2 and 4 were totally changed between the June and October 1975 versions, with the text of "Examples" also changed (1975a, 13–16; 1975b, 18–22). More significantly, Tables 1 and 2, which appeared in the October 1975 version, were elided in the published 1977 version of the paper.

The "Discussion" section was changed almost completely between the June and October versions (1975a, 17; 1975b, 22–23); the October version of that section appeared in the 1977 version. The wording of the "Summary and Conclusions," however, was *not* changed between the June and October 1975 and the 1977 published versions (1975a, 18–19; 1975b, 23–24; 1977, 486–87). There were also minor changes to the Appendix. For example, a section on "Computations for the infinite period problem" was added in the October 1975 version, which also appeared in the published version. The "Notes" section saw changes between the June 1975 version as mentioned above, with changes in text and the addition of footnote 11 in the October 1975 version. Finally, references were added to the October 1975 version which also appeared in the published version, including Haavelmo (1960), Gould (1968), Lucas (1967a, b), Phelps and Taylor (1975), Sargent (1973), Taylor (1975), and Treadway (1969).

Dynamic optimal taxation

A somewhat lesser-known paper that flowed out of the Kydland–Prescott research program was on dynamic optimal taxation and rational expectations. In a paper dated November 1977 and revised in May 1978, entitled "Rational expectations, dynamic optimal taxation and the inapplicability of optimal control," they first distinguished between the "behavioral" and "maximizing rational expectations" approaches. They examined the issue of "optimal policy selection" in the context of a "rational expectations competitive equilibrium framework" by examining optimal taxation. The August 1979 version of the paper was published in JEDC in 1980, under a slightly different title. A comparison of the 1978 revised paper and the 1980 published paper shows that while there are formal changes in the text, the published version places much more emphasis on the implications of time inconsistency for "optimal policy plan" in general, and "optimal taxation" in particular (1980d, 80). Indeed, they wrote that despite the issue of time inconsistency, they thought that optimal policy determination was still an interesting problem (1980d, 80).

From "Time inconsistency" to "Time to build"

The "key example" in their seminal 1977 paper, as Kydland put it, was the "investment-tax-credit example." What is important to realize is that this example encompasses a "two-period time to build approach" reflecting "the fact that time is required to expand capacity, and investment expenditures occur over the entire time interval" (1977a, 482), as recognized by both Kydland (2005b, interview) and Prescott (2006d). This is a crucial point in the evolution of the Kydland–Prescott approach, for it illustrates the inherent linkage between their 1977 and 1982 papers.

In recent correspondence (2006d), Prescott has also stressed the dynamic general equilibrium nature of the "Rules vs. discretion" paper. After acknowledging that the investment-tax-credit example did "exploit the rental price of capital theory of Jorgenson and of Jorgenson and Hall," he continued on to say

> but what is important is that it exploits the theory developed in "Investment under uncertainty" to derive the equilibrium process given the policy rule. Unlike Bob's [Lucas] "Neutrality" paper, there is capital accumulation so it was truly dynamic. Lucas comes up with the mapping from an investment tax policy rule to the equilibrium process of the economy ... Finn and my analysis introduces maximizing households, so we have a dynamic general equilibrium analysis.

What is the "formal" linkage between the "Time Inconsistency" and "Time to build" papers? In the conclusion of "Time Inconsistency," Kydland–Prescott state the following (1977a, 486–487):

> We have argued that control theory is not the appropriate tool for dynamic economic planning. It is not the appropriate tool because current decisions of economic agents depend upon expected future policy, and these expectations are not invariant to the plans selected...
>
> The structures considered are far from a tested theory of economic fluctuations, something which is needed before policy evaluation is undertaken. The implication of this analysis is that, until we have such a theory, active stabilization may very well be dangerous and it is best that it not be attempted. Reliance on policies such as a constant growth in the money supply and constant tax rates constitute a safer course of action.
>
> When we do have the prerequisite understanding of the business cycle, the implication of our analysis is that policymakers should follow rules rather than have discretion...
>
> If we are not to attempt to select policy optimally, how should it be selected? Our answer is, as Lucas (1976) proposed, that economic theory be used to evaluate alternative policy rules and that one with good operating characteristics be selected.

In their 1977 paper, Kydland and Prescott show that rules rather discretion are optimal in dynamic environments when agents form expectations about future policy rules, asserting that stabilization policy must be based upon on a "tested theory of economic fluctuations." In their 1982 paper, they construct a model which they test by matching the moments with the data. The policy implication of "Time to build" is that observed fluctuations are due to the dynamic response of a market economy to technology shocks. In their 1982 model, there is no role for discretionary fiscal or monetary policy, and the observed fluctuations are not due to such factors. Their 1977 paper says that such discretionary policy is sub-optimal. So how should optimal policy—which must be rule-based—be determined? In their view, this must be determined via examining the quantitative implications of different theoretical models. In other words, their 1977 paper contains the "core" of their research program, and also fits in with the Lucas critique and the role of rules versus discretion.

The 1978 NBER "Bald Peak" conference paper

The transitional phase in the development of the Kydland–Prescott approach reached its penultimate stage with the presentation of a paper by Kydland and Prescott at the 1978 NBER conference on rational expectations and economic policy. The story surrounding this watershed paper is enigmatic, to say the least. This is because those who attended the conference and commented, or who commented in correspondence with the authors on the paper, such as Fischer Black, did not realize its significance, as will be seen below; this is not unique, as the same phenomenon occurred when Muth's original Rational Expectations paper was presented at an Econometric Society meeting in December 1959 (see Young and Darity, 2001). Moreover, the evolution of the 1978 conference paper itself, from its initial form, through the draft presented at the conference, to its final published version in the 1980 NBER Conference volume, is a key element in the "Time to Build" story.

In order to understand the importance of this paper in the ongoing intellectual process that culminated in the 1982 "Time to Build" paper, however, we must first turn to how Lucas—and Kydland—perceived what occurred at the conference where the Kydland–Prescott paper on "Stabilization Policy" was given. There are two versions of Lucas's recollections regarding the NBER conference held at the Bald Peak Colony Club, New Hampshire, October 1978 (Fischer, 1980). In his "Professional Memoir," Lucas wrote (2001, 28):

> At that conference, Ed Prescott presented a model of his and Finn Kydland's that was a kind of mixture of Brock and Mirman's model of growth subject to stochastic technology shocks and my model of monetary shocks. When Ed presented his results, everyone could see they were important but the paper was so novel and complicated that no one could see exactly what they were. Later on, as they gained more experience through numerical simulations of their Bald Peak model, Kydland and Prescott found that monetary shocks were just not pulling their weight: By removing all monetary aspects of the theory, they obtained a far simpler and more comprehensible structure that fit postwar U.S. time series just as well as the original version. Besides introducing an important substantive refocusing of business cycle research, Kydland and Prescott introduced a new style of comparing theory to evidence that has had an enormous, beneficial effect on empirical work in the field.

Lucas published "Present at the creation: reflections on the 2004 Nobel Prize to Finn Kydland and Edward Prescott" in the *Review of Economic Dynamics* (2005). Lucas wrote (2005, 777):

> The first public presentation of "Time to build..." occurred at an Oct. 1978 conference sponsored by the Federal Reserve Bank of Boston. You might picture the scene as something like the New York appearance of King Kong,

> when the theater curtain is drawn and the 40-foot ape is revealed, struggling with his chains. But it was nothing like that. The paper … was too hard to be read in advance, and Ed's presentation was technical and confusing.

He continued (2005, 778):

> I should say that this paper was not the version that was published in Econometrica in 1982. The 1978 version had a kind of nominal wage stickiness, related to my 1972 information-based model (Lucas 1972). This feature is now interesting mainly as evidence that Ed and Finn did not start out by attempting to show that business cycles were real in origin or that monetary influences were unimportant. Their substantive aims at the time were pretty standard. But their methods were brand new, and it was only after much experimentation with the model that they were led to the *discovery* [his emphasis] that the real, technology shocks were doing all the work, and the sticky wage part was contributing nothing.

In his Nobel autobiography, Kydland also recalled events surrounding the 1978 NBER conference paper. As he put it (2005, autobiography):

> For an NBER conference in 1978, we wrote a paper that was somewhat schizophrenic. It contained a business cycle model, but also evaluated stabilization policy. The main idea behind the latter was that changes in taxes were costly as a way to balance the government budget over the cycle. Instead the "slack" should be picked up by fluctuations in government debt. In the end, we were asked to reduce the length of the paper for the resulting conference volume published by the NBER in 1980, and we had to leave out much of that material.

Detailed comments on the Kydland–Prescott conference paper were made by Feldstein, Hall, and Taylor, and published in the conference volume (1980, 187–194). The general discussion appearing in the volume also cited comments by Blinder and Nelson, among others.

Nelson, for his part, had perhaps the clearest recollections of the NBER conference, while also making significant comments on the Kydland–Prescott paper. As he recalled (2002):

> It was a great conference and I remember the general scene vividly (including noticing that Paul Samuelson was reading the St. Louis Fed weekly newsletter on money supply, and it had his name as addressee on it!). I can't really say that I recall the Kydland–Prescott paper making a splash, but we all had our personal reaction. Mine was that sources of lags they mention, particular [*sic*] time to build, did not seem sufficient to account for the very great persistence of business cycle fluctuations as implied by their AR equation on page 171 [of the conference volume]. My comment is directed to the

> fact that the sum of coefficients is quite close to unity, so in light of the Dickey–Fuller problem of downward bias (which I was working on at the time in connection with the Nelson–Plosser paper), it is not clear that the sum is significantly below unity. The Nelson–Plosser view was that if it is unity than the cycle is not just long-lived but possibly not stationary. Of course, what we argued in our paper was that the unit root—sum equal to one—could not be rejected, so detrending may be entirely artifactual and the trend process may account for variation that the Kydland–Prescott's simple linear detrending attributes to the cycle. Indeed we argued that perhaps all the variance in output is attributable to trend, leaving no transitory "cycle" to explain.

Above, we used the term "enigmatic" to describe the story of the 1978 Kydland–Prescott paper. Close inspection of the comment by Taylor on the paper published in the conference volume reveals the following anomaly. In his comment, Taylor wrote (1980, 193):

> Kydland and Prescott build their equilibrium business cycle model upon the assumption of utility maximization. That is, they posit a representative household utility function which depends on consumption, leisure, and *government expenditures*, and they assume that households maximize this utility function subject to budget constraints [my emphasis].

However, in the utility function in the version of the paper as published in the conference volume, government expenditures do not appear (1980a, 174, 177). When asked about this, Kydland replied (2006):

> We wrote a paper for the NBER conference containing a business cycle model (not unlike, as I recall, that in the paper I had written up in preparation for my "job talk"—that is, converting my one-year visiting position to permanent—at CMU that same spring) along with an application to public finance. That application would have shown that fluctuation in the desired provision of public goods, combined with cyclical fluctuations otherwise, implied that the fluctuation ought to be picked up primarily by changing government debt and not by changing tax "rates". In other words, the paper had somewhat of a dual focus (often not a good idea), as reflected also in its title. After the conference, the editor (Stan Fischer, as I recall) told us the paper was too long for the volume and had to be cut. So we more or less omitted the portion emphasizing cyclical public finance (with a heavy heart, because we thought the message was really interesting and innovative). Of course, with that emphasis removed, there was no longer any point in keeping government purchases in the utility function.

In fact, in a letter dated 2 November 1978, Stan Fischer wrote to Ed Prescott commenting "on the Bald Peak paper." In this letter, Fischer focused on what he considered as the problem of “exposition” in the version of the paper as delivered by Prescott at the conference. He wrote:

> My comments are largely expositional, and on details. However, there is one overall comment—namely that it is difficult to figure out where a lot of your results are coming from. I checked the 1977 *JPE* article, and guess that you’ve expanded on the model of section V of that article. I wonder whether either you could make the present paper more explicit in the text, or else present parts of the earlier paper in an appendix. I’d have a slight preference to doing it in the text if you can conveniently fit it in; you refer to a number of interesting results that one would like to see proved. Please let me know if you think the model would take up too much space, or if there is any other reason it might be better not to include it. Please call me … if you have any problems with what I’ve suggested, particularly if you think it impossible to have a brief exposition of the model on which you’re relying for your conclusions.

And indeed, a “brief exposition” of the 1977 Kydland–Prescott model was “expanded” on and included in the revised version of the paper (1978d), with the section on “financing fluctuating government expenditures” (1978c, section 3, 16–19) elided. However, this “expanded” model also included elements of the model presented in their April 1978 “Persistence” paper (1978a), as will be discussed below.

But more is involved than simply the elision of material from the version of the conference paper as presented by Prescott, and commented upon, by Taylor, among others. There are, in fact, *five* versions of the 1978 Kydland–Prescott conference paper: four drafts (1978a, b, c, d), and the published version (1980a). Finn Kydland has kindly provided the author with some of these drafts. Kydland has also explained—in an extensive interview (2005b, interview)—their significance and relation to the published version of the conference paper, and the relationship of the conference paper to other work in the context of what can be called the “Time to build research program,” all within the framework of the overarching Kydland–Prescott research program.

According to Kydland (2005b, interview), the “first draft” of the October 1978 NBER paper—that is to say “Time to build”—as Lucas put it (2005), was a draft paper by Kydland and Prescott entitled “Persistence of unemployment in equilibrium,” dated 19 April 1978 (1978a). This draft was the basis for the “Time to build” research program, in Kydland’s view (2005b, interview), as it was the first modern real business cycle paper, in that it was quantitative and encompassed models of people and businesses (1978a, 5). The catalyst for this paper was that both Kydland and Prescott were “bothered by ‘persistence’ based upon rigidities and adaptive expectations” (Kydland 2005b, interview). The draft included an explicit time to build feature in “the basic model” (1978a, 5–6) and a quadratic utility function, in addition to the possibility of monetary shocks (1978a, 9). However, as Kydland also noted (2005b, interview), while the April 1978 “Persistence of unemployment in equilibrium” paper had “most of the features of 'Time to build', it did not start with *exponential forms of utility and production functions that enabled calibration*" [Kydland's emphasis]. On the other hand, Kydland maintained that the April 1978 "Persistence" paper and the October 1979 "Time to build" paper "*formed one research program*"[his emphasis]. Moreover, he also recalled how he and Prescott "struggled" in trying to develop the "quantitative part of Time to build."

According to Kydland (2005b, interview), the April 1978 draft is linked to both the 1978 Kydland–Prescott NBER paper and to the paper by Kydland entitled "Analysis and policy in competitive models of economic fluctuations" (1980). A notable feature of the April draft was that according to the title page it was "preliminary and incomplete" and comprised "Background material for GSIA Seminar, April 19th, 1978." He also recalled that he gave this seminar as he was being considered at the time for a tenure track position. The model presented in this April 1978 draft was the basis for the model that appeared in the published version of the 1978 Kydland–Prescott paper, as will be shown below. There is no government expenditure in the utility function in the April 1978 draft, and "the driving terms of the model are productivity and possibly tastes" (1978a, 11). The model is in a "dynamic competitive equilibrium" (dynamic general equilibrium) framework (1978a, 11–13).

The "draft" entitled "On the possibility and desirability of stabilization policy" actually had two draft versions: the first was a "preliminary" version (1978b) dated September 1978, the second an amended version with the same title which was presented at the NBER conference, also dated September 1978 (1978c). According to the title pages, both were "Prepared for the NBER conference on rational expectations and economic policy, October 13–14, 1978." The major differences between the preliminary version (1978b) and that submitted to and presented at the NBER conference by Prescott (1978c) were the inclusion in the latter of a number of important illustrative examples and the addition of two figures. The final version was dated: "October 1978, revised Dec. 1978" (1978d). According to the title page, the title was changed to "A competitive theory of fluctuations and the feasibility and desirability of stabilization policy." This was also the title of the paper as published in the conference volume.

There are a number of differences, both formal and substantive, between the amended September 1978 version (1978c), which was that presented at the conference—on the basis of John Taylor's comment, Finn Kydland's recollection, and Stan Fischer's letter to Ed Prescott—and the October–December 1978 revision (1978d). In addition, there is one minor—albeit significant—difference between the October–December 1978 revision and the version published in 1980 (1980a), in the form of an additional reference in a note in the text, as will be seen below.

Moreover, the October–December 1978 revision contained an abstract, absent from the September 1978 amended version, which reads as follows:

> A competitive theory combining elements of Lucas' (1972, 1975) monetary shock theory with a model of equilibrium capital accumulation, under

> uncertainty is developed. The model assumes that multiple periods are required to build new capital goods. The resulting equilibrium process displays both the observed co-movements of economic aggregates and observed serial correlation of real output from trend. A conclusion is that the tax rates should be constant over the cycle. This does not minimize fluctuations but does minimize the burden of financing government expenditures.

The difference between the references in the September 1978 amended version, October–December 1978 revision, and the 1980 published version include citation, in the latter versions, of published papers by Debreu (1954) and Friedman (1948), working papers by Brock (1978a, b, c) and Prescott and Mehra (1978), and two 1978 Carnegie-Mellon Working Papers by Kydland and Prescott, including their paper "Persistence of unemployment in equilibrium." Moreover, to the note (1978d, 10 note 5; 1980a, 175 note 5) referring to the passage "Ours is a competitive theory which combines the Lucas (1972) monetary shock model with a model of capital accumulation in an environment with shocks to technology," the following was added in the 1980 published version: "Black (1978) has argued that real factors can explain aggregate fluctuations"; more about the reason for this below.

But the *crucial* difference between the September 1978 amended version (1978c) and the October–December 1978 revision (1978d) and 1980 published version (1980a) can be seen in the model of the latter versions; a model which also emanates from the Kydland–Prescott "Persistence" paper of April 1978 vintage (1978a), that is, in Kydland's view, as cited above, the first modern real business cycle paper. Indeed, as Prescott recalled (2008) "I remember the summer of 1978 when Finn and I figured out how to use the neoclassical growth model and the growth facts to restrict the parameters of the linear-quadratic economies. That changed everything."

A cross-fertilization aspect of this stage in the Kydland–Prescott story is manifest in the comments provided to them in February 1979 by Fischer Black, which dealt with the October–December 1978 revised version of the conference paper (1978d). His comments were attached to a letter to Kydland and Prescott dated 13 February 1979. Black started by saying "my paper is listed in your bibliography, but there seems to be no reference to it in the paper." He went on to question the nature of the supporting evidence relating to the importance of the effects of monetary shocks on real aggregates, and asked "Does such evidence exist?" His next substantive comment related to the Kydland–Prescott treatment of plant and equipment, the nature of capital and the capital good, and the time period needed to "build a new capital good." Black noted that on one page, Kydland and Prescott had limited the focus of their model to plant and equipment, while on the next page the model involved "a single kind of capital," and he asked "Which is it?" Black then dealt with their presentation of a "time ... to build" notion: "You talk about more time being required to build a new capital good. I think it would be better to talk about the 'optimal' length of the production period."

Finally, Black said that while Kydland and Prescott talked "about the time between starting and finishing a plant," they also talked "about a time that runs into the period during which the plant is used," and asked "Isn't the latter more relevant in explaining persistence?" In his covering letter, Black wrote "Here are the comments on your paper. I guess my overall reaction to this draft is that it needs a lot of work..

In his reply, dated 26 Feb. 1979, Prescott wrote

> Thank you for your comments.... We had planned to, and in the published version will, cite your paper as another general equilibrium analysis emphasizing the importance of real shock as a cause of business fluctuations. I apologize for the goof up.

He went on to say:

> The studies of Barro and Sims were the ones we thought "supportive" of the importance of monetary shocks. This is not to say any theory with real shocks only would imply the absence of the correlations they found.

He continued:

> You suggest we should have considered a multi-capital good growth model. In subsequent analysis we plan to build in more features of the economy such as the distinction between capital in the household and capital in the corporate sector. With this paper we had a time deadline and a length constraint so we considered only the simplest examples to get order of magnitude effects and I am confident of our conclusions from a single capital model.
>
> Making the length of the capital good production period endogenous is something we considered. It would have presented a number of technical difficulties and we knew of no evidence that the construction period of new plants varies much over the cycle. Do you know of any evidence that it does?

Prescott concluded by saying

> I have found our discussions very useful in clarifying issues. My view is that a good theory of fluctuations should make assumptions consistent with empirical findings in the other applied areas such as labor, finance, growth, etc. Otherwise there is not enough discipline and it is too easy to explain any set of observations.
>
> Thanks again for the comments. Finn and I will be discussing the issues you raised at length.

Prescott also provided detailed retrospective assessments of the history and the impact of the 1978 and 1982 "Time to build" papers. Because of their significance, they are cited at length here. He wrote (2001, 2002):

> the 1978 paper did not have much of an impact. In fact Finn and my 1982 paper did not have much of an impact. At the time ... the only person who thought it was important was Bob Lucas. The big break in Finn and my thinking ... came [in 1978] when [we] decided to begin with the growth model with the leisure decision endogenous ... [and] to use the growth model to study fluctuations. The beauty of growth theory is the connection between it and the system of national accounts. Restricting our linear-quadratic economy so that it behaved in the same way as the growth model when not too distant from the steady state seems little in retrospect, but was a major [breakthrough] ... At the time we ... were convinced that monetary shocks were the cause of business cycle fluctuations ... Finn and my paper forced me to change my mind. Prior to writing the paper, and finding that the productivity shocks were of the right magnitude and persistence, I was certain that monetary shocks were the factor giving rise to business cycle fluctuations and the problem was to find the propagation mechanism for these shocks. We were searching for a propagation mechanism for monetary shocks along lines suggested by ... Frisch many years before. At the time ... Black and ... Plosser ... [were] the only people I know who would argue that real shocks are all important ... Finn and I (1982) were surprised when we found that persistent changes in the factors that affect the steady state of the deterministic growth model gave rise to business cycle fluctuations. Finn and I in this paper broke a taboo against general equilibrium in macro.

Optimal policies, control theory, and economic stabilization, 1977

In the January 1977 issue of the *Carnegie-Rochester Series on Public Policy*, Prescott published "Should Control Theory be Used for Economic Stabilization?" In the introduction, Brunner and Meltzer dealt in detail (1977a, 1–6) with the points Prescott made in his paper, in which he distinguished "between the control and equilibrium approaches" (1977a, 32). Prescott reviewed a number of issues (1977a, 15–32): (1) control theory in the context of econometric models; (2) the existence of a "policy invariant law"; (3) control theory in the context of "long-term contracts and rational expectations"; (4) "non-neutralities with anticipated policy"; (5) "testing the alternative paradigms."

With regard to (5), Prescott wrote (1977a, 31): "Many suggested 'tests and applications' of the use of control theory for macro stabilization have appeared in the literature." He went on to describe the "tests" conducted in the "investment tax credit" example in Kydland and Prescott (1977a), and said (1977a, 31–32):

> Distributed lags were introduced by assuming that capacity expansion required two periods, with some fraction of the expenditures occurring in the first, and the rest in the second period. We simulated the use of optimal control in such an environment...

> The tests found that the iterative process typically converged. For some examples, this simulated application of control theory improved economic performance initially (e.g. early iterations) but then had detrimental effects. ... For other examples, the iterative process did not converge, and each iteration resulted in a less stable economy. Insofar as this iterative process captures the essence of what is happening, these tests indicate that the use of control theory for macro stabilization is hazardous and can very well increase economic fluctuations.

Prescott concluded (1977, 32–33):

> The use of optimal control is predicated upon the existence of a policy invariant law of motion, which economic theory predicts will not exist if expectations are rational.... The implication of the equilibrium view of business fluctuations is that until a tested theory of the business cycle is available it is best that active stabilization not be attempted. Reliance on a policy of maintaining a relatively stable currency price and constant tax rates is appropriate. Once a tested theory is available, the implication of the equilibrium view is that economic theory be used to predict the economy's operating characteristics under alternative policy rules, and that one with good characteristics be selected.

According to Brunner and Meltzer (1977, 4): "Franco Modigliani and John B. Taylor were invited to discuss" Prescott's paper, and "John Bryant submitted a comment to clarify the computational problem in relation to the issues raised by Prescott."

In his comment, Modigliani (1977, 85–91) strongly criticized Prescott's views on the non-applicability of control theory, the Kydland–Prescott (1977) approach to "the inconsistency of optimal plans," and Prescott's advocacy of the use of rational expectations to explain macroeconomic phenomena. Modigliani wrote (1977, 85):

> The intent of this [Prescott's] paper is to answer the question posed by Prescott in the title with an unequivocal and resounding no. Unfortunately, the attack against the use of control methods is so vehement and indiscriminate that it tends to obscure the valid, if not entirely novel, message that one can, in principle, conceive of circumstances under which conventional control methods cannot be readily utilized in the design of stabilization policies, and, if utilized nonetheless, would lead to less than optimal solutions. Whether or not such cases are empirically relevant is, of course, an entirely different matter on which the paper throws hardly any light.

With regard to rational expectations and its place in macroeconomics, Modigliani said (1977, 89–90):

> The reason why the ... paradigm has not been widely accepted in macroeconomic analysis and policy—except at the level of interesting logical exercises—is that its broad relevance here appears most doubtful.... There are many and, by now, well-known reasons for this. For one thing, the simple straight-forward model of rational expectations and frictionless competitive markets that provides such a good approximation to speculative markets does not work at the macro level, as is evidenced by the high serial correlation in unemployment or in the deviations of output from "full employment". One must then shade the meaning of rational expectations and allow for market imperfections and frictions in the process of adjustment to equilibrium. By this time, the paradigm no longer has sharply differentiable implications. Certainly, one can accept the view that expectations are rational without accepting the proposition that, therefore, they must be modeled as the forecast implied by the model, in which, furthermore, expectations have been so modeled. And, even if one were gullible enough to accept the view that the average unemployed worker has an efficient and unbiased forecast of the wage rate that would clear the labor market given expected monetary policy, one's gullibility might not extend to the point of believing that the worker has the power to enforce that wage.
>
> In the end, the only empirical evidence offered by Prescott in favor of rational expectations is the behavior of inflation in recent years, which interprets as the result of an attempt at exploiting a falsely perceived trade-off between employment and inflation. I would radically disagree with his interpretation of the causes of inflation in the last decade.

Modigliani concluded (1977, 90):

> To summarize, many of the arguments adduced by Prescott to support the thesis that control theory should not be used for stabilization do not appear to stand up under close scrutiny. This holds in particular for his examples in which a consistent plan was supposed to be nonoptimal.... There remains the crucial question as to whether situations in which control methods are inappropriate are empirically important in the stabilization context. On this issue, unfortunately, Prescott has failed to provide any evidence, and I am, therefore, inclined to retain my initial view that they are not. Still, I am happy to have acknowledged that Prescott's provocative paper has sensitized me, and will undoubtedly sensitize the reader, to a potentially important problem.

Taylor (1977, 93–98), on the other hand, in his comment, made a number of salient points. Among these were (i) Prescott actually distinguished between "optimal control" and "optimal design," where the latter "should be used to find policy *rules* which generate the best operating characteristics for the economy"; and (ii) that the incorrect use of "optimal control theory" is "inappropriate for stabilization problems" (1977, 94).

In his rejoinder, Prescott focused (1977, 101–102) solely on Modigliani's critique. Again, because of its importance, we cite from it at length here. Prescott started by saying (1977, 101): "That there is a fundamental conflict between the tradition of nearly all existing dynamic econometric models and the tradition of equilibrium theory cannot be denied." He went on: "The major point of my paper is that, if dynamic economic behavior (e.g. fluctuation in economic activity) is viewed as an equilibrium phenomenon, with agents forecasting efficiently conditional on their information sets, then optimal control is inappropriate."

Prescott concluded:

> The use of control theory is predicated on the existence of a stable policy invariant structure that specifies current decisions as a function of past and current variables. Is there any empirical evidence that such a structure exists? Econometricians have not been successful in finding stable structures over even the sample period for which the model is estimated. This assumption is also inconsistent with the generally accepted view that announced permanent and temporary tax changes will have different effects. There is an abundance of examples ... of political events causing agents to revise future policy expectations, a process which in turn affects current decision. These observations are inconsistent with the assumption justifying the use of optimal control for stabilization.

3 Kydland–Prescott and Long–Plosser

Development and cross-fertilization

There are a number of ways to analyze the developmental process characterizing how seminal papers in scientific research programs reach the publication stage. One is based upon textual analysis of variorum draft manuscripts. A second is analysis of the interaction of papers with complementary work in the research field. A third is analysis of the impact of professional colleagues, such as commentators on drafts, journal editors, and referees.

In Chapter 2, the early years of the Kydland–Prescott research program was dealt with in detail by focusing specifically upon the process of what Lucas called putting "all the pieces together" (2005, 777). Textual analysis of variorum drafts was supplemented with the recollections of the authors and others, so as to comprehend the origins and evolution of their research program, the connection between elements in their approach (such as their critique of control theory), and the development of their "Time Inconsistency" (1977a) and "Competitive Theory of Fluctuation" [1978 Bald Peak "Time to build"] (1978a-d, 1980a) papers.

This chapter deals with how the "cross-fertilization" of ideas occurred in the work of Kydland–Prescott and Long–Plosser on the business cycle. This is done by surveying the reactions of informal and formal commentators regarding the respective contributions in the form of: (1) comments of colleagues on drafts, (2) editors' and referees' reports on versions submitted to journals, and the resultant amendments to these drafts and submitted versions, and (3) cross-citation and presentation patterns of the respective papers themselves.

This chapter is divided into three parts. The first focuses on the development of the Kydland–Prescott 1982 "Time to Build" paper from its 1979 form onwards, the impacts on it, such as Lucas's "Understanding Business cycles," and cross-fertilization in terms of the written comments of colleagues and correspondence relating to these comments. The second part deals with the cross-fertilization between Kydland–Prescott and Long–Plosser via a "clearinghouse" for ideas in the form of Fischer Black. The final part utilizes referees' comments and authors' correspondence with editors, and others, to show how Kydland–Prescott (1982) and Long–Plosser (1983) came to be published in the form that they took. In addition, patterns in cross-citation and seminar presentation of the respective papers will be dealt with.

The Long–Plosser paper, for its part, is based solely on a real business cycle foundation. It should also be recalled here that there is no "precedence issue" involved when dealing with the Kydland–Prescott and Long–Plosser models, as they are not competitors, but "alternative"—that is to say, complementary—models for dealing with business cycles (Long and Plosser, 1983, 45 note 8).

It should be recalled that Kydland–Prescott is based upon a *one-sector model* and its methodology is aggregative. Long–Plosser, on the other hand, is a *multi-sector model*. When placed in the perspective of its subsequent development, as manifest in the King–Plosser and King–Plosser–Rebelo research program—characterized by *one-sector models*—this becomes important due to the associated loss of analytical "richness" involved in the movement from a multi-sector to a one-sector model, as will be seen in Chapter 4. In this chapter, the focus is on the *interaction* between the research programs and papers of Kydland–Prescott and Long–Plosser as manifest in the process of "cross-fertilization" that characterized the nature of their development—that is to say, the interaction between the authors, commentators, and referees.

Three additional points have to be dealt with here. They are: (1) the role of Solow's 1956 and 1957 papers; (2) the influence of Lucas's 1972 paper "Expectations and the neutrality of money"; and (3) the impact of Lucas's paper "Understanding business cycles" on the Kydland–Prescott program. With regard to Solow's papers, from the October 1979 draft of "Time to build" to the 1982 published version of the paper, neither of Solow's papers is cited. According to Kydland (interview, October 2005), while they are not mentioned because they were not directly utilized, the influence of the Solow papers was "at the back of their minds." This is clearly evident in Prescott's Nobel lecture (2004, 379). With regard to Lucas (1972), while the paper is cited in both the October 1979 and December 1980 versions of "Time to build" it is not cited in the 1982 published version. Despite this, Kydland asserted (interview, October 2005) that it was very influential on his thinking, and that he had originally been introduced to it in Lucas's Spring 1970 class on "Economic fluctuations," where an early version was taught. Kydland's explanation (interview, October 2006) of why it was not cited in the published version of "Time to build" is that this version put "monetary shocks" to one side and concentrated on "real shocks," whereas the October 1979 version included a shock that "mimics the effect of a Lucas (1972) monetary shock" (1979, 2), and the reference was brought over into the December 1980 version; however, as such a shock did not appear in the 1982 published version of "Time to build" the reference to Lucas (1972) was elided.

"Understanding business cycles": Lucas's 1976 and 1977 versions

More important, however, is the role of Lucas's "Understanding business cycles." It was originally presented at the June 1976 Kiel Conference on Growth without Inflation (Lucas, 1976b) and, according to the introductory note in its published version, was revised in August 1976 (1977, 7). There are some significant textual differences between the original and revised versions, which will now be dealt with.

These differences consisted of changes, elisions, and additions to the text. For example, in the 1976 version, Lucas wrote "the de-emphasis on money was on empirical grounds: econometricians from Tinbergen on discovered that money just did not 'matter'" (1976b, 7). In the 1977 published version, this was changed to "econometricians from Tinbergen on discovered that monetary factors did not seem very important empirically" (1977, 11), adding in a note that "Tinbergen, as did most subsequent macroeconometricians, used the significance of interest rates to test the importance of money" (1977, 11 note 7).

Lucas then went on, in both versions, to give what was the central message of his paper: "One exhibits understanding of business cycles by *constructing a model* [his emphasis] in the most literal sense: a fully articulated artificial economy which behaves through time so as to imitate closely the time series behavior of actual economies" (1976b, 7; 1977, 11). He wrote that Keynes had "sidestepped" the problem of fluctuating labor supply based upon household choice "in the face of moderately fluctuating nominal wages" by postulating "rigid nominal" wages (1976b, 8; 1977, 12), and then elided a paragraph dealing with disequilibrium theory in the 1976 version (1976b, 8–9), and in its place added two paragraphs in the 1977 version (1977, 12) as follows:

> This decision on the part of the most prestigious theorist of his day freed a generation of economists from the discipline imposed by equilibrium theory, and, as I have described, this freedom was rapidly and fruitfully exploited by macroeconometricians. Now in possession of detailed, quantitatively accurate replicas of the actual economy, economists appeared to have an inexpensive means to evaluate various proposed economic policy measures. It seemed legitimate to treat policy recommendations which emerged from this procedure as though they had been experimentally tested, even if such policies had never been attempted in any actual economy.
>
> Yet the ability of a model to imitate actual behavior in the way tested by the Adelmans (1959) has almost nothing to do with its ability to make accurate *conditional* forecasts, to answers questions of the form: how *would* behavior have differed had certain policies been different in specified ways? This ability requires *invariance* of the structure of the model under policy variations of the type being studied. Invariance of parameters in an economic model is not, of course, a property which can be assured in advance, but it seems reasonable to hope that neither tastes nor technology vary systematically with variations in countercyclical policies. In contrast, agent's *decision rules will* in general change with changes in the environment. An equilibrium model is, by definition, constructed so as to predict how agents with stable tastes and technology will *choose* to respond to a new situation. Any disequilibrium model, constructed by simply codifying the decision rules which agents have found it useful to use over some previous sample period, without explaining *why* these rules were used, will be of no use in predicting the consequences of nontrivial policy changes [Lucas's emphases].

Finally, Lucas both added and elided text in the conclusion of the published version of his paper. The conclusion of the 1976 version read (1976, 29–30):

> As long as the business cycle remains "in apparent contradiction" to economic theory, the possibility that real well-being can be increased by sufficiently clever manipulation of the books of financial intermediaries will appear to many to be an open one. In the absence of an understanding of the mechanism by which geese produce eggs, a kill-the-goose policy appears reasonable, perhaps even "optimal". After all, interest rates *are* positive, and in the long run we *are* all dead [Lucas's emphasis].

The conclusion of his 1977 published version was (1977, 26):

> The economically literate public has had some forty years to become comfortable with two related ideas: that market economies are inherently subject to violent fluctuations which can only be eliminated by flexible and forceful government responses; and that economists are in possession of the body of scientifically tested knowledge enabling them to determine, at any time, what these responses should be. It is doubtful if many who are not professionally committed hold, today, to the latter of these beliefs. This in itself settles little in the dispute as to whether the role of government stabilization policy should be to reduce its own disruptive part or actively to offset private sector instability. As long as the business cycle remains "in apparent contradiction" to economic theory, both positions appear tenable. There seems to be no way to determine how business cycles are to be dealt with short of understanding what they are and how they occur.

Interestingly enough, while the June 1976 version is not mentioned, the 1977 published version of Lucas's paper is cited a number of times in the Kydland–Prescott April 1978 draft "Persistence of unemployment in equilibrium," which is the first draft of the later "Bald Peak" paper (Lucas's "Time to build" paper)—or, as Kydland put it, the first draft of "Time to build" (interview, October 2005). Moreover, as Kydland said (interview, October 2005), they had made Lucas (1977) operational, and thus brought about a change from the methodological approach they took in their April 1978 "Persistence" draft to that in their "Time to build" draft of October 1979, which, in Kydland's view, forms one research program. In the October 1979 version of "Time to build," according to Kydland (interview, October 2005), Lucas's 1977 statement that "one exhibits understanding of business cycles by constructing a *model* [Lucas's emphasis] ... a fully articulated artificial economy which behaves ... so as to imitate closely the ... behavior of actual economies" (1977, 11) became one of the methodological precepts for the "Time to build" approach. Indeed, according to Kydland, it was the operationalization of Lucas's modeling prescription which brought about, in his recollection (Kydland interview, 2005), the change from the introduction written for the April 1978 "Persistence" paper to the introduction written for the

October 1979 "Time to build" version of the paper, both of which will be presented below.

Evolution and development of the 1982 "Time to build" paper

Much has been written about the impact of the published version of the 1982 "Time to build" paper in the form of the subsequent Kydland–Prescott research program that emanated from it. However, the evolution and development of the 1982 paper itself has not been dealt with. As in the case of their 1978 NBER paper discussed in Chapter 2 above, and its final version as published in 1980 (1980a), the evolution of the 1982 Kydland–Prescott "Time to build" paper is characterized by a number of draft versions and the final 1982 published version.

Because of their importance for an understanding of the phases in the development of Kydland and Prescott's "Time to build" paper, the introductions to the April 1978, October 1979, December 1980, and September 1981 versions of "Time to build" will be cited at length here, so as to illustrate the differences between these versions of the paper. The introduction to the April 1978 paper, entitled "Persistence of unemployment in equilibrium," read:

> Kareken (1978) argues that two major revolutions have taken place in aggregate economics in the last decade or so. One is the resurgence of monetarists as opposed to Keynesians, emphasizing the effects of monetary policy or monetary shocks on real aggregate variables. The other revolution is emphasis on microeconomic foundations. Some economists have of course contributed to both, such as Lucas (1972, 1973, 1975), whose theories of the business cycle based on microeconomic foundations emphasize monetary shocks as an explanation of the observed movements in aggregate variables.
>
> Although there appears to be general agreement that monetary shocks have important effects on real aggregates (and such shocks will indeed be investigated in this paper), we think there are good reasons to explore the hypotheses that real shocks to tastes, and in particular to technology, may be of major importance in triggering economic fluctuations. To a large extent, of course, such shocks net out across individuals or firms, but there are also shocks whose effects clearly do not net out. We shall concentrate on technology shocks...
>
> Some of the regularities among co-movements of aggregate time series that a theory of the business cycle should be consistent with, are (see, e.g., Lucas (1977), Sargent (1978)): (i) Output movements across broadly defined sectors go together. (ii) Production of consumer and producer durables exhibits *much* greater amplitude than does production of nondurables. (iii) Monetary aggregates and velocity measures are procyclical. (iv) Output per man-hour generally moves weakly procyclically, and appears to lead output movements. (v) There is little evidence of either pro-or counter-cyclical movements in real wages.

> It has generally been the belief that prices and output move procyclically (see Lucas (1977) and Sargent (1978)). Recent empirical results by Hodrick and Prescott (1978) for the period 1947–1977 indicate, however, that deviations from trends in the two series are negatively correlated. This is true even when the years after 1973 are excluded. This observation would hardly be consistent with monetary shocks being the major cause of fluctuations. In view of this it appears appropriate to look to real shocks, such as technology shocks, as an explanation of this perhaps surprising phenomenon.
>
> A final important empirical regular is the persistence of deviations of aggregate output or employment from trend. These persistent deviations have by many been taken as an argument against the use of equilibrium models assuming rational expectations to explain business cycle phenomena.
>
> In our model persistence of deviations from trend will derive essentially from capital-type elements of the model. The work by Jorgenson (1963, etc.) and recent estimates by Hall (1977) indicate that the average lag from the time when plans are made for capital expansion and until the new capital starts yielding services is about two years. Thus, an important feature of our model is a distributed lag in accumulation of durables within an equilibrium framework. Lucas and Rapping (1969) and Ghez and Becker (1975) found ample evidence that leisure in different periods are good substitutes. This suggests that intertemporal substitution is an important feature of people's preferences. To model this explicitly, we introduce a capital-like element which measures how much workers have worked in the past, with relatively more weight on the most recent past. The higher the value this variable is in a given period, the more utility is derived from leisure in that period.

The introduction to their October 1979 version, whose title had been changed to "Time to build and equilibrium persistence of unemployment," read:

> That wine is not made in a day has been recognized by economists (e.g., Böhm-Bawerk [1890]) for a long time. But, neither are ships nor factories built in a day. The thesis of this essay is that the assumption of instantaneous construction, or single-period construction for discrete time models, is neither necessary nor, for purposes of understanding fluctuation in aggregate economic activity, innocuous. Previously, no one, to the best of our knowledge, has introduced this element into a competitive equilibrium model that was designed to explain the serial correlation properties of the cyclical component of aggregate output.
>
> The objective of this research is to develop a theory of the covariances and autocovariances of the cyclical components of certain important aggregate economic series. This development is at an early stage and should be judged as such. As we are designing a model to explain the second moments of the cyclical components, implicitly we are constrained to a preference-technology-information structure for which the equilibrium

process implied by the model is linear. One discipline, then, of this analysis is that quantitatively the model's covariances are not only of the correct sign but also that the magnitudes are comparable to those for the U.S. economy in the post-war period.

Our theory assumes a representative infinitely-lived household. Multiple periods are required to build a new capital good and only finished capital goods are part of the *productive* capital stock. Each stage of production requires a period and utilizes resources. Half-finished ships and factories are not part of the productive capital stock even though U.S. National Income Accounts treat them as such. Section 2 contains a short critique of the commonly used investment technologies and presents evidence that single-stage production is inadequate. The preference-technology-information structure of our model is presented in Section 3.

The steady state for the model is determined in Section 4, and quadratic approximations are made which result in an "indirect" quadratic utility function that values leisure, the capital goods, and the negative of investments. Most of the relatively small number of parameters are estimated using findings in other applied areas of economics or steady state considerations. For example, the degree of risk aversion is selected to be consistent with the market price of non-diversible risk reported in the finance literature; the number of periods required to build new productive capital is of the magnitude reported by business; the parameters of preferences for leisure and consumption streams are not inconsistent with the finding of labor economics. The small set of free parameters plus considerations such as these impose considerable discipline upon the inquiry—more than making an exhaustive search of the parameter space to find the point which minimizes the sum of the squared innovations. The estimated model and the comparison of its predictions with the empirical regularities of interest are in Section 5...

Our structure has no monetary sector so monetary shocks are not formally a part of the model. We do introduce a shock to the indicator of an "island's" productivity that is correlated across islands. Insofar as this shock mimics the effect of a Lucas (1972) monetary shock, our model can be viewed as a theory of monetary shock propagation. Decisions to initiate new investment projects and to allocate labor to production activities are made contingent upon this indicator which is the sum of a "monetary shock" and a productivity shock. Unlike Lucas (1975), agents learn the value of the shock at the end of the period so that the gradual diffusion of information about unobserved capital stocks is not a principal cause of persistence. Of course, like his analysis and that of Blinder and Fischer (1978), capital plays a crucial role in creating persistence.

Kydland and Prescott revised the paper in December 1980, and entitled it "Time to build and the persistence of unemployment." This version was sent to *Econometrica*. Its introduction read as follows:

> The thesis of this essay is that the assumption of multiple-period construction is crucial for explaining the serial correlation properties of the cyclical component of real output. A model of economic fluctuations is developed and estimated using U.S. quarterly data for the post-war period. The serial correlation of cyclical output for the model match well with those observed for the U.S. economy in that period. The standard deviations and correlations with output of the other variables determined by the model are also consistent with U.S. data.
>
> Our approach integrates growth and business cycle theory. Like standard growth theory, a representative infinitely-lived household is assumed. As fluctuations in employment are central to the business cycle, the stand-in consumer values not only consumption but also leisure. The most important modification to the standard growth model is that multiple periods are required to build new capital goods and only finished capital goods are part of the productive capital stock. Each stage of production requires a period and utilizes resources. Half-finished ships and factories are not part of the capital stock. Section 2 contains a short critique of the commonly used investment technologies, and presents evidence that single period production, even with adjustment costs, is inadequate.... The exogenous stochastic components in the model are shocks to technology and imperfect indicators of productivity. The two technology shocks differ in their persistence.

The introduction to the September 1981 revision, now entitled "Time to build and aggregate fluctuations," was the finalized version of the introduction, and also appeared in the 1982 published version of the paper. It read:

> A thesis of this essay is that the assumption of multiple-period construction is crucial for explaining aggregate fluctuations. A general equilibrium model is developed and fitted to U.S. quarterly data the post-war period. The comovements of the fluctuations for the fitted model are quantitatively consistent with the corresponding comovements for U.S. Data. In addition, the serial correlations of cyclical output for the model also match well with those observed.... A crucial feature of preferences is the non-time-separable utility function that admits greater intertemporal substitution of leisure.
>
> Findings in other applied areas of economics are used to calibrate the model. For example, the assumed number of periods required to build new productive capital is of the magnitude reported by business, and findings in labor economics are used to restrict the utility function. The small set of free parameters imposes considerable discipline upon the inquiry. The estimated model and the comparison of its predictions with the empirical regularities of interest are in Section 5.

The differences between the respective versions of the introduction not only reflect the operationalization of Lucas (1977), but also the impact of Taylor's comments as a referee for *Econometrica*, as will be seen below.

Now, the link between the April 1978 Kydland–Prescott paper, entitled "Persistence of unemployment in equilibrium," and their 1982 "Time to build" paper is seen in what Kydland considers (2005b, interview), to be the first "formal draft" of their 1982 paper—that is, the October 1979 revised draft version entitled "Time to build and equilibrium persistence of unemployment." According to Kydland, this draft was just circulated for comment, "probably to Lucas." The term "equilibrium persistence of unemployment" remained in the title in the October 1979, September 1980, and December 1980 versions, and was changed to "aggregate fluctuations" only in the September 1981 revision, after comments by the referees of the December 1980 version.

What is also important about the October 1979 revised version is that it contains handwritten amendments and additions attesting to the interaction between Prescott, who was then at Minnesota and Northwestern, and Kydland at Carnegie-Mellon. For example, Prescott changed the original term "the relative demand shift" to "productivity shock" (1979, 3), added "adjustment costs" 1979, 7; 1982, 1348), and added a footnote regarding "beginning of period stocks" (1979, 9; 1982, 1349). But more important was the utilization, in this version, of an exponential "constant relative risk aversion utility function" (1979, 12), which is made quadratic in the September 1980 version (1980b, 12). According to Kydland (2005b, interview), the September 1980 version should be regarded as the first complete version; it was issued as a GSIA Working Paper (No. 28–80–81) and sent to Cornell for a seminar given by Kydland (2005, Nobel autobiography). In Kydland's opinion (2005b, interview), the September 1980 version also contained the central message of the 1982 Kydland–Prescott paper in the form of the sentence "Our approach integrates growth and business cycle theory" (1980b, 2; 1982, 1345); this, according to Kydland (2005b, interview) and Prescott (2004, 376 note 1) follows from the 1978 and 1980 versions of the Hodrick–Prescott paper (1978, 1980).

The December 1980 revision of "Time to build" was submitted to *Econometrica* under the title "Time to build and the persistence of unemployment." The manuscript of the 1982 Kydland–Prescott paper was received by *Econometrica* in January 1981, and the revision was received a year later, in January 1982 (1982, 1369). Publication of the paper was announced in the list of accepted manuscripts that appeared in the July 1982 issue of *Econometrica* (1982, 1085), and the paper eventually appeared in the November 1982 issue.

Moreover, the September 1980 version of the paper (1980b) was given by Prescott at the University of Chicago Money and Banking Workshop. While Becker did not attend, Prescott sent him a copy of the paper. In a letter to Prescott dated 24 November 1980, Becker said that he found the Kydland–Prescott draft to be "interesting" and "the right way to go," and was "impressed" by the sample calculations in their paper relating to "how much" of business fluctuations could "be generated from delays in the time to build." Becker went on to make a number of cogent points regarding the outcome of "Time to build":

> As a general matter, it would appear that *long* delays in building time will tend to moderate cycles rather than contribute to them.... Even if one is not sure whether a shock is permanent or temporary, one could discontinue investments if the shock turned out to be temporary when it was anticipated to be permanent. The cost of such discontinuation would be smaller, the smaller the outlays required over the first year or two relative to the total eventual outlay.

Becker concluded:

> Of course, if the lags are just of the right length, not too long and not too short, they can, it appears from your paper, produce cycles of the kind we have observed. There must be a nonmonetonic function relating the length of lags to the implied cyclical fluctuations, such that fluctuations rise as lags increase from zero to some value, and then begin to fall. Am I right on some of these inferences?

The September 1980 version was revised in December 1980, but the title "Time to build and the persistence of unemployment" remained. The revised December 1980 version was submitted to *Econometrica*, and received in January 1981, with Lucas and Taylor acting as referees for the paper. The September 1980 version was further revised in September 1981, and was titled "Time to build and aggregate fluctuations." This version was presented at the NBER economic fluctuations group meeting held at the University of Chicago, 9–10 October 1981, organized by Lucas. The Kydland–Prescott Paper was discussed by Taylor (NBER Report, 1981, 27), who was also the referee for *Econometrica*, as noted above. As will be seen below, re-statement of comments made by Taylor in his referee's report regarding the September 1981 revision brought about a final revision in December 1981, sent for publication in *Econometrica*. This revision was received January 1982 (1982, 1369). Publication of the paper was announced in the list of accepted manuscripts that appeared in the July 1982 issue of *Econometrica*, and it was published in November 1982.

The importance of the October 1981 NBER fluctuations group meeting cannot be understated. During the two-day meeting, besides "Time to build," a number of other important papers were presented and discussed. Among these were "The behavior of money, credit and prices in a Real Business Cycle" by King and Plosser, discussed by Azariadis; "The roles of money and credit in macroeconomic analysis" by B. Friedman, discussed by Barro; "Money, real interest rates and output" by Litterman and Weiss, discussed by Shiller; "Forecasting the forecasts of others" by Townsend, discussed by Futia; and "Stopping moderate inflation: the methods of Poincare and Thatcher" by Sargent, discussed by McCallum (NBER Report, 1981, 27–28).

Indeed, anticipating methodological questions regarding the paper at the meeting, Prescott had prepared remarks to accompany his presentation of "Time to build," entitled "Remarks on methodology for aggregate analysis." Because of its importance for an understanding of the rationale underlying the methodology of "Time to build," his "Remarks" are cited at length below. He said:

> An important methodological question that I anticipated would be posed is the following: Since your theory puts restrictions upon the general linear vector autoregressive model, shouldn't statistics be used to test these restrictions? The anticipated follow-up to this question is given that you do not rely upon the statistical discipline, what discipline are you using and is it adequate? These prepared remarks address these two questions.
>
> The world is complex and the art of scientific discovery is to make it understandable. This requires that our models of the world be sufficiently simple so that we can derive the models' implications that are of concern. This severely restricts the set of artificial economies that can be used to mimic the economic phenomena which are of interest. Our theory is designed to explain the covariances of the deviations of aggregate economic series from their smoothed paths while also being consistent with the covariations in the smoothed series. That is, ours is an attempt to integrate growth and fluctuation theory. The theory is not designed to make accurate period ahead forecasts.

Prescott went on to say:

> Another reason not to test our models versus the less restrictive linear vector auto-regressive model was data problems. The correspondence between our model's variables and those reported in the national income accounts is less than perfect. It is true that the national income accounts could be revised in order that they conform more closely to our theory but this is hardly warranted. Even with revisions in the national income accounts to make them more in line with the model, there would still be non-trivial measurement errors about which our knowledge would be insufficient to model them as being generated by some set of probability laws as required for the application of the statistical discipline. We do not have a set of true and a corresponding set of measured values which can be used to construct a good probability model of the measurement errors. Still another problem is that economic activity takes place in continuous time with new data becoming available periodically while the model is in discrete time. Because of these problems, our model is poorly suited for short-run forecasts of the reported data.

He then said:

> As previously stated our theory was constructed to explain the covariances and the fluctuations. For these numbers the noise introduced by measurement errors and modeling approximation should not be large relative to the signal—at least that is our hope. This raises the second question that I

mentioned at the beginning of these remarks. Does explaining these numbers provide sufficient discipline or would almost any set of numbers be consistent with theoretical construct? Without the additional discipline of cross paradigmatic verification, this would be the case.

Prescott continued:

> The requirement that certain model's statistics such as of average labor shares and the capital-output ratios be on average equal to the corresponding averages for the post-war U.S. economy imposed considerable additional discipline. Cross-sectional observations impose additional constraints on parameter selection. If, for example, we found that assuming 16-day or 16-year construction periods for new capital was necessary in order to explain the covariances, this would be grounds for rejecting the model. If we found that to explain the high variability in employment relative to productivity, it was necessary to use a parameter value in the utility function that implied the standard household allocated 95% of its time to non-market activities, this also would be unacceptable. These implications are inconsistent with micro observations.
>
> A related issue is what observations would falsify the theory? We found that high persistence of the technology shock was crucial to explaining the persistence of economic fluctuations. If there were some economy for which the shocks were clearly not persistent and the behavior of the economy were not different in the way predicted by the theory, the theory would be falsified.
>
> Another feature of the model which was crucial and not strongly supported (nor conflicted) by micro studies was the assumed non-time separable utility function that resulted in higher intertemporal substitution of leisure. This feature was needed in order that both fluctuations in employment be large relative to fluctuations in productivity and the share of the household endowment of time allocated to market activities not be ridiculously small.

Prescott concluded:

> Discussion of scientific methodology quickly became tedious and tended to evoke extreme reaction. Even though we made little use of the statistical discipline, I am not arguing it is done without its use. The controlled experiment paradigm has been invaluable in biology particularly in developing better plants and fertilizers for agriculture. Sampling theory has been used to obtain much of the aggregate data that we used to test our theory. Statistics clearly has played an important part in many applied areas of economics. What I am suggesting is that its use is limited in testing our theory of aggregate fluctuation and that the discipline of cross paradigmatic verification is well suited for the task.

The Kydland–Prescott, Black, and Long–Plosser nexus: cross-fertilization

As regards the influence of Black on the development of Kydland–Prescott, while Prescott wrote in correspondence (2002) that he "did not influence my thinking on business cycles," Black's November 1979 MIT Working Paper entitled "General equilibrium and business cycles" was cited in both the December 1980 and December 1981 revisions of the Kydland–Prescott "Time to build paper," and in the 1982 published version. An earlier 1978 version of Black's working paper was cited in the drafts and published version of the Kydland–Prescott NBER conference paper, as seen above. There are actually five versions of Black's paper. The original appeared in April 1978 as an MIT Working Paper, which was first revised in September 1978 and later revised in November 1979. A 1978 version of Black's paper was not cited in the Kydland–Prescott NBER conference paper draft dated September 1978, but was cited in the Kydland–Prescott draft dated October 1978 and revised December 1978, and also appears in the Kydland–Prescott paper as published in the NBER conference volume (1980a, 196). Interestingly enough, the third version—that is the November 1979 revision of Black's 1978 paper—was cited by them as early as in the September and December 1980 revisions of "Time to build," and also in the published version of the "Time to build" paper (1982, 1369). The fourth version appeared in August 1982, as an NBER Working Paper. The fifth and final version was published in his 1987 book. But much more is involved here than citation of Black's paper, for, as in the case of their Bald Peak conference paper discussed above, Fischer Black was a "clearinghouse" to which Kydland and Prescott sent their draft paper entitled "Time to Build and the Persistence of Unemployment" for comments. Moreover, as will now be shown, he was the key player in the process of "cross-fertilization" between Kydland and Prescott and Long and Plosser.

Despite their complementary development, up to now cross-fertilization between the ongoing work of Kydland and Prescott and Long and Plosser before publication of their papers has not been established. Now, documentary material provided by Finn Kydland shows that while the models were independently discovered, there was some correspondence between the authors themselves at the draft stages of the papers, and that they interacted with Fischer Black, who played the role of both clearinghouse and commentator, bringing together their ideas, and, as will be seen below, even suggesting, at one point, a combination of their respective approaches.

In February 1981, Fischer Black sent three pages of detailed comments to Ed Prescott on the Kydland–Prescott draft entitled "Time to build and the persistence of unemployment," which dated from December 1980 (1980c). This was also the version they submitted to *Econometrica*, as will be seen below. Black opened his comments by saying that the Kydland–Prescott paper was "full of insights" and "interesting results." He then said that he believed that there were "many ways to generate the qualitative features of business cycles," such that a model could be described as one of "competitive," "real," or "general equilibrium" type. According to Black, the Kydland–Prescott paper gave not "one," but "many examples," and this, he said, "because some parameters" in their model "did not matter much," thus providing "an example for each set" of a parameter values. Black then counter-pointed the Kydland–Prescott approach to that which he had taken in the November 1979 revision of his paper "General Equilibrium and Business Cycles" (1979b). He wrote in his comments:

> Another way to do it, I believe, is with adjustment costs. The adjustment cost models you reject are not complex enough to give the kind of behavior you are looking for. For example, in the model in my paper, a key feature is that there are many sectors and the shocks to different sectors are somewhat independent. With that feature, I believe you can generate a complex autocorrelation pattern for output.

In fact, the November 1979 revision of his paper not only comprised "many sectors," but was "a multisector model with unemployment" (1979b, 2). Moreover, in the 1979 version, Black clearly explained how "shocks to different sectors" occur:

> Starting with unemployment at its average level, suppose there is a burst of technological change in certain sectors, so that the values of [the state variable] in those sectors goes up sharply. This will increase utility, but the transfer of resources into those sectors will also increase unemployment in this model.
>
> (1979b, 8).

In a note to this, Black continued: "In a more general model, we might assign a different unemployment cost to resource shifts resulting from good shocks and bad shocks. The job search resulting from good shocks is often done while the individual remains employed" (1979b, 19 note 14).

In his comments on the Kydland and Prescott draft, Black continued on to make the very interesting suggestion that illustrated the degree to which "cross-fertilization" characterized his views, which advocated the combination of the Kydland–Prescott model with his and that of Long and Plosser. In Black's words:

> Actually, though, I think the best model would be one combining "time to build" and "adjustment costs". And other features, such as those in the Long–Plosser paper, as well. There are virtues to simplicity, but the world is not simple. If we want the model to explain micro behavior and macro behavior at the same time, it will have to have a lot of structure, I think.

After discussing the possibility of utilizing Alchian's treatment of adjustment costs, the Kydland–Prescott definition of the price of capital goods, and their discussion of depreciation, Black returned to compare their approach to his own regarding unemployment, as manifest in his November 1979 paper:

> I think it is useful to distinguish two kinds of unemployment: search-type unemployment and layoff-type unemployment. I take my paper as dealing with search-type unemployment, and yours as dealing with layoff-type unemployment. The two are related, of course, both economically and statistically.

Black, however, was somewhat critical of the Kydland–Prescott treatment of "current productivity":

> I can't convince myself that you really need ignorance about current productivity to get your results. Any more than I can believe ignorance about the current money supply is needed. If the decay rate for permanent shocks is higher than you have assumed, is the ignorance still needed? Which features of your model is it crucial to?

On the other hand, Black "especially liked" how Kydland–Prescott dealt with "the intertemporal substitution of leisure" and their "concise discussion of policy."

Black then posed a series of questions, and made a number of observations, regarding the Kydland–Prescott approach. Among these were the implications of combining the related notions of "Time to build" and "cost to build" in a model. In this case, Black wrote:

> If you have a model where "time to build" and "cost to build" are related, I think you may not have to single out inventories as a special kind of capital. You may be able to have a single kind of capital, or, better, to have many kinds of capital that are all factors of production, but without the need to say which is which.

He also posed the following questions: "How would your model be affected if you used a labor-augmenting productivity shock rather than the kind you use? Or if you used both?"

After stating his belief that "wages are procyclical, at least with longer measurement intervals," and that "wages were certainly low in the depression," he went on to ask:

> What is the economics of a negative correlation between the capital stock and output? How is the capital stock measured?… If people slept 16 hours a day and worked 8 hours, would you still use the fractions 1/3 and 2/3 in your utility function?

Black concluded his comments by saying "Anyway, as you can imagine, I am very enthusiastic about the thrust of your paper. There's no monetary policy, and no fooling with countercyclical tax policy. Just pure, optimal, business cycles."

Black's comments were the start of a significant cross-fertilization of ideas. Prescott sent his responses to Black's comments in a letter dated 25 February 1981. In the body of the letter he wrote:

> Thanks for the extensive comments and the kind remarks on Finn Kydland's and my "Time-to-Build and the Persistence of Unemployment" paper. Enclosed are responses to the comments. I found preparing these comments a very useful exercise for clarifying my views.

He continued his letter: "Enclosed are two papers. One is a copy of Lucas's 'Method and Problems in Business Cycle Theory' paper. I interpret his arguments as supporting our methodology. Enclosed also is Hodrick's and my descriptive investigation of post-war U.S. business fluctuations." Prescott's responses consisted of two pages of detailed paragraph-by-paragraph replies to Black's comments. In response to Black's comment regarding the importance of the multi-sectoral approach, Prescott replied "Possibly multi-sector models, at least if they represent multistage production, could give rise to more complex serial correlation properties. I suspect, by relabeling variables, our model could be viewed as a multi sector model." Regarding the Long–Plosser paper, Prescott wrote "I have not yet seen a copy of the Long–Plosser paper. Do they have a model that mimics the behavior of the economy and that could be used to predict the effect of various exogenous interventions?"

Prescott then turned to the issue of periods of construction:

> This is just the Austrian business cycle story. I know of no evidence that construction periods are cyclically variable and even if they are I would be surprised if a model incorporating this feature would behave much differently than ours. Neither Finn nor I know how to incorporate this feature into a model that can be quantitatively analyzed. Computational costs become essentially infinite.

He went on to say:

> With constant returns to scale the shadow price of capital is the market price of the firm. In fact stock prices probably vary more than our model predicts. We conjecture that having new technology embodied in new capital might resolve this anomaly as well as the model's overly high correlation between productivity and output. That we are able to discuss issues such as these is, I think, a virtue of our methodology.

After replying to Black's point regarding depreciation, Prescott also dealt with the issue of "search equilibria," and wrote "I always felt search equilibria difficult to analyze. Bob Lucas and I failed in our attempt to extend our equilibrium search paper to environments which would in equilibrium display aggregate fluctuations." Prescott then turned to the problems raised by Black regarding the Kydland–Prescott treatment of "ignorance" about "productivity," and the possible introduction of "cost to build" into their model:

> Crucial to our model is uncertainty as to future productivities. The auto makers in this country were surprised when they found the demand (i.e. value of output) less than expected. I think the stock market is a very good indicator of the expected present value of future returns upon existing capital. There is no reason why this need move with expected future productivity though I expect a model could be constructed for which it would.

He continued:

> To introduce the Austrian-Alchian 'cost to build' construct into a general equilibrium framework necessitates the introduction of many more capital goods. Capital in construction must be indexed not only by periods from completion but also by how long it takes to construct using the chosen technology. Problems of corners arise. It's the computation problem again.

Prescott that then turned to the observations made by Black: "with our model, technological change is neutral and, possibly non-neutral technological change would also resolve the anomalies mentioned." He went on to say:

> the real wage does not move over the business cycle much. Some people argue that it is pro-cyclical and others counter. I would not label the depression a business cycle. My expertise on the depression is limited but my impression is that the real, as opposed to nominal wage did not vary that much in the depression. With respect to growth, the real wage is highly correlated with real output per capita.

He continued: "If the capital stock is low, the optimal decision is to accumulate capital rapidly (high investment). Investment is the most pro-cyclical component of real output varying in percentage terms four or five times as much as consumption." Finally, Prescott wrote:

> Becker in coming up with the 2/3 of time allocated to leisure activities, does not include sleeping time in the endowment of time. Consequently if leisure was zero, then I would not include leisure as an argument of utility function; i.e. I would use 1 and 0 in our utility function.

Two weeks later, on 9 March 1981, Black again wrote Prescott and said "Your replies are so stimulating that I can't resist another round." In answer to Prescott's assertion that, under Prescott's assumption of different stages of production, Kydland–Prescott could be considered a multi-sector model, Black wrote:

> You have one way to link your model and a multi-sector model. But what if the sectors represent different consumption goods and services rather than different stages of production? What if the issue is not "time to build", but rather "time to complete a shift of resources from one sector to another"? Won't that give the same kinds of behavior that your model gives?

Black then turned to the Long–Plosser paper and said "Long and Plosser don't talk much about exogenous interventions. Neither do you. What kinds of interventions do you think can be analyzed in your model?"

He then returned to the issue of construction periods: "I didn't mean to suggest that construction periods be made cyclically variable. I think of the Alchian story as providing an even-more-micro basis for your story. I did not mean that it would give different results." Black then counter-pointed his model to the Kydland–Prescott approach:

> If a change in market value of existing capital is due to physical deterioration in your model, then I can see why you won't have stock prices varying too much. This is a crucial difference between your model and the model in my head, some of which is in my paper. In my multi-sector model with adjustment costs, changes in tastes and technology cause changes in the market value of existing capital.

He then replied to Prescott regarding "search equilibria":

> Perhaps I'm cheating, but I simplified the job of analyzing search equilibrium by changing the problem to one with adjustment costs. I think of the cost of changing jobs as arising largely from the cost of search. I do not analyze the details of the search process.

Black then replied to the issue of "surprise": "How does the automakers' surprise fit into a model? As a change in productivity? In my model it is a shift in the allocation of demand across sectors (and possibly across time)."

Black turned to the relationship between output, investment, and capital stock:

> I thought you said in the paper that output (not investment) was negatively related to the capital stock. Why would that be? Because investment is high when capital stock is low? But isn't investment high when the capital stock (as measured by stock prices) is high?

Black ended this part of his letter, regarding the utility function, by saying "I forgot about weekends and holidays and vacations. Possibly because of some work habits I am trying to change."

Black then turned to Lucas's paper "Methods and Problems in Business Cycle Theory":

> First, this, like almost all his work is sharply reasoned and insightful. This paper disproves his apparent assertion that good theoretical work must involve highly abstract models. Second, though he generally avoids reference to "testing" a model, he does use that word in the second paragraph of his paper. I am coming more to the view that testing is a notion from classical statistics that may be useful in physics, but that Bayesian estimation is more useful than "testing" in economics. Experimental data can be used to test a theory. But time-series data?

Black went on to provide comments on the Hodrick–Prescott paper and wrote "Does your method give substantially different results from a method that simply starts with percentage differences of growing variables?" He then asked:

> Do you have reasons to believe that a business cycle involves 'overshooting' of some kind? Your arguments … seem to imply that you expect a positive deviation at one point to be followed by a negative deviation (not just a smaller positive deviation) at a later point.

He continued: "is labor productivity observable in a world of uncertainty? I think you might say that you are relating conventional measures of the variables of interest, rather than the true variables." He then wrote: "Again, if you measure the capital stock using market values, I think you will find a positive relation with output, especially when you include lagged values of the capital stock." Finally, Black said "I regard your paper [Hodrick–Prescott] as presenting the correlations among certain variables of interest without attributing any causal structure to the correlations. That, I think, is the right way to do empirical work!"

A fortnight later, on 19 March 1981—after Plosser has presented the Long–Plosser paper at MIT—Black sent a letter to Kydland regarding the difference between the Kydland–Prescott and Long–Plosser approaches to separatibility and substitutability. Black copied this letter to Prescott, Long, and Plosser respectively. In it, he wrote:

> Charlie Plosser and I were discussing the intertemporal substitution of leisure when he was here to give his paper. He and John Long feel that all you need is a high elasticity of substitution between leisure and goods in consumption. I said that I think you need a non-separable utility function, as you and Ed have.

A few days later, on 24 March, Prescott sent a letter to Plosser. Because of its importance to our story, the text of letter is cited in its entirety below [spelling corrected and insertions made for clarity]:

> Thank you for the copy of John Long's and your "Real Business Cycles" paper. I thought the basic question of the business cycle was why the

> consumption of leisure moved *counter* cyclically yet the real wage (or marginal product of labor) varies little over the cycle. I thought your crucial statement was on page 27. If, however, producers substitute between inputs (as relative prices change) less readily than consumers substitute between commodity and leisure consumption, then the above analysis suggest ... employment ... will be positively associated with commodity outputs...
>
> First I assume you mean commodity consumption and not commodity output for some output is for investment purposes. Second is this consistent with your assumptions concerning preferences and technology (i.e. (3.1), (3.2), (2.3) and (2.4))? In the single consumption good case, Finn and I were unable to get employment to vary enough over the cycle within your framework...
>
> I think a special version of your technology is essentially the same as our time to build technology ... so I anticipate that you will have no trouble accounting for the serial correlation properties of output.
>
> I also like your technology much better than those which assume adjustment costs. With them, more of the variation in output is associated with variations in productivity rather than in the labor input. To repeat, the fundamental puzzle of the business cycle is why the labor supplied varies so much given the small variation in productivity.
>
> I think you find the extension to the government sector difficult. Once the invisible [hand] fails, computing the equilibrium can become more difficult. Finn has made some progress on this problem in a recent paper. Introducing money is even more difficult.
>
> That for your model sectionally independent shocks to production in each sector result in positive serial correlation in output and positive cross-sectional correlations is interesting. Your random walk example does not satisfy assumption (IX) page 9. It has a high degree of serial dependence. This is not to argue that introducing serial dependence this way is not a good procedure. After all, technological inventions have a persistent effect upon the production possibility set.

On 26 March, Prescott sent Black a copy of his letter to Plosser, and also replied to the "hypothetical test" proposed by Black in his letter of 19 March. Two days later, on 28 March, Prescott again wrote Black, with further replies to the points Black raised in their earlier exchange of ideas, and this time, included a response to Black's comments on the Hodrick–Prescott paper. He first took up Black's point regarding exogenous interventions (Black to Prescott, 9 March 1981):

> One exogenous change might be a change in the process governing the ability of a small country to transform some good that it produces into goods it consumes via trade. Another exogenous change might be a policy of a balanced budget rather than having it balanced on average over the cycle.

Prescott then answered Black's query regarding "surprise":

> I was trying to follow the Chicago principle of loading as much as possible into the constraints and as little as possible into preferences. Due to the increase in the relative price of a complementary product, the output of the auto firms valued in terms of the composite consumption good was smaller. The difference here is more semantic than substantive.

He then turned to the relationship between capital stock, investment, and output raised by Black:

> Here I was thinking of the capital stock as the number of machines and the market value of a machine as reflecting the expected present values of its net rental. When capital stocks are low, investment, an important component of output, is high. The market value of existing capital is high because returns on capital are expected to be above average until the capital stock is no longer low. This is what Finn and I found though the variability in the value of existing capital for our model was lower than the observed variability in stock prices. Possibly firms are insuring the returns on human capital and in the boom insurance payments are low. This is consistent with the procyclical movement in capital share.

With regard to Black's comments on the Hodrick–Prescott paper, Prescott wrote:

> Differencing nicely eliminates the growth component but it forces one to think in terms of rate of changes rather than levels. It is not at all robust to the measurement errors—at least those that are not highly serially correlated. Further, it tends to eliminate too much of the power associated with the business cycle frequency.

He continued:

> If people are over (or under) accumulating capital, it is rational for them to offset these errors by accumulating capital at a slower (or faster) rate once the error is recognized. If on the other hand there are no errors, then there is no need to offset past errors. Behavior of inventories suggests there are errors. Our argument … [is against] the finding of growth theorists that growth rates were not constant over the period. I would be wary in interpreting the reported impulse response functions as supporting overshooting. The analysis does suggest there may be less persistence than commonly assumed.

Prescott ended his letter by saying: "Thanks for the encouragement. The reviews on this paper [Hodrick–Prescott] have been mixed … with most on the negative side." As a result, Hodrick–Prescott was not published until 1997, as mentioned in Chapter 1.

Referees, editors and revisions, 1980–1982: the case of "Time to build"

As noted above, the Kydland–Prescott paper was received by *Econometrica* in January 1981. This version of the paper [the December 1980 draft] was entitled "Time to build and persistence of unemployment." In a letter to Ed Prescott dated June 26, 1981, Chris Sims, then co-editor of *Econometrica*, wrote:

> Both referees like your paper with Kydland "Time to build and the persistence of unemployment". One, however, has some suggestions, which are enclosed. He is particularly concerned about what he calls points 3 and 4. Point 3 is that he is made uneasy by your trend-adjustment procedure. It reflects a general difficulty with the paper: it is clear that in some sense you are giving up at the start on the possibility of fitting all aspects of the time series behavior of the data series you use. (These are quarterly, aren't they? The time unit should be explicit.) This may be a reasonable thing to do, but you should provide some indication of what your model misses. You should explain how the drift in your model differs from the observed time series drift. You should summarize in what sense you miss the fine structure of the dynamics. This latter could be done by fitting VAR's to the artificial and actual data and displaying the largest observed differences. Or it could also be done by estimating, say, the first two autocorrelation matrices and drawing attention to the largest differences observed. You may think of other or better ways to accomplish the same thing, but some effort in this direction seems essential to the paper's scientific value.
>
> I assume that the data used are exactly as in Hodrick and Prescott and are given source citations there.
>
> I'll look forward to seeing a revision.

The two referees of "Time to Build" were, in fact, Robert Lucas and John Taylor (personal communication, 21 October 2006). In a letter dated 23 January 1981 to Sims that comprised his report, Lucas wrote:

> I am familiar with the Kydland–Prescott paper, so I can give you my reactions quickly. There is no need to protect my anonymity, though you may if you wish. The paper is very original, both in the business cycle theory it contains and in the way it relates theory and observation. The authors estimate as many parameters as they can from simple sample averages (e.g., factor shares) and informally used "prior" information. Then they fiddle rather unsystematically with remaining parameters to obtain a reasonably close match between certain theoretical moments and the corresponding sample moments. The fiddling is done by a very sophisticated numerical simulation.
>
> The virtue of this procedure is that the model itself is very coherent theoretically, and the data are not permitted to throw estimates into ranges where economic interpretation is difficult or impossible.

> I found the paper very stimulating, especially in the direction of trying to guess at the nature of the statistical model which might rationalize this procedure.
>
> I would strongly recommend publishing this.

In his report on the paper—as Sims noted in his letter to Prescott dated 26 June 1981—Taylor requested revision and clarification of a number of points. Because of its importance for understanding the process of revision of the Kydland–Prescott paper, Taylor's report is cited in full below, in the context of an analysis of its impact on "Time to build." But before doing this, the issue of whether Sim's suggestions were taken into account in the Kydland–Prescott revision of December 1981—which became the published version—must be dealt with.

In a new opening to Section 5 of their revised paper—the section re-titled as "Test of the theory"—Kydland and Prescott addressed some of the points raised by Sims. For example, despite his suggestion, they wrote that they "chose not to test" their model against the "less restrictive vector autoregressive model" (1981, 24; 1982, 1360). On the other hand, they did deal with Sims's points regarding the shortcomings in their model, and its treatment of "the fine structure of dynamics." In the revised subsection entitled "Results" they said that one "possible explanation" for problems in the results they obtained could have been the "oversimplicity" of their model (1981, 31; 1982, 1365). They went on, as Sims put it in his letter to Prescott of 26 June 1981, "to summarize in what sense" they missed "the fine structure of the dynamics" when they wrote in the revised version "Thus, even though the overall fit of the model is very good, it is not surprising, given the level of abstraction, that there are elements of the fine structure of dynamics that it does not capture" (1981, 32; 1982, 1366).

Taylor, for his part, sent Sims a detailed three page referee report on the paper, consisting of four major points. Because of its impact on the form and substance of the final version of "Time to build" this report is cited in full here, and we will show how it brought about the changes between the December 1980 version submitted to *Econometrica*, the September 1981 revised version, presented by Prescott at the October 1981 NBER meeting, as described above, and the final December 1981 revision sent for publication. Taylor opened his report (Taylor, 1981) by saying:

> This paper represents a systematic attempt to show that an *equilibrium* growth model with intertemporal substitution of labor and serial correlation in investment due to *gestation* lags is capable of fitting U.S. business cycle data fairly well [Taylor's emphasis]. It is an extremely well-written paper with the approach carefully laid out, the theory well developed, and with a serious attempt to confront the predictions of the model with statistical regularities. I recommend that it be published in *Econometrica* but have a number of suggestions or questions which I feel the authors should attempt to address before publication.

His first point dealt with the "form" of the model and "calculation" of equilibrium:

> Rather than exclusively state their model in linear quadratic form as is common in rational expectations models, the authors of this paper develop their model in nonlinear form and calculate the equilibrium through linear approximations about the steady state. This alternative approach involves considerable calculation and approximations and in some respects it is difficult to get a feel for how accurate these approximations are. The authors state they do not use a Taylor's series approximation because they want their model to fit well for all points and given realizations. But this leaves one with no measure of goodness of fit of the approximation. At the minimum the authors should indicate why they chose the nonlinear specification and subsequent approximation rather than specify the linear quadratic approach at the beginning. While their approach is unusual for rational expectations modeling, it is not unusual for conventional econometric modeling and the techniques they develop could potentially be useful in other contexts.

Taylor's second point dealt with the "estimation" of the Kydland–Prescott model:

> Section V of the paper is called "Model Estimation". However, rather than estimate the model, the authors obtained information from other sources as to likely parameter values. Although this is largely a matter of semantics, it seems to me that this procedure has been called "model calibration" in the literature and the authors might consider such a term in their analysis. For example, those who compute general equilibrium models for the purposes of evaluating taxes use the word "calibration" in obtaining the parameters of their utility functions and production functions. The use of the word "estimation" in this context does not seem appropriate.

In his third point, he turned to model "evaluation":

> In evaluating their model … the authors use an approach developed earlier by Hodrick and Prescott. Although there might be some advantage to this method of analyzing time series, I feel it is a disadvantage in this paper. The Hodrick–Prescott method for extracting the cyclical component from the slower moving trend component depends on the underlying time-series data. In other words, when the Hodrick–Prescott procedure is used to filter the results of the model, the trend components will be different than that obtained when filtering the actual U.S. data. Hence, the cyclical components which are the ultimate issue here will be different not only because the data is different, but also because the trend extracted from the data is different. It would be more useful if the same trend could be extracted from both data

> sets so that the underlying cyclical components would be the same. In other words, the Hodrick–Prescott procedure makes it difficult for an observer not familiar with these techniques to evaluate the accuracy for this particular model. If the authors do not feel it is possible to do their comparison using more standard types of model-free analysis such as the Sims innovation accounting procedure, then at least they should provide plots of simulations for some of the major variables. These then could be compared visually with the actual observed time series.

Finally, in his fourth point, Taylor focused on "gestation lags" and "technology shocks":

> The main objective of the paper as indicated in the title is to indicate to what extent the persistence of unemployment, or more generally, the persistence of deviations of output from secular movements, is due to the gestation lag in the investment process. However, the model contains a number of sources of persistence in addition to the gestation source. It contains not only the permanent shocks to technology, but it also contains the substitution between work at different points in time. Some attempts should be made to distinguish between these various components in explaining the persistence of unemployment. The results that are thus far reported make it difficult to determine whether for example, the persistence is due to the gestation lags or to the permanent shocks to technology. One possibility would be to stimulate the model with some parameter values for technology shocks and for labor leisure tradeoff over time, but moving the gestation lag to a much shorter time point; at the extreme, have no gestation lag. This would enable one to determine to what extent the gestation lag is important in explaining the persistence of output. This seems particularly important given the title of paper and the time spent in Section II of the paper arguing that the gestation lag model is a more accurate way to describe investment behavior than the more traditional cost of adjustment model.

Taylor's impact upon and changes in variorum drafts of "Time to build": 1980–1982

The drafts of "Time to build"—from that submitted in December 1980 to the final version sent for publication to *Econometrica* in December 1981—are characterized by amendments, additions, and elisions, based on Taylor's referee report, and also resulting from changes Kydland and Prescott implemented and incorporated into the paper, including the title of the paper itself.

Indeed, when asked in an interview (2005) about the title change, Kydland acknowledged that it was based upon Taylor's "Point 4," "or more generally the persistence of deviations of output from secular movements." Moreover, Kydland recalled that while the title of the paper submitted to *Econometrica* contained the phrase "persistence of unemployment" so as "*to catch the eye,*" as he put it, "*there was no unemployment variable in the model*" [Kydland's emphasis]. Thus, as he recalled, the decision to change the title was in accordance with Taylor's comment regarding "the persistence of output" and Kydland's emphasis on "the deviations of output"—that is to say "aggregate fluctuations."

The introduction to the paper was changed by Kydland and Prescott between the December 1980 and September 1981 versions, as noted above. Taylor's points influenced Kydland and Prescott in the following manner. In the introduction to the September 1981 version the following sentence was added (albeit only partially reflecting point 1 in his referee's report regarding their mention of the nature of the utility function): "A crucial feature of preference is the non-time-separable utility function that admits greater intertemporal substitution of leisure."

Moreover, the final paragraph of the introduction to the December 1980 was changed, in the September 1981 version—reflecting the impact of point 2 in Taylor's report regarding "calibration"—to read:

> Findings in other applied areas of economics are used to calibrate the model. For example, the assumed number of periods required to build new productive capital is of the magnitude reported by business, and findings in labor economics are used to restrict the utility function.

Specific sections of the draft also changed as per Taylor's report, and his comments on the September 1981 draft, presented at the October 1981 NBER meeting. Indeed, regarding the latter, point 1 in Taylor's referee report was only fully dealt with in the final December 1981 revision sent to *Econometrica* for publication. This is reflected in the comparison below between the relevant paragraph in the December 1980, September 1981, and December 1981 versions of the paper dealing with point 1. There was no change between the December 1980 and September 1981 versions of the material dealing with the general problem of "approximating" what Kydland and Prescott called the "approximate quadratic function." In the December 1981 revision the paragraph was totally re-written to reflect Taylor's first point (1981b, 19), and a very important addendum regarding their use of the "Taylor series" appeared in the form of a new footnote (1981, 43 note 11) which read:

> We experimented a little and found that the results were essentially the same when the second order Taylor series approximation was used rather than this function. Larry Cristiano ... has found that the quadratic approximation method that we employed yields approximate solutions that are very accurate, even with large variability, for a structure that, like ours, is of the constant elasticity variety.

As the revised text and footnote were only added in the December 1981, and not in the September 1981 revision, it would seem that Taylor, as discussant of that version at the October 1981 NBER meeting, repeated point 1 of his *Econometrica* referee's report in his discussion of the paper, and Kydland–Prescott only then addressed the issue in their December 1981 revision.

Other additions, amendments, and elisions in the drafts between December 1980 and December 1981 appeared in the section entitled "Preferences." In the December 1980 and September 1981 drafts, the relevant paragraph is as follows (1980,12; 1981a, 12):

> Non-time-separable utility functions are implicit in the empirical study of aggregate labor supply by Lucas and Rapping (1969). Grossman (1973) and Lucas (1977) discuss why a non-time-separable utility function is needed to explain the business cycle fluctuations in employment and consumption. Cross-sectional evidence of households' willingness to redistribute labor supply over time is the lumpiness of that supply. There are vacations and movements of household members into and out of the labor force for extended periods which are not in response to large movements in the real wage. Another observation suggesting high intertemporal substitutability of leisure is the large seasonal variation in hours of market employment. Finally the failure of Abowd and Ashenfelter (1981) to find a significant wage premium for jobs with more variable employment and earnings patterns is further evidence. In summary, it is difficult to rationalize the observed patterns of employment and wages (actually marginal products of labor) with a standard time-separable utility function.

In the published version they presented a new argument. As they put it (1982, 1351):

> The micro justification for our hypothesized structure based a Beckerian household production function is as follows. Time allocated to non-market activities ... is used in household production. If there is a stock of household projects with varying output per unit of time, rational households would allocate [this] to those projects with the greatest returns per time unit. If the household has allocated a larger amount of time to non-market activities in the recent past, then only projects with smaller yields should remain.... In summary, household production theory and cross-sectional evidence support a non-time-separable utility function that admits greater intertemporal substitution of labor—something which is needed to explain aggregate movements in employment in an equilibrium model.

Additional examples of the elisions and amendments are found in the sections entitled "Approximation about the Steady State" and "Computation of Equilibrium."

Now, in point 2 of his referee report on the December 1980 version submitted to *Econometrica*, Taylor talked about "Section V" of the paper, which was entitled "Model Estimation," and questioned the wording of the section. The

December 1980 version of "Section V" also included subsections entitled "Tests of the Model" and "Sensitivity of Results to Parameter Selection" (1980, 26–36). The December 1980 version of the latter read (1980, 36):

> All the considered values of the risk aversion parameter ... and the inventory-capital substitution parameter ... yield similar results.... This is true for somewhat smaller values of the intertemporal leisure and substitution parameters ... as well. The results are sensitive to the relative variances of the shocks. Only if the variance of the transitory shock to technology is small relative to the sum of the three variances and the size of the other two variances and the size of the other two variances comparable are the model's serial correlation properties consistent with those for the U.S. post-war economy. In other words, the confounding of the permanent shock to the technology with the noisy indicator is crucial to the model.

Based upon Taylor's recommendation, much of the December 1980 version of "Section V" was elided and replaced by new material. In the September 1981 version, the newly structured "Section V" was entitled "Test of the Theory," with the addition of two pages of text, and included new subsections entitled "Model Calibration," "Results," "Sensitivity of Results to Parameter Selection," and "Importance of Time to Build" (1981a, 26–42). Thus, with regard to "Sensitivity of Results...," the December 1980 version was changed in the September 1981 version as follows (1981a, 39–40):

> With a couple of exceptions, the results were surprisingly insensitive to the values of the parameters. The fact that the covariations of the aggregate variables in the model are quite similar for broad ranges of many of the parameters suggests that, even though the parameters may differ across economies, the nature of business cycles can still be quite similar.
>
> We did find that most of the variation in technology had to come from its permanent component in order for the serial correlation properties of the model to be consistent with U.S. post-war data. We also found that the variance of the indicator shock could not be very large relative to the variance of the permanent technology shock. This would have resulted in cyclical employment varying less than cyclical productivity which is in inconsistent with the data.
>
> Of particular importance for the model is the dependence of current utility on past leisure choices which admits greater intertemporal substitution of leisure. The purpose of this specification is not to contribute to the persistence of output changes. If anything, it does just the opposite. This element of the model is crucial in making it consistent with the observation that cyclical employment fluctuates substantially more than productivity does.

As noted, the September 1981 version also contained a new subsection with the title "Importance of Time to Build" (1981a, 40–42). This followed from

Taylor's point 4, regarding the importance of comparing the results of the "gestation lag" approach, as against the "cost of adjustment" approach, including the "polar case" of "no gestation lag" (1981a, 41). More significant, perhaps, was the change in text made in this subsection between the September 1981 and the final versions. The September 1981 version read (1981a, 41):

> The magnitude of the adjustment cost can probably best be judged in terms of the effect it has on the relative price of investment goods … Even when the adjustment cost is of this small magnitude, the covariance properties of the model are grossly inconsistent with U.S. data for the post-war period. In particular, most of the fluctuation of output in this model is caused by productivity changes rather than changes in work hours. The standard deviation of hours is 0.42, while the standard deviation of productivity is 1.46. This is just the opposite of what the U.S. data show.

In the published version, the results reported were as follows (1982, 1367): "The standard deviation of hours is 0.60, while the standard deviation of productivity is 1.29."

There were also changes made in the "Test of the Theory" subsection between the September 1981 revision and the December 1981 version sent to *Econometrica* for publication. For example, following from Taylor's point 3, Kydland and Prescott justified their use of data generated by the Hodrick–Prescott filter in the following paragraph, which was added in the published version (1982, 1362):

> The statistics reported in [Hodrick and Prescott, "Post-war U.S. business cycles: an empirical investigation," Working Paper, Carnegie-Mellon University, revised 1980] are not the only way to quantitatively capture the co-movements of the deviations. This approach is simple, involves a minimum of judgment, and is robust to slowly changing demographic factors which affect growth, but are not the concern of this theory. In addition, the statistics are robust to most measurement errors, in contrast to, say, the correlations between the first differences of two series. It is important to compute the same statistics for the U.S. economy as for the model, that is, to use the same function of the data. This is what we do.

Following on from this, they added an additional subsection on "The Smoothed Series," describing the results they obtained for "the smoothed output series" for U.S. post-war data, which they found "deviated significantly from the linear time trend." According to Kydland and Prescott, this matched "well with the predictions of the model," and "the smoothed output series" was "also consistent with the model" (1982, 1366). Moreover, wording was changed in the "Results" subsection between the September 1981 revision and the final version. For example, the September 1981 revision read (1981a, 38): "The most troublesome anomalies are the model's low variability of hours and the related problem of high correlation of productivity with output. Part of this discrepancy might be due to measurement errors." This was changed to (1982, 1365): "The model displays more variability in hours than in productivity, but not by as much as the data show. In light of the difficulties in measuring output and, in particular, employment, we do not think this discrepancy is large." An additional paragraph was also added to the "Results" section in the final version, which read (1982, 1366):

> We also examined lead and lagged relationships and serial correlation properties of aggregate series other than output. We found that, both for the post-war U.S. economy and the model, consumption and non-inventory investment move contemporaneously with output and have serial correlation properties similar to output. Inventory and capital stocks for the model lag output, which also matches well with the data. Some of the inventories stock's cross-serial correlations with output deviate significantly, however, from those for the U.S. economy. The one variable whose lead-lag relationship does not match with the data is productivity. For the U.S. economy it is a leading indicator, while there is no lead or lag in the model. This was not unexpected in view of our discussion above with regard to productivity. Thus, even though the overall fit of the model is very good, it is not surprising, given the level of abstraction, that there are elements of the fine structure of dynamics that it does not capture.

Some wording in the conclusion was also changed between the September 1981 revision and the final version of the paper. For example, the September 1981 version read (1981a, 44): "Another refinement is the estimation procedure. But in spite of the considerable advances recently made by Hansen and Sargent (1980), computational considerations still preclude the application of maximum likelihood or Bayesian estimation techniques." The final published version read (1982, 1369):

> Another possible refinement is in the estimation procedure. But, in spite of the considerable advances recently made by Hansen and Sargent (1980), further advances are needed before formal econometric methods can be fruitfully applied to testing this theory of aggregate fluctuations.

Finally, a new footnote was added in the final published version to the first sentence of the last paragraph in the paper. The sentence read (1982, 1369): "Models such as the one considered in this paper could be used to predict the consequence of a particular policy rule on the operating characteristics of the economy." The note read (1369 note 19): "examples of such policy issues are described in [21]," referring the reader to the published version of Kydland and Prescott's 1978 "Bald Peak" paper. The circle was now complete regarding the linkage between the variorum drafts of their "Time to build" approach.

Cross-fertilization, editorial role expansion, and revision: the Long–Plosser case

The interaction and cross-fertilization of ideas between Long and Plosser and Kydland and Prescott was significant, but it is not the only case of interaction between Long and Plosser and others working in related areas of research. This is evident from a letter dated 5 December 1980 from Brock, from the University of Wisconsin, to Long, at Rochester. Brock wrote (Brock to Long, 1980):

> I read your paper "Real Business Cycles" with interest.
>
> I wonder if you could put stocks into your model along the lines of the enclosed SSWP 275 ["Asset Prices in a Production Economy," California Institute of Technology, June 1978, Revised July 1979], especially p. 66, and explain stylized facts about the behavior of stock prices over the business cycle?
>
> It is interesting to note that your example in section 3 is closely related to my example in section 5 (page 53). I think I lectured on that in Barro's workshop two years ago. In any event, you should be able to calculate closed form solutions for stock market values of firms and stock prices along the lines developed on page 66 of SSWP 275.
>
> I might add that I developed the theory of those kinds of decentralized asset pricing models independent of Prescott and Mehra (PN) and (in my opinion) got better theorems. Yet I see (PM) cited ad nauseum while my work lies in the dust bin of the lagging Chicago Press production schedule. 'Tis discouraging.
>
> You might look at the two enclosed papers and judge for yourself how good the results are. They were both written in early 1978 and lectured on extensively in 1977–78.
>
> In any event, I enjoyed your paper and am gratified that my years of study of stochastic growth models were not wasted.

As shown above, there was constructive interaction between Chris Sims, the editor of *Econometrica*, and the authors in the Kydland–Prescott case. The revision of the Long–Plosser paper, for its part, was also based upon constructive interaction between the authors and Sam Peltzman, the editor of the *Journal of Political Economy*, whose role was actually expanded at their behest, as will be seen below. The process of revision in this case can be seen in letters from Plosser and Long to Peltzman over the period February–June 1982. The paper was sent to *JPE* on 16 February 1982. In a letter dated 1 April 1982, Peltzman sent his comments, and that of the referee.

On 9 April 1982, Long and Plosser replied to Peltzman:

> We appreciate your comments and those of the reviewer. We are especially pleased with the excellent turn-around time you provided. We are writing to you now to express our immediate reaction to the comments and to seek some further advice concerning appropriate revision of our paper.

Long and Plosser summarized the points raised by Peltzman and the referee:

> As we understand them, the major comments/suggestions are:
>
> (1) There is an inadequate link between the model ... and the simulation...
> (2) In particular, the dynamics ... seem to be independent of consumer preferences and utility maximization. The notion of business cycle dynamics resulting from maximizing choice should be emphasized.
> (3) Given the causal link between the sections ... and the apparent simplicity of the basic theoretical idea (that a production lag combined with any reasonable intertemporal preferences imply smoothing the effects of transitory shocks), the theoretical model ... is overdone and should be shortened and de-emphasized relative to the simulation...

Long and Plosser went on to address these points: "As a matter of expositional inadequacy, we fully agree with comments (1) and (2). There is, in fact, an intimate and exact link between the model and the simulation, but we clearly did not to make that link obvious." However, they continued that: "The dilemma we face concerns comment (3). We are entirely willing to attempt some shortening ... but we believe that if comments (1) and (2) are addressed, *substantial* shortening will be inappropriate." They then described the connection between their model and the dynamics of the "model economy." As they put it:

> The link between the model and the dynamics analyzed ... is this: Section 3 presents an exact "closed-form" solution for equilibrium quantities and relative prices in a particular example of the type of economy generally described in section 2. [This solution is itself unique. To our knowledge, no one else has ever presented such a closed-form solution without either assuming quadratic preferences and linear technology or approximating actual preference/technology with a quadratic-linear form.] The joint time-series behavior of outputs expressed in equation 4.1 (page 26) is *not* an ad hoc specification. Equation 4.1 is the *exact formula* for output behavior *in the model economy of section 3*. Is obtained by directly substituting the equilibrium utility maximizing input rules from Section 3 into the Cobb–Douglas production functions assumed in the section 3 economy. The A matrix is the matrix of exponents from those production functions. The constant vector k determines the "steady state" vector of expected outputs. This vector depends on all of the parameters of the utility function assumed in Section 3 (a point that we neglected to mention, much less emphasize). Without the detailed model of section 3 the dynamics analyzed in section 4 would be, at best, an ad hoc analogy between observed multi-sector output behavior and the behavior of vector autoregressive processes As a purely descriptive conjecture, this analogy is commonplace and not, in itself, very informative with respect to the *economic* principles that generate such a process. Our section 3, however, both makes the analogy exact and fully

> specifies the autoregressive parameters in terms of the preferences and technological parameters of the economy [emphases of Long and Plosser].

Long and Plosser then gave two additional reasons for their objection to cutting back the sections on their "formal model":

> The first is a matter of emphasizing economic interpretation. Section 4 characterizes the dynamics of our example economy primarily in terms of its probabilistic properties (e.g., covariance structure, impulse response functions, etc.) and in terms of the correspondence between these properties and alleged regularities in actual business cycles. We regard this as an essential part of the paper but, by itself, it is only a summary of the "outcomes" of the underlying economic forces at work in our model economy. The bulk of our analysis of those underlying economic forces is in sections 2 and 3. The present length of those sections is in fact due to our (perhaps inept) attempt to make them as widely accessible as possible (compare the density of mathematics in our presentation with that in Lucas' 1975 *JPE* article "Equilibrium Business Cycles".) We fear that a substantial shortening of the sections will make them less readable and/or de-emphasize the economic principles that give rise to "business cycle" behavior.

They went on to say:

> This fear would be unwarranted, of course, if the economics of the model were so simply straight-forward that it did not require any lengthy discussion. We don't believe that this is the case, however, and this is our final reason for questioning the reviewer's suggestion that presentation of the "basic idea" be substantially shortened. It is not true that (in the reviewer's words) "the one-period production lag, combined with any type of utility function which would imply smoothing across time and commodities, will generate the desired result". As we point out in the paper, smoothing behavior that *would* occur in response to shocks at *constant* relative prices may *not* occur in equilibrium when one accounts for the changes in relative prices induced by the shocks. An immediate and extreme example of this is a special case of our example (Sections 3–4) economy in which labor is the only input in production. In that case shocks are not smoothed across either time or commodities even though the opportunity to smooth is available and our representative consumer would smooth at constant relative prices. It takes a rather close examination of the basic "smoothing" idea to usefully characterize the *combinations* of preferences and technology that lead to the kind of fluctuations observed in actual business cycles (see, for example, our conclusions about labor employment, pp. 21–22). We believe that our analysis of this issue in sections 2–3 contains some non-obvious implications of the "basic idea" that are not evident in the discussion of dynamics in section 4 [emphases by Long and Plosser].

Long and Plosser then turned to Peltzman to ask for his assistance in the revision process:

> We are most anxious to work with you in revising our paper. We would appreciate your reaction to our comments and welcome any additional advice you could offer as to how we might go about preparing a revision that you would find acceptable.

Two months later, on June 15, 1982, Long and Plosser sent Peltzman their revised version of the paper. In the covering letter, they wrote:

> We have done a considerable amount of rewriting and reorganizing in an effort to shorten and improve the manuscript. Overall, we managed to shorten the paper by over 25%. Specifically, we have made a number of changes in response to your comments and those of the referee:
>
> (i) Section 2, which previously discussed the "general model", has been substantial shortened and from over 8 pages to 4 pages. As now written Section 2 quickly lays out the major assumptions and notation of the model as a minimal introduction to the example worked out in Sections 3 and 4.
> (ii) Section 3 has been shortened by eliminating some redundant and tangential passages…
> (iii) The logical link between the utility-maximizing allocation rules (page 11) and the dynamic behavior of outputs has been emphasized.… We have also explicitly noted (page 17–18) how and where the utility parameters appear in the stochastic difference equations governing outputs.
> (iv) Section 4, which presents the simulation of the example, has not been significantly shortened, but some minor stylistic changes have been made.

They ended their letter by saying: "We believe that the revised version of the paper is a better and more economical exposition of our basic ideas and we hope that you will agree. The suggestions made by you and your referee were most helpful."

Citation analysis is usually applied to assess the impact of a paper on the respective field of economic inquiry and on the economics profession as a whole. An analysis of cross-citation, for its part, can provide some information regarding the interaction between research programs and associated papers. The pertinent case here is that of the relationship between the published versions of Kydland–Prescott (1982) and Long–Plosser (1983), as there was indeed cross-citation—albeit of unpublished working papers. Kydland–Prescott (1982, 1368 note 17; 1370), for its part, refers to a November 1980 University of Rochester Working Paper version of Long–Plosser. Long and Plosser (1983, 44–45; 69), for its part, cites a "September 1981 Carnegie-Mellon Working Paper" version of Kydland–Prescott. The title of the September 1981 Kydland–Prescott working paper cited by Long–Plosser was that of the 1982 published version of Kydland–Prescott—that is, "Time to build and aggregate fluctuations." As shown above, the version of Kydland–Prescott received by *Econometrica* in January 1981 was "Time to build and the persistence of unemployment," which was the title of the December 1980 version of Kydland–Prescott (1980c). The December 1981 revision of Kydland–Prescott, received by *Econometrica* in January 1982 (1982, 1369), was submitted with the revised title, which appeared in the published version of the paper, as noted in Chapter 2.

As for the impact of working papers and their interaction, one prominent example from this context should suffice. This involves the relationship between Prescott–Mehra and Long–Plosser. In December 1977, Prescott and Mehra circulated a draft paper entitled "Recursive competitive equilibria and capital asset pricing" (Prescott and Mehra, 1977). In 1978, this paper was revised and given the title "Recursive competitive equilibrium: the case of homogenous households," and circulated as a Columbia University Graduate School of Business Working Paper. The paper was eventually published in the September 1980 issue of *Econometrica.* The 1978 draft of the paper was received in December 1978, and the final corrected version in December 1979 (1980, 1378). In their 1977 draft, Prescott and Mehra further developed the recursive competitive equilibrium framework originally presented in Lucas and Prescott (1971). Moreover, they extended it to the analysis of the cases of "many consumers" and "small fluctuations in aggregate output." In the former case, their analysis was of "an economy with many consumer classes, where each class has different preferences, but the same discount factor" (1977, 21). The latter was an analysis of the case where "fluctuations in aggregate output are but a few percent" (1977, 22). They concluded "These difficult and important extensions and applications will be the subject of future inquiry within our recursive competitive equilibrium framework" (1977, 23).

This case is an important one, since—based upon the 1977 draft, as cited above—if all agents have the same discount rate, and if conditions satisfy that a competitive equilibrium Pareto Optimum is ensured, then, as Prescott and Mehra later wrote (1980a, 1365), "equilibrium processes for economic aggregates and prices [for some heterogeneous consumer economy] will be observationally equivalent to those for some homogeneous consumer economy." Moreover, that fluctuations in aggregate output is mentioned in their 1977 draft is also significant, although there is no mention of this in the 1980 version. The importance of the 1977 and 1978 drafts of Prescott and Mehra lies not only in it being the linkage between Lucas and Prescott (1971) and their 1980 paper, but because of their impact, it would seem, on Long and Plosser's 1983 paper—that is to say, on the 1980 draft of Long and Plosser.

In their 1983 *JPE* paper, Long and Plosser wrote (1983, 43 note 4):

> The model we employ is quite similar to the model described in Prescott and Mehra (1980). Their remarks (p. 1365) about the identical consumers

> assumption (i.e. it is not quite as restrictive as it may appear) and their treatment of the optimality of competitive equilibrium are particularly relevant. They do not, however, explicitly consider the business-cycle implications of their models.

In correspondence with Mehra (2005a, b, c), he acknowledged that Long had seen the 1977 version of Prescott–Mehra at a Rochester "job seminar" that took place in "late 1977 or early 1978." The Prescott–Mehra paper was published in September 1980. Now, the earliest citation of what was to become the Long–Plosser paper found by this author dates to 1980, as cited in the August 1980 draft of the now classic "Two Charlie's paper" (Nelson and Plosser, 1980). This implies that unless either Long or Plosser, or both, were referees of the 1980 Prescott–Mehra paper—which is doubtful—it can be surmised that Long and Plosser most probably extended the 1977 and 1978 Prescott and Mehra approach.

Long–Plosser was presented at a number of places, including Wisconsin, USC, Stanford, Washington, Carnegie-Mellon, and MIT (1983, 39), and elicited the written comments of Black; the November 1980 Long–Plosser working paper was also cited in versions of Kydland–Prescott and King–Plosser. As seen above, then, the interactions between authors, referees, and editors were instrumental in bringing the papers to their published form, which brought about the research program. The Long–Plosser case, however, deserves attention due to its "metamorphosis" from a multi-sector to a one-sector approach. And it is to the King–Plosser and King–Plosser–Rebelo papers that we now turn.

4 Themes, variations, and initial extensions

In previous chapters, we dealt with the origins and evolution of the watershed Kydland–Prescott (1982) and Long–Plosser (1983) papers. This chapter deals with the research programs they generated. In the first part of the chapter, the extension of Long–Plosser in the form of the King–Plosser model (1981, 1982, 1984a) is discussed. We then proceed to its further development in the King–Plosser–Rebelo "class of models" (Plosser, 1989c, 14 note 7; King *et al.*, 1986; 1987; 1988a, b; 2002). The ongoing efforts of Long and Plosser (1987) and Plosser (1989a, b, c; 1990) to explain their approach is then dealt with. The second part of the chapter deals with extensions, variations, and the initial critique of "Time to build." This includes extensions by Sumru Altug, Gary Hansen, Thomas Cooley, Kydland and Prescott themselves, the critique of Heckman, and Kydland's reply. The focus here is on Altug's econometric estimation of Kydland–Prescott and its utilization in Heckman's critique of Kydland and Kydland–Prescott, Hansen's extension in the form of "indivisible labor," Kydland and Prescott's "workweek of capital," and the contributions of Cooley to the story.

From Long–Plosser and King–Plosser to King–Plosser–Rebelo

In June 2007, Robert King was interviewed on "the evolution of thought" regarding the transition from the Long–Plosser approach to the King–Plosser and King–Plosser–Rebelo frameworks (2007b, 29 June). He reported that a "paper trail" from the 1980s regarding their development was not to be found, at least in his files, as when he "left the University of Virginia to move to Boston University," he "apparently threw away everything about this period ... including drafts of various papers, correspondence and so forth" (2007a, email 28 June). Despite this, some papers emanating from the King–Plosser research program did appear in the form of Rochester Center for Economic Research (RCER) and NBER Working Papers before publication, and the ongoing work of King and Plosser, and that with Rebelo, was cited in these as "manuscripts in progress" (e.g. King and Plosser, 1984b, "Production, Growth and Business Cycles," cited in King and Plosser, 1986). King's recollections will therefore be integrated here with the material reflecting the development of King–Plosser and King–Plosser–Rebelo extant, so as to provide some insight into their origins and evolution.

King on Long–Plosser

When interviewed in 2007, King recalled the "first presentation of Long–Plosser at the Rochester Macro Workshop," organized by Robert Barro. King recalled that "at this presentation there were substantial discussions" regarding (1) "how large are productivity shocks," and (2) "what could be done to eliminate the fixity of employment and 100% depreciation." King also recalled that while for Long and Plosser it was "clear that the multi-sectoral approach" was the "way to do things," and that while "everybody recognized that multiple sector models were interesting," they "were hard to solve" and demanded "specific assumptions." King also remembered Grossman asking "why should I be interested in a business cycle model where employment is constant?" In the interview, King went on to say that the "Real Business Cycle" approach was "not an overnight or an immediate success," and that within the framework of the NBER Summer Institute Program on "economic fluctuations" in July 1982, King and Plosser "organized a small discussion group on it, consisting of King, Plosser, Kydland, Prescott, Black, and Christiano" (interview, 29 June 2007).

King and Plosser, 1981–1984

The earliest version of King and Plosser was their 1981 University of Rochester Working Paper entitled "The Behavior of Money, Credit and Prices in a Real Business Cycle" (1981a). According to King (interview, 29 June 2007), it was presented in the Spring of 1981 at an "informal seminar" at the University of Rochester, and was also presented at the University of Chicago and the University of Pennsylvania. In June 1981 the paper was also presented at a meeting at the University of Konstanz (1981b). King (interview, 29 June 2007) thought this presentation was "crucial" as it was "the first outside of Rochester."

The paper was then presented at the October 1981 NBER fluctuations group meeting held at the University of Chicago, and was discussed by Azariadis. Interestingly enough, as noted in Chapter 2, the Kydland–Prescott "Time to build" paper was also presented at this meeting. The description of the King–Plosser paper in the report of the meeting read as follows (NBER Report of Chicago meeting, 1981, 27):

> The paper by King and Plosser describes an initial attempt to account for the money-output relationship through the operation of the banking system and the monetary authority, in a business cycle that is fully "real" in origin. Broadly, the real sector drives the monetary sector, in contrast to the traditional view of monetary movements as business-cycle impulses. The theoretical analysis focuses on the banking system's central position in the

> economy while deemphasizing the role of central bank policy response. Preliminary empirical analysis at the annual interval provides general support for this focus, since much of the correlation between monetary measures and real activity is apparently with inside money.

According to King (interview, 29 June 2007), the October 1981 version of his paper (1981c) with Plosser was sent to the NBER for circulation as a working paper after the October 1981 meeting. In February 1982, the King–Plosser paper appeared, under the same title as their October 1981 paper, as NBER Working Paper 853 (1982). The abstract of their 1982 NBER paper is very similar to the description of the October 1981 version. The abstract read:

> This paper analyzes the interaction of money and the price level with a business cycle that is fully real in origin, adopting a view which differs sharply from traditional theories that assign a significant causal influence to monetary movements. The theoretical analysis focuses on a banking system that produces transaction services on demand and thus reflects market activity. Under one regime of bank regulation and fiat money supply by the monetary authority, the real business cycle theory predicts that (i) movements in external monetary measures should be uncorrelated with real activity and (ii) movements in internal monetary measures should be positively correlated with real activity. Preliminary empirical analysis provides general support for this focus on the banking sector since much of the correlation between monetary measures and real activity is apparently with inside money.

After describing their model as "a stochastic growth model with a single final product" (1982, 4), King and Plosser referred to the November 1980 Long–Plosser working paper in the following terms (1982, 4): "Stochastic growth models of a more general variety have recently been employed to study business cycles by Long and Plosser (1980)." Their NBER Working Paper also referred to Nelson and Plosser's *Journal of Monetary Economics* article as "forthcoming." The King–Plosser paper was published under the title "Money, Credit and Prices in a Real Business Cycle" in the June 1984 issue of the *American Economic Review* (1984a). In this version of the King–Plosser paper, the published versions of Kydland–Prescott and Long–Plosser were cited, but not the working papers of either.

In the interview (29 June 2007), King recalled the origins of his paper with Plossser. According to him, "while Kydland–Prescott and Long–Plosser advanced the view that production shocks were dominant, the correlation between monetary shocks and real activity showed that money should also he dealt with in real business cycle theory"; and this, as the real business cycle, could "be seen as a model driven by production shocks or as a model that 'delivers' business cycles." King also said that they wanted to attempt to prove Tobin's (1970) "reverse causation" in a general equilibrium environment by emphasizing the banking system, following on from Tobin (1963). King stressed that "people build models to display a core point." He said that in the Long–Plosser model, as "the stress was on co-movements," the model "needed a rich production structure." In his view, the King–Plosser model, on the other hand, was a "model for macroeconomists." Moreover, King said that the paper was "designed to produce a 'sharp reaction' from the 'old style Keynesians' and supporters of the 'new style' sticky wage approach as seen in Fischer (1977)." King recalled that while his paper with Plosser "started well after" the Kydland–Prescott and Long–Plosser papers, it was completed "early enough for simultaneous conference presentation" with the Kydland–Prescott paper, as described above. King also recalled that his paper with Plosser was first submitted to the *Journal of Political Economy*, then edited by Robert Barro, and while "it had positive reports on two rounds," it was formally "declined" for publication there. A substantially revised version of the paper was then sent to the *American Economic Review*, edited by Robert Clower, who "accepted" the paper and it was "published almost immediately." A comparison of the 1982 and 1984 versions is presented below.

NBER and AER versions of King–Plosser

The 1982 NBER Working Paper version of King–Plosser underwent a number of changes—both formal and substantive—before it was published in 1984 in the *American Economic Review*. The title was changed, with the phrase "The behavior of" elided, and the introduction was also changed, with some material put into long footnotes. According to King and Plosser, their analysis of "the model economy" employed "a stochastic neoclassical growth model in which movements in money and real activity respond to variations in real opportunities ..." with a "single final product" (1982, 2,4). And this, in contrast to "stochastic growth models of a more general variety"—which, in the words of King and Plosser, "have recently been employed to study business cycles by Long and Plosser (1980)"—incorporated "many final products ... a more general pattern of production interrelationships," thereby generating "richer patterns of variation in economic activity" (1982, 4). In their view, "the main aspects of the interactions of money, credit and prices with a real business cycle" could "be outlined" in the "simpler framework" of their "present" model (1982, 4).

What is more significant, in light of King's recollection regarding their objective of producing a "sharp reaction" from Keynesians and supporters of the "sticky wage" approach, was the change in language between the 1982 and 1984 versions of the paper regarding this. In the 1982 version they wrote (1982, 3):

> Our motivation for pursuing this line of research is to produce an equilibrium model that is capable of explaining the joint time-series behavior of real quantity variables, relative prices, the price level, and alternative monetary measures. It is a common observation, however, that such models must include a causal role for money [e.g., Lucas (1977)]. Yet, economic

> theory has yet to provide a convincing rationale for such a "nonneutrality" of money. Traditional explanations focus on central, but implausible market failures: Keynesian models most obviously so and recent equilibrium theories in terms of the use of information, particularly contemporaneous monetary information ... Consequently, it seems worthwhile to consider alternative hypotheses concerning money and business cycles.

In a note to this paragraph they said (1982, 40 note 3):

> Not surprisingly this single sentence dismissal of received doctrine on the relationship between money and business cycles has provoked a sharp reaction from a number of readers. Although a footnote is not an appropriate vehicle for a survey of contemporary macro theory, some additional comments are perhaps in order. Keynesian models typically rely on implausible wage rigidities, from the textbook reliance on exogenous values to recent, most sophisticated efforts of Fischer (1977) and Phelps and Taylor (1977) that rely on existing nominal contracts. As Barro (1977) points out, a key feature of the Fisher—Phelps–Taylor model is that agents select contracts that do not fully exploit potential gains from trade.

In the 1984 *American Economic Review* version they wrote:

> Our proposed explanation of the correlation between money and business fluctuations stands in sharp contrast to traditional theories that stress market failure as the key to understanding the relation and interpret monetary movements as a primary source of impulses to real activity. Given the controversy surrounding the main contending hypotheses concerning money and business cycles—the incomplete information framework of Lucas (1973) and the Keynesian sticky wage models as revitalized by Stanley Fischer (1977)—it seems worthwhile to consider alternative hypotheses.

In a note to this paragraph they said (1984a, 363 note 3):

> In our view, there are good reasons for dissatisfaction with existing macroeconomic theories. Keynesian models typically rely on implausible wage or price rigidities, from the textbook reliance on exogenous values to the recent more sophisticated effort of Fischer (1977) that relies on existing nominal contracts.

Other additions to the 1984 paper include text and notes referring to the "recent real general equilibrium theories of the business cycle" which "illustrate how these models can mimic the key elements of business cycles, including complex patterns of persistence and comovements in economic time series" (1984a, 363 note 1; 364). Moreover, an important section entitled "Households" was added (1984a, 365–366) and parts of other sections rewritten (1984a, 367–368). Other changes included the addition of parameters and variables, such as real wages, resulting in the revision of a number of equations to include the real wage (defined by King–Plosser as "average hourly earnings divided by the producer price index" (1984a, 365, table 1)). Their inclusion of the real wage was important in their view, for, as they wrote: "although not included in many other studies, the real wage enters these equations in a manner that is consistent with our theory" (1984a, 377–378). On the other hand, sections in the text of the 1982 version were elided, such as the section on "Asset returns" (1982, 7–8), as were major portions of the 1982 sections on "Industry" and "Equilibrium prices and quantities" (1984a, 8–10). However, while some aspects of the two versions are different, as shown above, the conclusion of the 1982 and 1984 papers stressed the same basic points. Indeed, in a somewhat prescient final paragraph King and Plosser wrote (1982, 39; 1984a, 378–379):

> some individuals have argued that market failure is central to both the understanding of cyclical fluctuations and the primary reason for economists to study these phenomena. Our view is that widespread market failure need not be a necessary component of a theory of business fluctuations, and that real equilibrium business cycle theory promises to make important contributions to positive economics. This perspective, however, is not inconsistent with the view that the accumulation of scientific knowledge may lead to the design of more desirable policies toward business fluctuations (such as tax and expenditure policies) or toward the regulation of the financial sector.

From King–Plosser to King–Plosser–Rebelo: "production, growth and business cycles," 1984–1988

In his 2007 interview, King asserted that what distinguished King–Plosser–Rebelo I and II (1988a, b) was that "the researcher is told how to solve the model by solving efficiency conditions by using a linear systems approach, which can also be applied outside the real business cycle framework." Moreover, the King–Plosser–Rebelo approach was designed "to provide a broad based platform," so as to also enable its utilization in "new Keynesian type environments" and deal with "imperfect competition" and "tax shocks" (interview, 29 June 2007). Indeed, as they put it (1988b, 327):

> Many economists believe that analysis of economies with suboptimal competitive equilibrium is necessary for understanding various macroeconomic phenomena. Distorting taxation, externalities, market incompleteness, increasing returns to scale and imperfect competition are often invoked as key ingredients in explaining certain features of the data or as a rationale for policy interventions. The objective of this section [1988b, section 4, pp. 327–335] is to explore methods that allow us to incorporate some of these alternatives.

Now, as noted above, "Production, Growth and Business cycles" (1984b) was cited as a "manuscript in progress" by King and Plosser in their July 1986 Rochester Center for Economic Research Working Paper "Nominal Surprises, Real Factors and Propagation Mechanisms" (King and Plosser, 1986). In this paper, King and Plosser outlined the approach they were taking in their "manuscript in progress" version of "Production, Growth and Business Cycles" in terms of "propagation mechanisms" such as "various types of labor market capital" (1986, 17). A manuscript version of "Production, Growth and Business Cycles" including Rebelo as co-author was cited in Long and Plosser's May 1987 *American Economic Review* paper "Sectoral vs. Aggregate Shocks in the Business Cycle" (1987, 336), which was presented at the American Economic Association meeting the year before, and which will be discussed below.

The King–Plosser–Rebelo research program "Production, Growth and Business Cycles" is based upon three components. Two papers were published in the *Journal of Monetary Economics* in 1988 subtitled "The Basic Neoclassical Model" and "New Directions." In their introduction to the 1988 *Journal of Monetary Economics* issue, King and Plosser noted that the papers were presented at a June 1986 conference on Real Business Cycles held in Lisbon, Portugal. They described the papers as follows (King and Plosser 1988, 191):

> King, Plosser and Rebelo provide an introduction to the neoclassical model of capital accumulation and show how it can be used as an integrated model of economic growth and of business fluctuations. They conclude that the framework provides a good basis for understanding many of the characteristic features of business cycles, but also exhibit some shortcomings. In particular, shocks to technology must be highly serially correlated if a model with exogenous growth is to match the serial correlation properties of postwar U.S. economic time series. Alternative specifications and extensions are considered in the second King, Plosser and Rebelo paper discussed further below.

In the first King–Plosser–Rebelo paper, this description was extended to include shocks emanating from other causes. They wrote (1988a, 196):

> Real business cycle theory, though still in the early stages of development, holds considerable promise for enhancing our understanding of economic fluctuations and growth as well as their interaction. The basic framework developed in this essay is capable of addressing a wide variety of issues that are commonly thought to be important for understanding business cycles. While we focus here on models whose impulses are technological, the methods can be adapted to consider shocks originating from preferences or other exogenous factors such as government policies and terms of trade. Some of these extensions to the basic framework are developed in the companion essay [1988b].

They went on to say:

> To many readers is it must seem heretical to discuss business cycles without mentioning money. Our view, however, is simply that the role of money in an equilibrium theory of economic growth and fluctuations remains an open area for research. Further, real disturbances generate rich and neglected interactions in the basic neoclassical model that may account for a substantial portion of observed fluctuations. The objective of real business cycle research is to obtain a better understanding of the character of these real fluctuations. Without an understanding of these real fluctuations it is difficult *a priori* to assign an important role to money.

However, there were two items that were not cited in either of the *Journal of Monetary Economics* papers. The first was the King–Plosser 1984 *American Economic Review* paper; the second was the "Technical Appendix" to the papers. Regarding the former, this was an oversight, as King recalled (interview, 2007). The story of the "Technical Appendix," however, is somewhat more involved. According to the University of Rochester Library Catalog, it is dated May 1987. It was later circulated in June 2001, with an abstract as follows (King *et al.*, 2001):

> The methods used in our two survey papers on real business cycles (King, Plosser and Rebelo [1988a, b]) are detailed in this document. Our presentation of the basic neoclassical model of growth and business cycles is broken into three parts. First, we describe the model and its steady-state, discussing: the structure of the environment including government policy rules; the nature of optimal individual decisions and the dynamic competitive equilibrium; technical restrictions to insure steady state growth; comparable restrictions on preferences and policy rules; stationary levels and ratios in the steady state; and the nature of a transformed economy. Second, we detail methods for studying near steady-state dynamics, considering: the linear approximation approach; the rational expectations solution algorithm; the nature of alternative solutions; and the special case of the fixed linear model. Third, we discuss the computation of simulations, moments and impulse responses.

The "Technical Appendix," it should be noted, was only published in the October 2002 issue of *Computational Economics* (King *et al.*, 2002).

Long and Plosser, and Plosser, 1987–1990: extensions and explanations

In an important extension to their 1983 paper, Long and Plosser (1987) presented the results of the further analysis of "Sectoral vs. Aggregate Shocks in the Business Cycle." They first reiterated what they had done in their 1983 paper (1987, 333):

> In multisector versions of these models (1983), we show that even if random productivity shocks are independent across sectors, agent's choices will cause comovement of activity measures from different sectors. Thus, observed comovements do not logically dictate the presence of a common or aggregate disturbance.

They then described what they intended to present in their 1987 paper:

> The purpose of this paper is to look directly at the comovement in commodity outputs in an attempt to determine the extent to which it can be characterized as resulting from a common aggregate shock from a more diverse set of independent disturbances.

They summarized their results as follows (1987, 336):

> The data we have investigated suggests that the explanatory power of a common aggregate disturbance for industrial outputs is significant, but not very large for most industries. This result arises even though our factor analysis procedure attributes all correlations among industry innovations to a common factor. If any part of the observed comovement of industry output innovations is attributed to independent disaggregate influences like regionally specific shocks, then the implied explanatory power of an aggregate factor is less than we have estimated.

Plosser's survey "Understanding Real Business Cycles" appeared in the Summer 1989 issue of *Journal of Economic Perspectives* (1989a). In it, he made the important observation that "analytical solutions for decision rules under uncertainty are rare" and noted that (1989a, 57 note 10):

> Long and Plosser (1983) provide an example. Unfortunately, their example possesses some special features that limit its usefulness for business cycle research. In particular, they require 100 percent depreciation to obtain the analytical solution. This results in hours worked being invariant to variations in productivity. As suggested by Long and Plosser and demonstrated by King, Plosser and Rebelo (1988a), this result does not hold when the assumption of 100 percent depreciation is relaxed.

The first draft of Plosser's paper "Money and Business Cycles: a Real Business Cycle Interpretation" was originally prepared in September 1989, and presented at the St. Louis Fed in October 1989. The second draft is dated December 1989, and appeared in the same month as Rochester Center for Economic Research Working Paper 210, and in January 1990 as NBER Working Paper 3221 (Plosser, 1990). In the abstract to this paper he wrote:

> This paper focuses on the role of money in economic fluctuations. While money may play an important role in market economies, its role as an

> important impulse to business cycles remains a highly controversial hypothesis. For years economists have attempted to construct monetary theories of the business cycle with only limited empirical success. Alternatively, recent real theories of the cycle have taken the view that to a first approximation, independent variations in the nominal quantity of outside money are neutral. This paper finds that the empirical evidence for a monetary theory of the cycle is weak. Not only do variations in nominal money explain very little of subsequent movements in real activity, but what explanatory power exists arises from variations in endogenous components of money.

To sum up then, the Long–Plosser approach (1983) is a *multi-sector* log linear model. The King–Plosser (1982, 1984) approach is a *one-sector* model with money. The King–Plosser–Rebelo approach has two versions. Version I (1988a) is a one-sector model *without* government "and heterogeneity of preferences and productivities" (1988a, 200). Version II (1988b) is also a one-sector model, but *with* government, heterogeneity, and other "departures from the strict representative agent model" of Version I, and thus includes "government expenditures and distorting taxes, productive externalities and heterogeneity of preferences and productivities" (1988a, 200). To reiterate, according to King (interview, 2007), the important characteristic of Versions I and II "is that the researcher is told how to solve the model by solving efficiency conditions by using a linear systems approach," which "can be also applied" to models "outside the real business cycle" approach, including "New Keynesian" elements, as in Version II.

Competitive models of fluctuation and the role of money in business cycle models: Kydland and Prescott, 1980–1989

The final paragraph of Kydland and Prescott's 1982 "Time to build" paper read as follows (1982, 1369):

> Models such as the one considered in this paper could be used to predict the consequence of a particular policy rule upon the operating characteristics of the economy.[19] As we estimate the preference-technology structure, our structural parameters will be invariant to the policy rule selected even though the behavioral equations are not. There are computational problems, however, associated with determining the equilibrium behavioral equations of the economy when feedback policy rules, that is, rules that depend on the aggregate state of the economy, are used. The competitive equilibrium, then, will not maximize the welfare of the stand-in consumer, so a particular maximization problem cannot be solved to find the equilibrium behavior of the economy. Instead, methods such as those developed in [20] to analyze policy rules in competitive environments will be needed.

Note 19 in the paragraph above read, in part, "examples of such policy issues are described in [21]." Reference [21] was to Kydland and Prescott's NBER conference paper as published in the volume edited by Fischer (1980), discussed in Chapter 2. Reference [20], on the other hand, was to Kydland's "Analysis and policy in competitive models of business fluctuations," a Carnegie-Mellon Working Paper, "revised April 1981." But, for our story, the history and evolution of this paper by Kydland is much more significant than its simple citation at the end of "Time to build."

The first "preliminary and incomplete" draft of the paper, dated May 1980, was prepared for presentation at the "Conference on Economics and Control" in June 1980. (Kydland, 1980). A year later, in April 1981, the paper was revised as Carnegie-Mellon Working Paper 74–79–80, but was still described on its title page as "incomplete" (Kydland, 1981). As the paper is an important element in his effort to "extend" the Kydland–Prescott approach, a summary of its central message is given below.

There are slight changes in text, notation, and equations between the May 1980 in April 1981 drafts. For example, in the April 1981 version, π the "vector of policy variables," is added to equations. More important, however, is the emphasis that Kydland places upon monetary shocks and the inclusion of money in the model he proposes (1980, 22–32). Indeed, in both versions Kydland mentions the necessity for dealing with "three cases" of shocks: real, monetary, and simultaneous real and monetary shocks (1980, 30; 1981, 30).

But, again, more is involved here than an unpublished working paper citation.

First, Kydland thought his GSIA working paper "Analysis and policy in competitive models of business fluctuations" important enough to include it, along with the September 1981 revision of his GSIA working paper with Prescott, "Time to build and aggregate fluctuations," on the 1981 course outline and reading list for course number 47–817 "Dynamic Competitive Analysis," which he taught at Carnegie-Mellon. The outline described the course as follows:

> The central theme of this course will be a methodology for analyzing dynamic economic models with uncertainty though the techniques are appropriate for analyzing deterministic phenomena as well. Throughout, discrete rather than continuous time models will be considered. The emphasis will be on characterizing the equilibrium or market solutions. Often times, the equilibrium path converges to the stationary solution which is relatively easy to characterize.

Second, as seen above, as early as mid-1980, he had written about the necessity of modeling with both real and monetary shocks. However, he put the paper aside until he visited the Hoover Institution. There, in 1983, he again revised it, changing its title to "The role of money in a competitive theory of fluctuations," and circulated it as Hoover Working Paper No. E-83–10 (Kydland, 1983a). In May 1983, while there, he also circulated a paper entitled "Non-separable utility and labor supply" (Kydland, 1983b), which he later presented at the NBER Conference on Macroeconomics, in Cambridge, Massachusetts in July 1983(but more about that later).

In June 1983, Prescott circulated Working Paper 239 of the Federal Reserve Bank of Minneapolis' Research Department, entitled "Can the cycle be reconciled with a consistent theory of expectations—A progress report on business cycle theory." He wrote (1983, 4):

> One conclusion of this report is that the stochastic growth structure economy in which technological change is random displays business cycle behavior remarkably similar to that experienced by the U.S. economy in the post-war period. With respect to the monetary shock models, the models are not sufficiently well developed, particularly with respect to their propagation mechanisms, to subject them to empirical tests of this variety. Progress in this respect is being made as will be apparent in the Kydland ... review.

Prescott went on to cite Kydland's 1983 Hoover Working Paper accordingly (1983, 8).

At Carnegie-Mellon, in December 1987, Kydland circulated a revised version of the April 1981 and 1983 drafts under the new title "The role of money in a business cycle model," noting that "an early version of the paper was entitled 'Analysis and policy in competitive models of business fluctuation'," based on research he "partly carried out" while visiting Hoover. The abstract of the December 1987 version read as follows (Kydland, 1987):

> This paper investigates the quantitative implications of two hypotheses regarding the role of money in a real business cycle theory. One is the form of aggregate price shocks when there is heterogeneity across individuals or groups of individuals ("islands"). The price shocks affect the accuracy of information that can be obtained from observed wage rates. Another, perhaps complementary, hypothesis is that the demand for money varies over the cycle due to a trade-off between real money and leisure. This leads to price fluctuations even when the money stock does not fluctuate. The resulting comovements of aggregate variables are discussed and compared with post-war U.S. data. The role of propagation mechanisms from preferences and technology for the behavior of nominal variables is emphasized.

The paper finally appeared as Discussion Paper 23, circulated by the Institute for Empirical Macroeconomics of the Federal Reserve Bank of Minneapolis, in December 1989. In a note he wrote:

> An earlier version of this paper appeared as Hoover Institution Working Paper No. 83–10. Previous drafts include a section describing a direct method for computing dynamic aggregate equilibrium in models of the type considered in this paper in which solving a stand-in planner's problem is inappropriate. That section has since been published in Kydland (1989a).

The abstract to this final version of the paper read (Kydland, 1989a):

> Two mechanisms are considered through which money can play a role in a real business cycle model. One is a form of aggregate price surprises when there is heterogeneity across individuals or groups of individuals ("islands"). These shocks affect the accuracy of information about real compensation that can be extracted from observed wage rates. Another, perhaps complementary, mechanism is that the amount of desired liquidity services varies over the cycle due to a trade-off between real money and leisure. This mechanism leads to price fluctuations even when the nominal money stock does not fluctuate. As in the case of the U.S. economy over the postwar period, the price level is then countercyclical. A key finding is that with neither mechanism do nominal shocks account for more than a small amount of variability in real output and hours worked. Indeed, output variability may very well be lower the larger the variance of price surprises is.

A comparison of the introduction to the December 1987 and December 1989 versions of Kydland's paper is both instructive and important for an understanding of the direction in which the post-1982 Kydland–Prescott research program was moving. The introductory paragraph of the December 1987 version read:

> In the last decade or so, much research on aggregate equilibrium models, to a large extent inspired by the seminal papers of Lucas (1972, 1975) and carried further by Barro (1976) and others, has dealt with the implications of various information structures for aggregate fluctuations. This research was particularly important because it demonstrated the potential for monetary shocks to create real fluctuations in equilibrium. For this purpose, it was not as yet essential to go into much detail about propagation mechanisms due to preferences and technology.

The introductory paragraph to the December1989 version was changed to:

> In the past decade or two, increasingly the language of dynamic general equilibrium theory has been used for discussing the role of monetary shocks or price shocks for business cycles. Most models of that type use imperfect information about the shocks as a way of generating real effects. In particular, imperfect information has the implication that people initially react to price shocks as though they were real changes. The early papers ... are mainly concerned with demonstrating the theoretical possibility of real effects resulting from nominal shocks.

The introduction to *both* versions went on to say that:

> real propagation mechanisms are important for understanding quarterly fluctuations. Examples of model elements ... are multi-period investment

> technologies, inter-temporally non-separable utility in leisure, and the interaction of many sectors. To the extent that [they] are found to be important in accounting for aggregate fluctuations, they are also of considerable interest to the monetary theorist.

The December 1987 version then read:

> Combining these features with the informational structure is needed in order to make a quantitative comparison between the properties of the model and those of the data. Such a framework could be useful for assessing the additional importance of monetary shocks in generating business cycles.

The December 1989 version read:

> Combining monetary features with an explicit specification of preferences (or home production) and technology, whose parameter values can be measured or inferred with relatively little error, offers the potential for obtaining a good estimate of the additional role of normal shocks, over and above that of technology shocks, for cyclical fluctuations.

Interestingly enough, the introduction to the December 1987 version also read:

> The real model elements include inter-temporally non-separable utility in leisure and a time-to-build technology for producing durable goods. The paper is exploratory in the sense that we investigate the potential quantitative importance of money as modeled here and explore the possible importance of the interaction of money with the real economy depending on what assumptions are made about preferences and technology. The hope is that this exercise will point to the most promising avenues for further research along these lines. Such work would include the imposition of quantitative restrictions from outside the model so as to eliminate free parameters.

This paragraph, was, however, elided in the December 1989 version.

Non-separable utility, inter-temporal substitution, labor force heterogeneity, and the business cycle: extensions and debates, 1983–1988

Kydland's contributions: 1983–1984

In November 1983, Kydland presented a paper at the Rochester-Carnegie-Mellon Conference entitled "Labor force heterogeneity and the business cycle," which was published in the Conference Series in 1984. According to Kydland, the research on which this paper was based had begun while he was visiting the

Hoover Institution in 1983 (1984a, 173). Heckman commented on Kydland's paper (Heckman 1984, 209–224), and Kydland replied to his critique (1984b, 225–230) in the Conference Series volume entitled "Essays on macroeconomic implications of financial and labor markets and political processes" edited by Brunner and Meltzer (1984).

In concise and lucid terms, Brunner and Meltzer, in their introduction to the volume, described Kydland's paper and Heckman's comments as follows (1984, 4–5):

> Finn Kydland approaches the issue of inter-temporal substitution within the dynamic framework set out in his earlier work with Edward Prescott ... (1982). The present paper extends that framework by introducing some heterogeneity in the labor force in place of the homogeneous (aggregate) labor force in the early work.
>
> Kydland shows that there are sizable differences in the cyclical responses of skilled and unskilled workers. He adjusts manhours for worker efficiency and uses the modified variable to obtain estimates of the cyclical response of employment. The estimates are obtained using the same procedures as in the earlier paper with Prescott. He finds closer correspondence of the predictions to observed cyclical movements in employment. The basic data used as a benchmark are measures of cyclical deviations from fitted trends.
>
> Kydland also discusses the effect of the change in the model on other estimates of dynamic responses. He concludes that introduction of heterogeneity in the labor market does not greatly alter the dynamic responses computed in his earlier work. The principle differences are confined to the labor market...
>
> Heckman presents data to support his claim that cyclical fluctuations in employment are dominated by changes in employment, not in hours of work. He criticizes the use of the model based on a representative worker-consumer. Important differences in the employment experience of different groups of workers cannot be properly analyzed in the representative agent framework. Heckman is critical also of the methods used by Kydland to obtain his estimates.

But again, more is involved in the story of Kydland's Carnegie-Rochester paper, Heckman's critique, and Kydland's reply, as will now be seen.

In May 1983, while at the Hoover Institution, Kydland circulated a paper entitled "Non-separable utility and labor supply" as Working Paper E-83–10, which he prepared for the NBER Macroeconomics Conference in July 1983 (1983a). He revised the paper in August 1983 (1983b). As noted above, he gave a paper with the title "Labor force heterogeneity and the business cycle" at the Carnegie-Rochester conference in November 1983, which was published in the 1984 Carnegie-Rochester volume.

A comparison of Kydland's "Non-separable utility" working paper (1983b) and "Labor force heterogeneity" (1984a) paper shows that the latter paper was based, to a significant extent, on his earlier working paper. This is evident in the introduction, which is identical in both papers, and in large parts of text which were taken verbatim from the working paper and integrated into the Carnegie-Rochester paper (1983b, 1–2, 11, 15–19; 1984a, 173–174, 184, 187–189). Kydland duly cited his Hoover Working Paper in the references of his Carnegie-Rochester paper, and as noted above, acknowledged that he had started to work on the topic while at Hoover.

Interestingly enough, in his "Non-separable utility" paper (1983b), Kydland cited his joint paper with Hutz and Sedlacek, entitled "Inter-temporal substitution and labor supply," which was a Carnegie-Mellon Working Paper "revised 1982." In his "Labor force heterogeneity" Carnegie-Rochester paper (1984a), Kydland cited this joint paper as having been "presented at the annual meeting of the AEA, New York, 1982" (Kydland 1984a, 204). The paper was in fact presented on Tuesday 28 December 1982 at the AEA morning session "Applications of new methods in macro-econometrics" chaired by Gertler. Other papers presented were by Geweke on "Feedback between real and monetary sectors is the short and long run" and Bernanke on "The role of storable inputs in the business cycle." The discussants were Chow, Fischer, and Taylor, with Fischer discussing the Kydland *et al.* paper (Program of ASSA/AER meetings 1982, 23). The paper was revised in 1985, and was eventually published in *Econometrica* in March 1988 under the title "Intertemporal Preferences and Labor Supply." At this point, we turn to Heckman's critique of Kydland's approach in his Carnegie-Rochester paper, and Kydland's reply.

Kydland vs. Heckman, 1984

Heckman (1984) was highly critical in his comments on Kydland (1984a). He started by saying (1984, 209) that "Kydland claims that with a few minor repairs, a representative agent equilibrium business cycle model is a good account of the 'facts'." He went on to say (1984, 213):

> Kydland's paper carries on the agenda set forth in his joint work with … Prescott (1982) which developed an empirically tractable dynamic equilibrium model of the business cycle. The current paper discusses certain limitations of their model. The principle contribution of this paper is to recognize heterogeneity in skill endowments of workers.
>
> The issue of heterogeneity in worker skills is raised in order to solve a problem in the Kydland–Prescott paper—the discrepancy between predicted and actual variance in manhours of work … Kydland redefines the manhours variable in Kydland and Prescott to an efficiency units concept … This redefinition substantially reduces the discrepancy between predicted and actual variability in manhours and goes part way toward making the model mimic the observed correlation between output and productivity….
>
> By introducing heterogeneous agents into a dynamic equilibrium model, Kydland takes an important first step toward accommodating the wealth of

> microeconomic findings that indicate considerable microeconomic diversity in preferences and endowments.

Heckman then wrote (1984, 215–216):

> As already noted, by appealing to a representative consumer model or a variant of it, Kydland is forced to ignore labor-force and/or employment entry and exit decisions despite the fact that such choices are empirically important.... By inventing a fictional representative consumer... Kydland/Prescott and Kydland preclude any direct appeal to micro studies to reduce a scale of the estimation problem on aggregate data.... Similar remarks can be made about all sectors of the Kydland/Prescott model. The micro data contradicts representative worker, firm or consumer models. A macro fiction can be constructed that "explains" the data, but no micro counterpart of these fictional behavioral functions can be found ... The micro evidence against an efficiency-units model of the labor market cast serious doubt on the fixup of the Kydland/Prescott model proposed by Kydland.

But perhaps more significant for our story is the fact that Heckman then strongly criticized the method by which Kydland, and Kydland and Prescott, fitted their models to the data, by turning to the results of Altug (1983), on the one hand, and Kydland, Hotz, and Sedlacek (1982) on the other hand. Heckman wrote (1984, 216):

> I also question the informal and subjective "calibration" procedure used by Kydland and Kydland/Prescott for determining how their model fits the data. Using modern econometric methods, Altug (1983) finds that neither "time to build" nor "non-separable labor supply" explains the Kydland–Prescott data. Her work undermines a key premise of the Kydland paper—that the Kydland/Prescott paper comes close to explaining the macro facts and that with further refinement their framework may give a good account of macro time series data on aggregate fluctuations. The original Kydland–Prescott paper created the false impression that a simple cost-of-adjustment model could not explain the aggregate data...
>
> Neither the micro nor the macro evidence obtained from conventional econometric procedures supports the other pillar of the Kydland/Prescott argument: that lagged leisure is a substitute for current leisure. Altug (1983) decisively rejects the hypothesis, and the micro evidence reported in Kydland, Hutz, and Sedlacek (1982) is mixed. The non-separable preference function advocated by Kydland and Prescott is not required to explain the macro time series nor has it been shown to be consistent with the microdata. I am less sanguine than Kydland that the amended Kydland/Prescott model is an empirically fruitful one although it is surely of considerable theoretical interest.

Kydland opened his reply to Heckman with a note (1984b, 225) stating that:

> To the extent that this reply deals with those of Heckman's comments that are also directed at the joint paper with Edward Prescott, it has received extensive input from Prescott. This note was written while I was visiting the Hoover institution.

He then wrote (1984b, 225):

> There is apparently considerable confusion as to what has been learned from the research reported in the paper "Time to Build and Aggregate Fluctuations" and from the subsequent research that developed this line. These efforts are best viewed as accounting exercises. We are determining to what extent the post-war fluctuations of the United States economy can be accounted by the equilibrium stochastic growth model. Following Solow (1957), changes in output not accounted for by changes in inputs are interpreted as being technological shocks. Using shocks of the same magnitudes and with similar serial correlation properties as those residuals, we found that they, along with an extended growth model, accounted for most of the fluctuations in aggregate United States output and employment.
>
> We learned that simple naive versions of the stochastic growth model account for too little of aggregate fluctuations, especially hours' variability. Using a standard time separable utility function, about two-thirds of the fluctuations in the data were accounted for. If households are assumed to value leisure more if they have consumed less leisure in the past, the growth model explained nearly all.

He then dealt with Heckman's critique regarding adjustment costs and said (1984b, 227):

> Adjustment costs, if significant, spread out the effects of shocks, reducing their effect at any point and thereby reducing the variation in output accounted for by any given shock, whether it be technological or monetary. The microevidence for the time-to-build assumption is also overwhelming. It is hardly controversial that expansion in capacity requires allocation of resources over more than one quarter.

Kydland then turned to Heckman's use of Altug's (1983) results (1984b, 227–228):

> Heckman relies on Altug's estimates as key support for his position. Considering the fact that her model is different from the one Prescott and I used, this hardly seems warranted. She assumed a one-parameter specification of the relative weight distribution on current and past leisure choices and the utility function.... Furthermore, Altug does not include our indicator shock

> but instead assumes that the aggregate variables are subject to measurement errors that are independent over time. Especially for hours worked, my paper indicates that this is an unrealistic assumption. With regard to productive technology, she has a problem one usually runs into when formally estimating production functions, namely that the output elasticity of labor input becomes near one. Average relations in the model, such as the inventory-output ratio or the ratio of investment in structures and equipment for the model in which they are treated separately, differ from those in the data by factors of more than ten. It is hard for me to see, then, how these estimates give any basis for firm conclusions about the appropriateness of time-to-build versus cost-of-adjustment investment technology, or about intertemporally non-separable vs. separable utility functions, for that matter.

Kydland concluded (1984b, 228):

> We do not view our efforts as the definitive numbers—just the best that are currently available.... In other periods or in other countries, one may find less or more of the fluctuations accounted for by technological shocks. There is no shortage of candidates to account for the residual. Monetary and fiscal shocks come to mind first, as do shocks to the household technology. We have been concerned with peacetime cycles. Wartime shocks may affect the economy differently, and so may foreign-trade shocks. These are a few of the questions that warrant investigation.

Estimating and extending Kydland–Prescott type models: Altug and the econometric approach, 1983–1989

As noted above, Heckman based his main critique of the Kydland (1984a) and Kydland–Prescott (1982) results on the "econometric" findings of Altug (1983) (Heckman 1984, 260), as presented in her 1983 Carnegie-Mellon Working Paper entitled "Gestation Lags and the Business Cycle." According to Heckman's citation, it was "presented at the 1984 Summer Meetings of the Econometric Society" (1984, 221), while in his Carnegie-Rochester paper and his reply to Heckman, Kydland cited Altug's paper as having been a "presented at the NBER Macro Conference, Cambridge, 1984" (1984a, 202; 1984b, 229). It must be recalled here that Altug's paper was actually written as a chapter for inclusion in her Carnegie-Mellon PhD thesis "Essays in the equilibrium approach to aggregate fluctuations and asset pricing," awarded in 1985. Altug's paper was revised in September 1983. It was subsequently issued as Federal Reserve Bank of Minneapolis Working Paper 277, revised August 1986, under the title "Time to build and aggregate fluctuations: some new evidence." It was submitted to the *International Economic Review* in September 1986, and underwent additional revisions in October 1987 and October 1988. It was finally published in the November 1989 issue of *International Economic Review*.

Because of its relevance for our story, and its impact upon Heckman's critique of Kydland (1984a) and Kydland, *et al.*, (1982), below we survey the evolution of Altug's paper between 1983 and its publication in 1989. The introduction to the September 1983 revision of "Gestation Lags and the Business Cycle," which was the version most probably seen by Heckman—and was the main basis for his critique of Kydland's Carnegie-Rochester paper and Kydland–Prescott—read (Altug 1983, 2):

> This paper estimates and characterizes the dynamic properties of a "real" business cycle model. As in Kydland and Prescott ... the model is based on the one sector optimal growth model modified to include gestation lags in investment and non-time separable preferences with respect to leisure.... Using time series data, maximum likelihood estimates of the structural parameters are obtained and spectral methods are used to characterize these estimates. In interpreting the empirical results, the assumption that multiple time periods are required to build capital is emphasized for describing the behavior of output under fixed investment and investment in "structures" and "equipment", separately.

She went on to say (1983, 2–3):

> Expanding on these objectives, Section 2 describes the planning problem for two versions of the theoretical model that forms the basis for the subsequent empirical work. While both versions of the model feature gestation lags in investment, the first version includes a single type of capital subject to the "time-to-build" assumption. The second version incorporates two types of productive capital, structures and equipment, and assumes that only the production of structures requires more than one period.... Section 3 presents the derivation of an estimable version of the model described in Section 2. ... This is in contrast to Kydland and Prescott and Long and Plosser who provide some informal empirical evidence for their models but do not conduct a formal econometric analysis.

Altug then talked about the results she had obtained (1983, 4):

> The empirical results are presented in Section 6. For both versions of the model we find that the non time-separability in preferences is unimportant in explaining the joint cyclical behavior of per capita hours, output, inventories and investment (both as fixed investment and as desegregated as investment in "equipment" and "structures"). By contrast, the evidence for the gestation lag assumption is much stronger for the version of the model which includes two types of productive capital. In this case, not only does the model capture the time-series behavior of investment in "structures" but it is successful in replicating the persistence or serial correlation properties of aggregate output and, to a lesser extent, of aggregate hours. We also find

> that different lag structures characterize investment in "structures" versus fixed investment: while most of the resources required to complete a given project are expended in the first few periods for the latter, they are spread out more evenly over the different periods for the former.

Altug concluded (1983, 40):

> Using a simple dynamic equilibrium model with an interesting specification of preferences and investment technology, this paper has tried to explain the cyclical properties of a set of aggregate time series. Our results show that, for certain parameter values, the model exhibits patterns of serial correlation which are consistent with the movement of deviations of output, hours, and (disaggregated measures of) investment from a stochastic trend. However, our results also suggest there is a potential improvement. Without claiming to provide an exhaustive list of theoretical and econometric enhancements of the model, one such improvement lies in the modeling of finished goods inventories and inventories of raw materials and goods in process, separately, to capture the interaction among firms' output, investment and inventory decisions. Also, given that the greater inter-temporal substitution of leisure allowed by non-separable preferences does not seem important for explaining hours at the aggregate level, another extension lies in developing features that account for the behavior of this series. From a methodological perspective, some of the econometric issues in developing and empirically analyzing such models involve finding tractable ways of testing different model features against non-trivial alternatives: for example, testing the gestation lag model against adjustment costs involves non-nested testing procedures.

Given the above—that is to say, what Altug actually found and presented in her 1983 paper, it could be asserted that Heckman, having based his assertions on it, may have been too critical of Kydland's Carnegie-Rochester Paper, and the Kydland–Prescott approach overall. Indeed, this is supported by subsequent revisions to the text made by Altug, as manifest in the August 1986 Federal Reserve Bank of Minneapolis Working Paper version, and the October 1987 revision of the version submitted to *International Economic Review* for publication. The introduction to the Minneapolis Fed version read (1986, 1–2):

> This paper presents maximum likelihood estimates of a model that has the main features of Kydland and Prescott's model. It uses postwar U.S. data on the differences of per capita values of aggregate output, total hours worked, and investment expenditure for two types of investment, namely in structures and equipment. Contrary to Kydland and Prescott's assertion, I find that the model fails most drastically in its ability to explain the variability of the two investment series. The source of this failure is not the time-to-build feature, as might be expected. Instead, it is a more fundamental feature of

the model: the existence of a well-behaved neoclassical production technology describing the relationship between aggregate output and the inputs of labor and the two types of capital. More precisely, I estimate the parameter which determines the share of labor in aggregate output—and, hence, the elasticity of output with respect to labor—to be unity. With a constant returns to scale production function such a finding implies that the composite capital good involving the stock of structures and equipment is, in effect, driven out of the aggregate production function. As the model is specified, the behavior of the two investment series is directly linked to the behavior of the two capital series, but little role emerges for capital with a unitary share parameter. Thus, the model can generate only a fraction of the variability in the two investment series which the actual data or other similar specifications display.

She went on to say (1986, 2–3):

I do find however that the model explains quite well the behavior of the hour series under a time-separable specification of preferences. But the evidence for the dependence of current utility on past leisure choices is, at best, mixed...

Kydland and Prescott's approach and mine differ in several ways. Some concern the specification of the model and the so called etrending procedure.... Our two studies also use somewhat different data sets. My data set is slightly smaller than Kydland and Prescott's—it does not include series on consumption expenditures, aggregate inventories, capital stocks, or productivity—but it does contain a sufficiently diverse set of series whose behavior can be used to investigate the important features of Kydland and Prescott's model. The most important difference between the two papers concerns the estimation procedure. Kydland and Prescott calibrated a singular stochastic model using a small set of sample moments—the variances of the detrended series, their correlation with detrended output, and five auto-correlations of detrended output. By contrast, I derive, as an econometric specification, a restricted index model in which the innovation to the technology shock appears as the common latent factor, while serially uncorrelated measurement errors constitute specific disturbances.

The last paragraph in the introduction read (1986, 3–4):

One way to summarize my results, therefore, is to note that, when a major subset of the unknown parameters is freely estimated, using full sample information, many of Kydland and Prescott's conclusions disappear, and they disappear in ways difficult to predict on a priori grounds. This paper may be viewed in another way, however. It provides an empirical investigation of a real business cycle model, which is similar to Kydland and

> Prescott's, but which also allows for additional specifications describing the durability of leisure, accounts for potential differences in the behavior of the stock of structures versus the stock of equipment, and incorporates nonstationary behavior for the latent technology shock.

In the conclusion to the October 1987 revision of the paper, as submitted to *International Economic Review*, Altug wrote (1987, 32–33):

> One final question to ask is whether results in this paper support Kydland and Prescott's conclusion about the performance of the model…
>
> This paper asked a slightly different question, namely, having chosen values for major subsets of the unknown parameters by matching all the covariances for the different series according to the metric defined by maximum likelihood, could the innovation to the technology shock account for a major fraction of the total *explained* variance in each series, computed according to the estimated representations. The results of Section 5 showed that the model experienced most difficulty in accounting for the variability of per-capita hours. Seen in these terms, the empirical findings of this paper do not necessarily conflict with Kydland and Prescott's results … in so far as they point to the difficulties encountered in rationalizing the behavior of per-capita hours (considered jointly with other quantity variables or with real wages and productivity).… Likewise, Kydland and Prescott argued that non-time separable preferences were required in order to rationalize the relative variability of aggregate hours and productivity within their model. Hence, one contribution of this paper may be regarded as providing evidence that is complementary to such results. However, another contribution is in terms of developing and implementing a framework in which alternative models of growth, investment and of aggregate consumption and labor supply can be potentially estimated and tested.

Interestingly enough, the final paragraph in the 1989 published version of Altug's paper dealt with the extensions of her econometric approach (1989, 913):

> There are several ways in which the current paper could be extended. One possibility is to allow for variability in the average work week of labor and to explicitly account for the behavior of individuals who do not participate each period. Another possibility is to separately model such components of GNP that we took as exogenous, namely, net exports, inventory investment, and government expenditures. These extensions would probably allow for a better test of the underlying hypothesis that an aggregative model driven by persistent technology shocks can explain the cyclical movement of a set of key series around some (stochastically) evolving trend. But these extensions would also take us far from the framework Kydland and Prescott originally presented and are hence the topic for future research.

Labor and capital redux: "indivisible" labor, "hours worked," "workweek of capital," and "hours and unemployment variation," 1984–1991

Hansen's contributions, 1984–1986

Prescott set his graduate student, Gary Hansen, to work on issues related to labor supply and fluctuations in hours worked, in the context of his University of Minnesota PhD thesis (1986a) "Three Essays on Labor Indivisibility and the Business Cycle." In November 1984 Hansen circulated Chapter 1 of his thesis, entitled "Indivisible Labor and the Business Cycle" (1984), which was revised in June 1985 (1985a). It was published in the November 1985 issue of the *Journal of Monetary Economics*. The "breakthrough" of the paper was expressed by Hansen as follows (1985b, 309–310):

> In this paper, a simple one-sector stochastic growth model with shocks to technology is constructed in which there is high variability in the number employed and total hours worked even though individuals are relatively unwilling to substitute leisure across time. The model differs from similar models, such as Kydland and Prescott (1982), in that a non-convexity (indivisible labor) is introduced. Indivisible labor is modeled by assuming that individuals can either work some given positive number of hours or not at all—they are unable to work an intermediate number of hours. This assumption is motivated by the observation that most people either work full time or not at all. Therefore, in my model, fluctuations in aggregate hours are the result of individuals entering and leaving employment rather than continuously employed individuals adjusting the number of hours worked, as in previous equilibrium models.

He went on to say (1985b, 310):

> Equilibrium theories of the business cycle have typically depended heavily on intertemporal substitution of leisure to account for aggregate fluctuations in hours worked ... The theory developed here is able to account for large aggregate fluctuations in hours worked relative to productivity...

He concluded (1985b, 323–324):

> Therefore, this is an equilibrium model which exhibits unemployment (or employment) fluctuations in response to aggregate shocks. Fluctuations in employment seem important for fluctuations in hours worked over the business cycle since most of the variability in total hours is unambiguously due to variation in the number employed rather than hours per employed worker...
>
> This feature enables the indivisible labor economy to exhibit large fluctuations in hours worked relative to fluctuations in productivity. Previous

> equilibrium models of the business cycle, which have all assumed divisible labor, have been unsuccessful in accounting for this feature of U.S. time series.
>
> [T]his study demonstrates that non-convexities such as indivisible labor may be important for explaining the volatility of hours relative to productivity even when individuals are relatively unwilling to substitute leisure across time. They are also useful for increasing the size of the standard deviations of all variables relative to the standard deviation of the technology shock. Therefore, a smaller size shock is sufficient for explaining business cycle fluctuations than was true for previous models such as Kydland and Prescott's (1982). In addition, these non-convexities make it possible for an equilibrium model of the business cycle to exhibit fluctuations in employment. Therefore, non-convexities will inevitably play an important role in future equilibrium models of the cycle.

The importance of Hansen's work in the context of the extension of the Kydland –Prescott research program was significant. His 1985 *JME* paper reconciled an extension of their approach with some labor market "facts" that had not been accounted for by previous models. These included (1985b, 310): (a) "most fluctuation in aggregate hours worked is due to fluctuation in the number employed as opposed to fluctuation in hours per employed worker," and (b) "large fluctuations in hours worked" accompanied by "relatively small fluctuations in productivity (or the real wage)."

Moreover, in 1986, Prescott, in his important Carnegie-Rochester (and Minneapolis Fed *Quarterly Review*) piece "Theory Ahead of Business Cycle Measurement," wrote (1986a, 11):

> Economists have long been puzzled by the observations that during peacetime industrial market economies display recurrent, large fluctuations in output and employment over relatively short time periods. Not uncommon are changes as large as 10 percent within only a couple of years. These observations are considered puzzling because the associated movements in labor's marginal product are small.
>
> These observations should not be puzzling, for they are what standard economic theory predicts. For the United States, in fact, given people's ability and willingness to intertemporally and intratemporally substitute consumption and leisure and given the nature of the changing production possibility set, it would be puzzling if the economy did not display these large fluctuations in output and employment with little associated fluctuations in the marginal product of labor. Moreover, standard theory also correctly predicts the amplitude of these fluctuations, their serial correlation properties, and the fact that the investment component of output is about six times as volatile as the consumption component.
>
> This perhaps surprising conclusion is the principal finding of a research program initiated by Kydland and me (1982) and extended by Kydland and

> me (1984), Hansen (1985a), and Bain (1985). We have computed the competitive equilibrium stochastic process for variants of the constant elasticity, stochastic growth model. The elasticities of substitution and the share parameters of the production and utility functions are restricted to those that generate the growth observations. The process governing the technology parameter is selected to be consistent with the measured technology changes for the American economy since the Korean War. We ask whether these artificial economies display fluctuations with statistical properties similar to those which the American economy has displayed in that period. They do.

In a note to this, Prescott said (1986a, 11 note 1):

> Others [Barro (1981) and Long and Plosser (1983), for example] have argued that these fluctuations are not inconsistent with competitive theory that abstracts from monetary factors. Our finding is much stronger: standard theory predicts that the economy will display the business cycle phenomena.

In March 1986, Hansen gave a seminar on Chapter 2 of his thesis, "Growth and Fluctuations" (1986b), at the Minneapolis Fed. In November and December 1986, Hansen circulated two "preliminary" papers which were also thesis chapters. The first paper, "Growth and fluctuations" (November, 1986c)—Chapter 2 of his thesis—was later revised and circulated in 1989 under the new title "Technical progress and Aggregate fluctuations" as UCLA Economics Department Working Paper No. 546 (1989). It was eventually published in revised form in the *Journal of Economic Dynamics and Control* as "Technical Progress and Aggregate Fluctuations" in 1997 (Hansen, 1997). The second paper, "Fluctuations in Total Hours Worked: a study using efficiency units" (December, 1986d), was Chapter 3 of his thesis. It was revised in 1991, and circulated from UCLA under the title "The Cyclical and Secular Behavior of Labor Input: Comparing efficiency units and hours worked" (Hansen, 1991) It was published in the *Journal of Applied Econometrics* in 1993 (Hansen, 1993).

As noted, Chapter 2 of Hansen's thesis was only published in 1997. In a communication a decade later (27 November 2006), Hansen wrote:

> The chapter in my thesis that corresponds to the 1997 paper … had additional results concerning the indivisible labor model with non-separable utility and showed that the cyclical properties of the model were not affected by the value of the risk aversion parameter within the range of "reasonable" values. I never published these results, and I'm not sure why. I think that at the time I was putting together the 1997 published paper, I wanted to make the paper more focused on trend stationary versus random walk models of the technology shocks. Also, I thought the results with non-separable utility were known by the time I got around to publishing the material from this chapter.

Interestingly enough, in his 1985 *JME* Paper, which was Chapter 1 of his thesis, Hansen cited an "unpublished manuscript" dated 1984 by Kydland and Prescott written at the Minneapolis Fed entitled "The Workweek of Capital and Labor" (Hansen 1985b, 319, 327). Hansen wrote (1985b, 319):

> Kydland and Prescott (1982, 1984) follow a methodology for choosing parameter values based on evidence from growth observations and micro studies. This methodology will also be followed here. In fact, since they study a similar economy, some of the above parameters ... also appeared in their model. This enables me to draw on their work in selecting values for these parameters, thereby making it easier to compare the results of the two studies.

Moreover, Chapter 3 of Hansen's thesis—"Fluctuations in Total Hours Worked"—was cited in the October 1986 revised version of Kydland and Prescott's Minneapolis Fed Working Paper 267 entitled "The workweek of capital and its cyclical implications," which was based upon their 1984 paper that Hansen cited, and it is to this that we now turn.

Kydland and Prescott: extensions, 1986–1991

In their introduction to the 1988 special issue of *JME* on the Real Business Cycle, where Kydland and Prescott published "Workweek of Capital," King and Plosser described the paper as follows (1988, 192):

> Kydland and Prescott present an *augmented version* [my emphasis] of their earlier model, Kydland and Prescott (1982), that permits the capital utilization rate to vary. They incorporate this feature into the model by permitting the workweek to lengthen or contract in response to variations in productivity. They conclude that this increases the amplitude of fluctuations generated by the model in a way that closely mimics the actual post-war U.S. data.

The published version of "Workweek of Capital" noted that it had been "revised" in October 1986 and submitted as a "final version" in August 1987. As the comparison of these versions is instructive regarding the evolution of this paper, this is done below. It should be noted, however, that the August 1987 "final" version was at the same time issued in the form of Minneapolis Fed Working Paper 267. There were considerable changes made in the "Workweek of Capital" between the October 1986 revised version sent to *JME* for publication—after the paper was presented in June 1986 at the Real Business Cycle conference held at the Portuguese Catholic University in Lisbon—and the August 1987 version published in the *JME* in 1988. Large parts of the October 1986 text were elided (1986a, 7–11, 13–14, 16–17) and text was added to the August 1987 version (1987, 4, 8–10, 12–13). References were also elided, and others were added.

Interestingly enough, while the October 1986 version cites Hansen's 1984 working paper "Fluctuations in Total Hours Worked," the August 1987 version cites it as Chapter 3 of his 1986 PhD dissertation (1986a, 24; 1987, 25).

The importance of the "The Workweek of Capital" paper is that it is an example of the plasticity of the Kydland–Prescott modeling methodology—that is to say, its ability to be augmented, as King and Plosser indicated in their introduction to the *JME* special issue in which it was published, as cited above.

Another indication of this plasticity can be seen in the further extension of the Kydland–Prescott *JME* approach in their August 1989 Minneapolis Fed Discussion Paper 17 entitled "Hours and Employment Variation in Business Cycle Theory," later published in 1991 in *Economic Theory* (1991b). In their Minneapolis Fed Discussion Paper they wrote (1989, 24):

> We have developed a computable general equilibrium structure in which both the hours a plant is operated and the number of employees can be varied. This, we think, is a better structure for assessing the contribution of shocks, of whatever origin, to aggregate fluctuations. We use this theory to estimate the importance of Solow technology shocks and we find that they are a major contributor. We find that, if they were the only source of shocks, the variance of aggregate fluctuations would be about 70 percent as large as the corresponding one for the U.S. data.
>
> In the aggregate, leisure is more substitutable than at the individual level. In this sense, the economy behaves as if there were indivisibilities. It has been suggested that the indivisibilities of Hansen (1985) … were ad hoc. Our framework provides a theoretical foundation for [his] approach.

Kydland and Prescott also dealt with cyclical movements in labor input and its impact on the real wage in two papers. The first was their 1989 Minneapolis Fed Working Paper 413, the second was published in the Federal Reserve Bank of Cleveland's *Economic Review* in 1993 under the title "Cyclical Movements of the Labor Input and its Implicit Real Wage." They concluded (1993, 20):

> To the extent that the relative variability of hours and labor force input found … hold for the entire U.S. population, our findings call for major revision of the traditional view of the nature of business cycles. Rather than productivity and the labor input being slightly negatively correlated, they become strongly positively associated. The importance of variations in labor input in accounting for fluctuations in aggregate output is substantially reduced. Given that cyclical components of capital stocks and output are roughly orthogonal, variation in the Solow technology coefficient must account for much more business cycle fluctuations in output. This factor, then, is nearly as important as are variations in labor input.

In the introduction to his survey paper entitled "Business Cycles and Aggregate Labor-Market Fluctuations," Kydland wrote (1993, 126):

> Central to business cycle theory as well as to growth theory is the aggregate production function, which relates the nation's output of goods and services to the inputs of capital and labor. Of prime importance to business cycle theory is the behavior of the labor input. For growth, most of the output change is accounted for by changes in technology and in capital. In contrast, perhaps in the order of two-thirds of the business cycle is accounted for by movements in the labor input and one-third by changes in technology. Thus, most business cycle theorists agree that an understanding of aggregate labor market fluctuations is a prerequisite for understanding how business cycles propagate over time.

In a retrospective piece—"The Discipline of Applied General Equilibrium"—Kehoe and Prescott discussed the evolution of the Kydland–Prescott approach to the labor market over the period 1982–1989. They wrote (1995, 5–6):

> The Kydland–Prescott (1982) model ... [found] that the theory resulted in a variance in hours worked that differed significantly from the data. This finding led Hansen (1985) to modify the Kydland–Prescott formulation, in which workers were homogeneous.... Actually, the Hansen model overaccounted for the variance in hours. Yet a further development by Kydland and Prescott (1989) allows for variations in both the number of workers and in the number of hours per worker. This model is more successful than either the original Kydland–Prescott model or the Hansen model in matching the variance in hours found in the data.

They went on to say (1995, 6):

> This sort of interplay between theory and measurement is frequent in general equilibrium business cycle modeling, because failures of a model to match the data are easily interpreted within the context of a well understood theory, they point to obvious directions for future research. This characteristic represents a significant advantage of the applied general equilibrium approach over the alternative of "accepting" or "rejecting" models based on formal statistical tests, at least as they are usually employed.

Indeed, in a prescient note to the 1989 "Hours and Employment Variation" paper Kydland and Prescott wrote (1989, 25 note 2):

> Cooley and Hansen (1988) introduce money via a cash-in-advance constraint. Greenwood, Hercowitz, and Huffman (1988) permit the utilization rate of capital to vary. Hansen (1988) introduces positive growth. Danthine and Donaldson (1989) introduce an efficiency-wage construct. In all these cases the quantitative nature of fluctuations introduced by technology shocks changed little. Backus, Kehoe, and Kydland (1989) introduce interaction between domestic and foreign technology shocks and study the

> implications for foreign trade and for the comovements of the key output components in the U.S. and abroad. It will be interesting to know whether this feature affects the amount of fluctuations accounted for by such shocks.

These papers represent further extensions and augmentation to the Kydland–Prescott approach, which we will discuss in Chapter 5. Now, let us turn to the issue of the dissemination of the Kydland–Prescott approach, as seen in the volume edited by Cooley (1995).

Cooley and the dissemination of the real business cycle approach

While the real business cycle approach has become the "core" of both recent macroeconomic theory and policy making, this was not the case in the decade or so after the initial appearance of Kydland–Prescott and Long–Plosser. Cooley had begun his career by dealing with parameter and price estimation (1975, 1976, 1977), and collaborating with Prescott at Carnegie-Mellon writing papers on "adaptive regression models" (1973a,b,c) and estimation and stochastic parameter variation (1976). He later collaborated with Hansen (1989, 1991, 1992, 1997, 1998), and both joined Prescott (1994, 1995) in writing a paper further extending the Kydland–Prescott approach to capital utilization and labor market processes and characteristics entitled "Equilibrium business cycles with idle resources and variable capacity utilization."

Indeed, Cooley recognized the initial opposition of some in the economics profession to the Kydland–Prescott and Long–Plosser approaches, and he wrote about this in the preface to the 1995 collection of papers he edited, entitled *Frontiers of Business Cycle Research*. Because of the importance of his volume for the dissemination of the real business cycle approach, and our story, we cite from its preface at length here.

Cooley wrote (1995, xv–xvi):

> Beginning in the early 1970s, the methods used to study business cycles changed in an important way. In what is often referred to as the new classical revolution, economists, led by the path-breaking work of Robert E. Lucas Jr., began to study business cycles using the tools of competitive equilibrium theory.... Beginning in the 1980s, another important development occurred, which has changed the way many economists study business cycles. This was the emergence of the real business cycle approach, as represented by the work of Kydland and Prescott (1982) and Long and Plosser (1983). The most important aspect of the real business cycle development is that it established a prototype and a set of tools for carrying the equilibrium approach forward. It combines general equilibrium theory with a set of tools for computing the equilibria of artificial economies and studying their empirical properties.

> The real business cycle approach has been impossible to ignore. It has attracted much attention precisely because it offers a strong challenge to more traditional theories of the business cycle. Most important, the real business cycle approach changed the rules of the game by which we conduct quantitative research in macroeconomics. Most economists now accept as incontrovertible the notion that theories of the business cycle should be consistent with long-term observations about economic growth and with the principles of competitive equilibrium theory. These ideas have become part of the core curriculum for virtually all students of macroeconomics. Unfortunately, the teaching of this material has been hindered by the lack of a well-organized and careful exposition of the ideas and methods of dynamic general equilibrium modeling. This book attempts to fill that gap.... This approach to studying business cycles and growth has been one of the most active and fast growing in all of economics. By the time this book is in print, many new and important applications of these ideas will exist. Nevertheless, the ideas and methods described here have become standard tools for economists, and they will be useful for a very long time to come.
>
> Many people have been quick to dismiss real business cycle theory because of its emphasis on exogenous shocks to technology as a source of the fluctuations that we associated with the business cycle. The chapters in this book belie the oversimplified view of what modern business cycle research is all about.

Cooley's 1995 volume contains 12 papers and covers a wide area of issues related to real business cycle theory including: an introductory chapter written by Cooley and Prescott; a chapter on computing equilibria using recursive methods, by Hansen and Prescott; computing equilibria for nonoptimal economies, by Danthine and Donaldson; heterogeneous agents, by Rios-Rull; aggregate labor market fluctuations, by Kydland; household production, by Greenwood, Rogerson, and Wright; money by Cooley and Hansen; non-Walrasian economies, by Danthine and Donaldson; imperfectly competitive product markets, by Rotemberg and Woodford; asset equilibrium models, by Rouwenhorst; international business cycles, by Backus, Kehoe, and Kydland; and policy analysis, by Chari, Christiano, and Kehoe.

In the introductory chapter, Cooley was responsible, among other things, for the section on calibration (communication, 18 December 2006). Cooley expanded his treatment of calibration in a paper he presented at the 1995 World Congress of the Econometric Society entitled "Calibrated Models," published in the *Oxford Review of Economic Policy* in 1997. Both the introductory chapter with Prescott and the volume as a whole were highly successful. As Lucas wrote in his endorsement:

> [it] collects a number of papers that are standards on my graduate reading lists, and some others that soon will be. It adds two lucid introductory papers, one by Thomas Cooley and Edward Prescott and another on

> computing by Gary Hansen and Prescott. The result is an excellent volume that will be invaluable to macroeconomic researchers and a stimulating introduction for graduate students.

But who were, the "people ... quick to dismiss real business cycle theory," and what was the response of Kydland and Prescott? Moreover, what were the "new and important applications" Cooley was referring to? It is to these and other questions that we turn in Chapter 5.

5 Debates, augmentation, and variations on the theme

Prescott, Summers, and Rogoff

The Prescott–Summers "debate" is well known, and often cited (Prescott 1986b, c; Summers, 1986). What is important to recall here is that their initial exchange took place at the Summer meeting of the NBER Economic Fluctuations Group held in Cambridge, Massachusetts, in July 1986. According to the summary of the meeting that appeared in the NBER *Reporter* (Fall 1986, 22–23), Taylor and Mankiw organized the program. It included papers by Bernanke and Gertler, Greenwald and Stiglitz, Hartley and Walsh, Dornbusch and Fischer, Zeides, and Prescott, who presented his paper "Theory Ahead of Business Cycle Measurement." The discussants of the papers were Stephen King, Woodford, Robert King, Lucas, Hall, and Summers, who discussed Prescott's paper (NBER *Reporter*, 1986, 23). The account of Prescott's paper in the NBER *Reporter* is as follows (NBER *Reporter* 1986, 23):

> Models of economic growth and technological change were originally developed to explain secular changes in economic activity. Prescott argues that simple modifications of these growth models can be used to explain post-war U.S. cyclical behavior as well. Prescott combines a production function involving capital, labor, and a random technological disturbance, and an inter-temporal utility function involving consumption goods and leisure, to produce a simple dynamic general equilibrium model. By specifying a set of parameters of the production function, the utility function, and the stochastic process of technological change, data can be generated from the "artificial economy". Prescott chooses a set of parameters that are consistent with microdata and long-term relationships between the data. He finds that the artificial data generated display the same type of business cycle behavior found in the post-war U.S. economy.

Prescott then presented his paper at the Carnegie-Rochester Conference on Public Policy, which was published in the Fall 1986 Conference Series volume. Rogoff commented on Prescott's paper in the same volume. While it has also been widely cited, the nature of the questions raised in it by Rogoff are, in our view, prescient, and may be said to point to subsequent directions of development for the real business cycle approach. Rogoff opened his comment by saying (1986, 45):

> Ed Prescott surveys a line of business-cycle research which is both positive and important. Even if one has reservations about the predominance of real disturbances, is still possible to appreciate the general methodological approach.
>
> The basic premise of this paper, and of Kydland and Prescott (1982), is that it is a mistake to analyze separately business cycles and trend economic growth ... Kydland and Prescott argue that the simplification is not only wrong in principle, but that in ignoring trend growth patterns, macroeconomists have also been throwing out information which would be very useful in identifying and estimating key business-cycle parameters.

He went on:

> By re-emphasizing the relationship between factors which govern growth patterns and factors which determine the transmission of productivity disturbances, Kydland and Prescott are able to draw on a large body of microeconomic evidence pertaining to the parameters of growth models.

In a prescient way, Rogoff then turned to whether Prescott's approach could be applied to policy and international questions, foreshadowing issues relating to DSGE, on the one hand, and the international model of Backus–Kehoe–Kydland, on the other, which will be discussed below. He said (1986, 46) "Prescott ... shows that it is possible to explain certain characteristics of business cycles with a growth model driven solely by productivity disturbances. Whether such an approach is suitable for policy analysis is not as clear."

He continued:

> Suppose one finds that the elasticities of substitution and the share parameters differ across countries. Also, countries may have different average discount rates because of differing age structures or life expectancies. If there are such structural differences in the growth-model parameters, then Prescott's model can be used to generate explicit predictions about how business cycles will differ across countries. These predictions can be checked against the data. There are *many* complications, but if productivity shocks are indeed the dominant source of disturbances in most countries, then this exercise may yield interesting results.

Rogoff concluded—again, in a prescient manner (1986, 46):

> The basic methodological approach exposited by Prescott should be relevant to models in which monetary disturbances play a greater role.... The

early empirical results of the real business cycle research Prescott discusses are certainly provocative. It has been said that a brilliant theory is one which at first seems ridiculous, and later seems obvious. There may be many who feel that this research has already passed the first test. But they should recognize the definite possibility that it may someday pass the second test as well.

McCallum's critiques and Prescott's response: 1986–1989

In his October 1985 Money, Credit and Banking lecture, published in the November 1986 issue of the *JMCB*, McCallum distinguish between "real" and what he termed "sticky price" approaches to business cycle theory. In the published paper, McCallum was critical of the Kydland–Prescott approach and method, including "calibration" (1986, 399–340). On the other hand, McCallum claimed (1986, 410–411), that augmentation of the sticky price model, combined with his own earlier work (1980, 1982) could "provide a satisfactory theoretical realization for real macroeconomic responses to monetary actions." In 1987 McCallum completed two drafts of a paper he prepared for the volume edited by Barro, *Handbook of Modern Business Cycle Theory*. The first draft was entitled "Real Business Cycles" and was a Carnegie-Mellon unpublished manuscript (1987). The title of second draft was changed to "Real Business Cycle Models," and this was circulated as NBER Working Paper 2480, dated January 1988 (McCallum, 1988).

In the NBER Working Paper, McCallum attempted "to provide an evaluation of both strengths and weaknesses of the real business cycle (RBC) approach" (1988, Abstract). He distinguished between two types of RBC "position" regarding the "initiators of business cycle movements." As he put it (1988, 2):

> The weaker of the two is that technology shocks are quantitatively more important than monetary disturbances as initiators of business cycle movements, while the stronger is that monetary disturbances are of negligible consequence. The former position is compatible with monetary-misperceptions variants of equilibrium theory, as these have not involved denials of the role of supply shocks. The stronger RBC position, however—the hypothesis that monetary disturbances are an insignificant source of cyclical fluctuations—is clearly inconsistent with most alternative theories. In this form, the RBC approach presents a distinct challenge to mainstream macroeconomic analysis.

In section III of his paper, (1988, 13–27), McCallum presented his interpretation of what Kydland–Prescott (1982) and Hansen (1985) "developed and simulated" (1988, 13).

In March 1987, Prescott circulated "A response to Bennett T. McCallum's attack on Applied Real Business Cycle Theory." Because of its importance to our story, we cite from it at length here. Prescott wrote (1987, 1):

McCallum did not correctly represent what we did and what we claimed to have done. What Finn Kydland and I and Gary Hansen did is as follows:

> We began with the neoclassical growth model and calibrated it using the national income and product accounts and household time allocation studies. We then examined the nature of the Solow technology parameter process and for the estimated process computed the equilibrium stochastic process for that economy. Our finding was that this model displayed fluctuations of the nature and amplitude that the U.S. economy displayed in the post-war period.

Prescott continued (1987, 1–2):

> Counter to McCallum's implicit claim, we did not use theory to estimate the effects of terms of trade shocks. McCallum's statement ... that such effects are treated by their analyses as "residual shifts in the production functions" is wrong—and I might say irresponsibly wrong. Changes in the Solow technology parameter are by definition changes in output not accounted for by changes in inputs. In a version of the model with a foreign sector and terms of trade shocks and with no Solow technology shocks, there would be fluctuations. To the best of my knowledge applied dynamic general equilibrium theory has not been used to assess the quantitative aggregate implications of these shocks for fluctuations. I confidently predict that it will.
>
> Needless to say we do not have a theory of technological change. We do have a theory that can be used to predict the behavior of an economy given the technology change process—in particular how investment and savings rates, output, capital stocks, factor prices and employment will vary. This is the theory used.

He went on to say (1987, 2–3):

> McCallum mentions "labor hoarding" as a possible measurement problem but does not even define labor hoarding. Is it leisure on the job? If so, what evidence is there that leisure on the job moves counter cyclically? Or does it mean organizational specific human capital investment? The onus is on others to show that with this feature present, the best estimate of the Solow technology parameter uncertainty is significantly smaller and predicted fluctuations less. My guess is that they would be larger if anything. Why should on the job investment in human capital behave differently than other investments and move counter rather than procyclically? If it does, output, and therefore both productivity and real wages as well, are more procyclically variable than measured.

Prescott then said (1987, 3):

> McCallum totally ignores the work of Finn Kydland who finds strong evidence that there are important errors in measuring the labor input due to the

> changing composition of the labor force over the cycle. Given Kydland's finding that for prime age males the human capital weighted hours are only half as sensitive to the aggregate unemployment rate as are equally weighted hours, aggregate hours could well fluctuate a lot less than measured. This would imply that the correctly measured real wage (i.e. total labor income divided by total human capital weighted hours) is strongly procyclical, as it is for the model. It also would imply that productivity (which is for all practical purposes proportional to real wages in the model economy) is strongly correlated.
>
> One major defect of McCallum's review that he is not consistent. In comparing statistics for our model economy with those for the actual economy he implicitly assumes measurement errors are negligible. But when discussing my measure of the technology shock variance, he argues that they are not negligible. McCallum should be consistent.

He went on (1987, 3–4):

> Some thought that the conclusions would change if the workweek of capital were endogenized. This is what Finn and I did in our workweek of capital paper and found that the amount of fluctuations accounted for by shocks to the Solow technology parameter is larger—not smaller—with this feature present.

Prescott concluded (1987, 4):

> The real wage is labor income divided by the labor input and the real return on capital is capital income divided by the capital stock. The income numbers are obtained from the national income accounts, while labor is measured independently and the capital stock is obtained from past investment data along with assumptions concerning depreciation. My position counter to that of McCallum's is that the model economy's factor price behavior is consistent with best measurement. There is the need for better measurement with the greatest needs being for better measures of the labor input and the inclusion of on-the-job human capital investment as part of output.

RBC and the *Journal of Economic Perspectives*: 1989 and 1996

Mankiw's predictions regarding RBC, 1989

In 1989, Mankiw presented "a New Keynesian Perspective" on the RBC approach, calling it (1989, 79) "the latest incarnation of the classical view of economic fluctuations." He went on to say (1989, 79):

> My goal in this essay is to appraise this newly revived approach to the business cycle. I should admit in advance that I am not an advocate. In my view,

> real business cycle theory does not provide an empirically plausible explanation of economic fluctuations. Both its reliance on large technological disturbances as the primary source of economic fluctuations and its reliance on the intertemporal substitution of leisure to explain changes in employment are fundamental weaknesses. Moreover, to the extent that it trivializes the social cost of observed fluctuations, real business cycle theory is potentially dangerous. The danger is that those who advise policy-makers might attempt to use it to evaluate the effects of alternative macroeconomic policies or to conclude that macroeconomic policies are unnecessary.

Now, while Mankiw discussed and specifically cited "RBC theories with multiple sectors" such as Long and Plosser (Mankiw 1989, 86) and also discussed King and Plosser (Mankiw 1989, 88), he neither cited nor discussed Kydland–Prescott (1982), choosing rather to cite only Prescott (1986) in an attempt to reject the evidence of technology shocks in the form of "the Solow residual" (1989, 83–85). Mankiw concluded by writing (1989, 89):

> The choice between alternative theories of the business cycle—in particular, between real business cycle and new Keynesian theory ... will undoubtedly continue. Each school of macroeconomic thought will highlight its strengths while trying to improve on its weaknesses. My own forecast is that real business cycle advocates will not manage to produce convincing evidence that there are substantial shocks to technology and that leisure is highly substitutable over time. Without such evidence, their theories will be judged as not persuasive.... While real business cycle theory has served the important function of stimulating and provoking the scientific debate, it will, I predict, ultimately be discarded as an explanation of observed fluctuations.

But, what has actually occurred since Mankiw's prediction has been a convergence, and then a synthesis, between RBC and new Keynesian approaches as will be seen below.

Kydland–Prescott, Hansen–Heckman, and Cooley: 1994–1997

In August 1994, Kydland and Prescott circulated Minneapolis Fed Staff Report 178 entitled "The Computational Experiment: an Econometric Tool." It was published in 1996 in the *Journal of Economic Perspectives*. A comparison of the two versions shows that they rewrote major parts of the paper, putting emphasis on the model economy and how "the researcher then calibrates the model economy so that it mimics the world along a carefully specified set of dimensions" (1996, 69). They also took the opportunity to again reply to McCallum's published critique (1989) of their approach, something which Prescott had done earlier, as recounted above.

A comparison of the treatment of McCallum in their 1994 Minneapolis Fed Working Paper version with that in the 1996 published version of their paper illustrates the nature of the changes made. In the 1994 working paper they wrote (1994, 20):

> A widespread and misguided criticism of our econometric studies (for example, McCallum 1989) is that the correlation between labor productivity and labor input is almost one for our model economy while it is approximately zero for the U.S. post-war economy. If we had found that technology shocks account for nearly all fluctuations and that other factors were unimportant, the failure of the model economy to mimic the data in this respect would cast serious doubt on our findings. But we did not find that the Solow technology shocks are all-important. We estimate that these technology shocks account for about 70 percent of business cycle fluctuations. If technology shocks account for 70 percent, and some other shocks that are orthogonal to technology shocks account for 30 percent, then the theory implies a correlation between labor productivity and labor input near zero—just as in the data.... The fact that this correlation for our model economy and the actual data differ as they do adds to our confidence in our findings.

In their 1996 *JPE* paper, they wrote (1996, 75):

> Some have questioned our finding, pointing out that on one key dimension real business cycle models and the world differ dramatically: the correlation between hours worked and average labor productivity is near one in the model economy and approximately zero in U.S. post-war observations (McCallum, 1989). The detractors of the use of standard theory to study business cycles are correct in arguing that the magnitude of this correlation in the world provides a test of the theory. They are incorrect in arguing that passing this test requires the value of this correlation in the model and in the real world to be approximately equal. An implication of the theory is that this correlation is a function of the importance of technology shocks relative to other shocks. In particular, the less is the relative importance of technology shocks, the smaller this correlation should be. The reason for this is that the factors other than technology shocks that give rise to variation in the labor input result in productivity being low when hours are high. Given that the estimated contribution of technology shocks to fluctuations is 70 percent, the correlation between hours and labor productivity being near one in the data would have been grounds for dismissing our answer.

In the same issue of *Journal of Economic Perspectives*, Lars Hansen and Heckman published a paper entitled "Empirical Foundations of Calibration" (1996). They criticized the Kydland–Prescott approach to calibration as "vague" and stated that "their empirical foundations are not secure" (1996, 89–90). They also questioned the Kydland–Prescott approach of using micro-economic estimates for macroeconomic models, stating that (1996, 90): "There is no filing cabinet full of robust micro estimates ready to use in calibrating dynamic stochastic general equilibrium models." They then went on (1996, 90) to "outline an alternative paradigm that, while continuing to stress synergy between microeconometrics and macro simulation, will provide more credible inputs into the computational experiments and more accurate assessments of the quality of the outputs." This involved symbiosis, as they put it (1996, 101), between "calibrators and empirical economists in which calibration methods like those used by Frisch, Tinbergen, and Kydland and Prescott stimulate the production of more convincing micro empirical estimates." And, it was the synthesis of RBC and the New Keynesian Economics that provided the basis for the DSGE models that they talked about.

A year before the *Journal of Economic Perspectives* papers of Kydland–Prescott and Hansen–Heckman, a Panel Session on "The Use and Evaluation of Calibration Methods" took place at the 7th World Congress of the Econometric Society in Tokyo, on 24 August 1995. The Panel was chaired by Wallis, and Cooley, Gallant, Kydland, and Pagan participated (Program 7th World Congress 1995, *Econometrica*, March 1996, 478). When asked about the Panel Session, Cooley replied (personal communication, 23 May 2013):

> I remember it well. The paper appeared as "Calibrated Models" in the *Oxford Review of Economic Policy*, 1997. Pagan was definitely a bit hostile and insisting on the discipline of the likelihood function as I recall. I tried to give some discipline to the practice of calibration in the paper. I don't remember that Wallis said much. Most interesting was Ron Gallant who argued that calibration is a very useful methodology, widely used in other sciences and ought to be completely uncontroversial provided it was done sensibly. There was quite big audience for the session.
>
> Finn was very complimentary about my paper. I think I was the only one who had prepared a serious paper for the session, but it seemed important to me to be on solid ground since I was being pitted against these powerful econometricians some of whom I had done battle with before.

Cooley's 1997 paper is an important one, as it sets out in detail the methodology of calibration. Moreover, it also sets out the scope of questions that can be dealt with using calibrated models, and deals with the evaluation of such models.

Augmentation

International real business cycles, 1988–2000

From 1988 onwards, Backus and Kehoe, and Backus, Kehoe, and Kydland, brought about the transition of the Kydland–Prescott approach from closed to open economy "environments," enabling it to deal with the co-movements in the "open economy perspective" (Backus, *et al.*, 1991, 1).

In June 1988, Backus and Kehoe circulated a paper entitled "International Evidence on the Historical Properties of Business Cycles" (1988). This was followed by their 1989 Minneapolis Fed Working Paper 402 with the same title. Their Minneapolis Fed Working Paper 425 followed, entitled "International Evidence on Business Cycles." They were later joined by Kydland, and the Backus–Kehoe–Kydland Minneapolis Fed Working Paper 426R (revised) entitled "International Real Business Cycles" was circulated in October 1991 (1991a). The Backus–Kehoe paper "International Evidence on the Historical Properties of Business Cycles" was then issued as Minneapolis Fed Staff Report 145 in November 1991, and was published in the *American Economic Review* in 1992. In November 1991, the Backus–Kehoe–Kydland paper "International Real Business Cycles" appeared as Minneapolis Fed Staff Report 146 (1991b), and was published in the *Journal of Political Economy* in August 1992. The next year, in February 1993, the Backus–Kehoe–Kydland paper "International Business Cycles: theories vs. evidence" appeared in the Minneapolis Fed's *Quarterly Review*. In October 1993, the paper—with a slightly altered title: "International Business Cycles: Theory and Evidence"—was circulated as NBER Working Paper 4993. This paper was published in the volume edited by Cooley (1995).

The *three* papers, then, that illustrate the transition are (1) "International Evidence"; (2) "International Real Business Cycles"; and (3) "International Business Cycles: Theory and Evidence." With regard to Backus and Kehoe's "International Evidence," they acknowledge (1991, 2; 1982, 864) that their work "is an outgrowth of business cycle research" by, among others, Kydland and Prescott (1990) and Lucas (1977). In the introductory note to the version published in the *American Economic Review*, they also acknowledge that it was Prescott "who suggested this line of work" (1992, 864).

Interestingly enough, in their 1990 paper "Business Cycles: real facts and a monetary myth"—on which Backus and Kehoe (1991, 1992) were based—Kydland and Prescott criticized Mankiw regarding his assertion that price behavior was "procyclical" (Mankiw 1989, 88). According to Kydland and Prescott (1990, 4), Mankiw's criticisms of their work, and that of King and Plosser (1984a) "are based on what is a myth." Kydland and Prescott go on to "stress that during the 35 years since the Korean War, the price level has displayed a clear *countercyclical* pattern" (1990, 4; emphasis in original). Backus, Kehoe, and Kydland's "International Real Business Cycles" was circulated as a Minneapolis Fed Staff Report under two titles, as noted, and finally published in the *Journal of Political Economy* in 1992.

The story of their paper "International Business Cycles: Theory and Evidence" is a bit more involved, as there are *three* versions extant. In 1993, two versions appeared: one in the Minneapolis Fed *Quarterly Review* (Fall 1993), the other as NBER Working Paper 4993 (October 1993), which was the version published in Cooley's 1995 edited volume, and not the 1993 *Quarterly Review* version. Now, the introductory note in the *Quarterly Review* version (1993a, 14) read: "This article is a revision of the chapter prepared for a book *Frontiers of Business Cycle Research*, edited by Thomas F. Cooley, to be published by

Princeton University Press." And indeed, the *Quarterly Review* version differs from the October 1993 NBER version (1993b). Not only are there differences in the text, but the references of the NBER paper are more extensive. The *Quarterly Review* paper has about 40 references, while the NBER paper has more than twice that number.

In their "Theory and Evidence" paper, Backus, Kehoe, and Kydland introduced the concept of "price and quantity anomalies"—that is to say, fundamental differences between their model and the data (1993b, 2–3; 1995, 332–333). The former anomaly, according to them, is that their model cannot replicate the degree of volatility in terms of trade as that in the data; the latter is that their model cannot replicate the cross-country correlations of output as against consumption. Moreover, the latter "anomaly," which came to be called the "Backus–Kehoe–Kydland puzzle," originally appeared in their earlier paper "International Real Business Cycles."

In the *Economic Dynamics Newsletter* of November 1999, Backus was interviewed "on international business cycles." He was asked: "Can IRBC modeling shed its 'R', that is, say something about monetary phenomena...?" Backus replied: "I don't think there's much question that RBC modeling shed its 'R' long ago, and the same applies to IRBC modeling.... So we really need a better term than RBC. Maybe you should take a poll." The importance of this comment will be seen below. And, when queried as to what he saw "as the next challenge of IRBC modelling," Backus replied: "I think you want to separate challenges from approaches. Although one's approach may suggest interesting questions, the best questions are often interesting from lots of perspectives, whether RBC or something else." As will be seen below, an international DSGE approach was developed accordingly. Finally, when asked whether the price and quantity anomalies noted in Backus, Kehoe, and Kydland (1993b, 1995) were "solved," Backus replied:

> Honestly, I don't think they're solved, although we've certainly taken some large bites out of them. I'm extremely enthusiastic, though, about the state of the profession: the quality of work in international macroeconomics has never been higher. Given the pace of change in the world economy and the amount of human capital devoted to understanding it, I'm confident that the next ten years will be just as exciting as the last ten.

Obstfeld and Rogoff (2001) identified the Backus–Kehoe–Kydland "quantity anomaly" as one of the six major puzzles in international economics, and indeed, the Backus–Kehoe–Kydland "consumption correlation puzzle" and the "price (terms of trade) anomaly" have generated much research since.

Variations on the theme: Barro's contributions

Over the period 1979–1989, Barro made a number of very significant contributions to the understanding and dissemination of the Real Business Cycle approach, parallel to his ongoing contributions to the development of the "equilibrium approach" to business cycles. This is evident in papers such as "A Capital Market in an Equilibrium Business Cycle Model," which first appeared as NBER Working Paper 326 (1979a), was published in *Econometrica* in September 1980 (1980c), and appeared as Chapter 4 in his 1981 collection of essays (1981b). In 1980, he also circulated NBER Working Paper 490 entitled "Inter-temporal Substitution and the Business Cycle" (1980b), published in the 1981 Carnegie-Rochester Conference Series (1981a). In 1984, he co-authored, with Robert King, a paper entitled "Time Separable Preferences and Intertemporal Substitution Models of Business Cycles" (1982a), which also circulated as NBER Working Paper 888 (1982b) and was published in the November 1984 issue of *Quarterly Journal of Economics* (1984b). In 1984, Barro also published his *Intermediate Macroeconomics* textbook (1984a), but more about this below.

In July 1979, Barro circulated a paper entitled "Developments in the Equilibrium Approach to Business Cycles" (1979b), which he termed "preliminary and incomplete." As per its title, the paper surveyed the "equilibrium approach," considering it to be "a positive theory" (1979b, 1). Interestingly enough, Barro cited Kydland and Prescott (1977), and their as yet unpublished December 1978 "A Competitive Theory of Fluctuations" (1979a, 22); this, in the context of an analysis of "the investment tax credit program" of Kydland–Prescott (1977, 42–86), and "the timing of non-lump-sum taxation" as manifest in Kydland and Prescott (1978, 25). The paper underwent two additional revisions, in November 1979 (1979c) and March 1980 (1980a), the latter with the revised title "The Equilibrium Approach to Business Cycles," prior to its publication in Barro's collection of essays entitled *Money Expectations and Business Cycles* (1981b, 41–79). Perhaps the most important change between the November 1979 and March 1980 versions was Barro's recognition of the "time-to-build" element in Kydland and Prescott's 1978 "Competitive Theory of Fluctuations," published in the conference volume edited by Fischer (1980) which was discussed above.

In the November 1979 version, Barro wrote (1979c, 11): "An overall view is that there is no theoretical problem in incorporating persistence effects into equilibrium business cycle models, but the empirically important channels for persistence have not been convincingly isolated." In the March 1980 version this passage was elided and Barro added the following important paragraphs (1980a, 12–13):

> One empirical difficulty with some adjustment cost explanations for persistence is the implication that the responses of investment, etc. would peak contemporaneously with shocks and follow a persisting, but declining, pattern thereafter. Empirical evidence … suggests a period of several quarters of rising output (and investment) in response to monetary disturbances. It seems that this behavior can be explained by the model of Kydland and Prescott (1980), in which planning-type costs for capital projects imply a delay in the peak response of investment to shocks.

> The arguments for persistence that depend on stock variables like capital goods imply future periods in which excess capacity would deter investment. However, unlike the initial response periods in which rapid reactions to the perception of temporary profit opportunities are warranted, these later periods may involve a relatively small amount of contraction. This possibility may account for the empirical evidence, which does not indicate an important contractionary effect of monetary shocks on the levels of output and unemployment in the periods following the roughly two-year interval of net expansionary effect.
>
> Adjustment cost-type explanations for persisting effects tend also to lessen the impact effects on supply of relative price variables like the anticipated rate of return. Therefore the extensions to account for persistence may undermine the quantitative role of the underlying intertemporal substitution mechanisms as the basis for fluctuations in output and employment.

These paragraphs appeared in the final published version of Barro's paper (1981b, 48–49).

In two retrospective assessments, Barro recalled the evolution of his relationship to Kydland–Prescott, Long–Plosser, and RBC, and his assessment of their respective impacts on economics. Because of its crucial importance to an understanding of our story, we cite them at length below. In the first, Barro wrote (personal communication, 18 January 2002):

> I guess I understand this best by understanding the evolution of my intermediate macro book, *Macroeconomics*, first published in 1984. The core business cycle model in my book is an RBC model, I just did not call it that in the first edition. I added that description in the 2nd edition (1987) and referred there to the Long–Plosser paper. I said (p. 217 of 2nd edition) in discussing my framework:
>
> "...business fluctuations can arise in the model only because of supply shocks (that is, shifts in the production function) and perhaps from changes in preferences. Models that rely on these kinds of disturbances to explain economic fluctuations are called "real theories of business cycles" (Economists who use these models should perhaps be called "realists", as opposed to monetarists). Such theories have received a lot of attention from researchers..."
>
> I have been disappointed that the term "realists" did not catch on.
>
> I did not refer to Kydland and Prescott until my 4th edition (1993) where I referred to their 1990 Minneapolis Fed paper. I used this material early on in my book to present empirical regularities about business cycles (basically using what is now called the Hodrick–Prescott filter). Obviously I did not learn about RBC models from Kydland and Prescott, though probably I should have. When I did my Modern Business Cycle Theory book in 1989, which had surveys of the main areas of research, I got Ben McCallum to

prepare the piece on "Real Business Cycles". He mentions both Kydland–Prescott (1982) and Long–Plosser (1983) at the beginning. But when he gets to quantitative analysis, Kydland–Prescott is the dominant work.

Long and Plosser were my colleagues at Rochester in the early 1980s. I remember their presenting their paper and talking with them about it. However I cannot recall how their work influenced the preparation of the 1st edition of my Macro book, which began in 1981. I think my book and their work were largely independent.

I think Kydland and Prescott were more influential in the profession because they tied their analysis more directly to empirical regularities. Included here was lack of regularities that looked like Phillips curves, that is, the price level was countercyclical in the data. Also important was the central role of investment and the behavior of productivity. Then they argued that a quantitative version of their RBC model could explain many of these regularities. This linking of the theory with the regularities is what distinguished their work and made it important. Long and Plosser did not have this, although they had the attraction of considering the structure of production by sector.

In general the RBC model reflected the dissatisfaction with monetary analyses of business cycles. This included Keynesian sticky price and wage models AND rational expectations (Lucas-type) models with money and information lags. It seemed that none of these models were empirically satisfactory. Moreover, there was the view that the great effort to explain why money and sticky price were important—culminating in the elegant work of Lucas—was a misplaced effort. With monetary models deemphasized at the time, it seemed logical to focus on frameworks in which real disturbances were dominant. Here, it was also natural to look at market-clearing approaches—one did not have to struggle, as one did in monetary models, to explain why real shocks would have real effects. The central issue was whether real shocks were important enough at the aggregate level to explain a substantial part of observed fluctuations. This issue is still outstanding.

In his second communication, Barro presciently wrote (18 January 2002):

A couple more points. When I teach RBC material in the first-year graduate course, I have on the reading lists Kydland and Prescott 1982, 1990, and some more recent items, not Long and Plosser. That is again because Kydland–Prescott fits with the interplay between the model and the empirical regularities in the data, and that is to focus of my discussion in the course.

Also, when a Nobel Prize is given in this area, it seems clear that it would go to Prescott—and perhaps Kydland would be included. The only way Prescott would not get it is if he got one earlier for his work on rules versus discretion (which also involved Kydland).

And this is indeed what happened.

Conclusion

Summing up—"business cycle research"

In his October 1998 Minneapolis Fed Working Paper 590 entitled "Business Cycle Research: Methods and Problems," Prescott essentially summed up the origins and evolution of the Kydland–Prescott research program, and also provided a detailed survey of the literature, and problems, that emanated from it. He wrote (1998, 3):

> Growth theory with measures of the elasticity of substitution and transformations and share parameters is theory in the sense I am using it here. Growth theory provides instructions for constructing a model economy to address some question of interest. The quantitative answer to the question is *deduced* for the model economy. In business cycles studies, growth theory is the theory used. Indeed, business cycle research is largely drawing inference from growth theory for business cycle fluctuations.

He went on to say (1998, 4):

> The Solow growth model, with its exogenously determined savings rate, led the economic theorists Cass (1965), Koopmans (1965) and Diamond (1965) to develop a theory of the allocation of product between consumption and investment. Brock and Mirman (1972) extended this theory to stochastic environments.
>
> Lucas (1977) defined business cycles to be recurrent fluctuations of output and employment about trend. He wrote that the key business facts were the comovements of the economic time series. Hodrick and I (1980) developed a statistical definition of the business cycle component of an economic time series.

Prescott continued (1998, 6):

> Exploiting Arrow-Debreu language, recursive methods, and computational methods, Kydland and I (1982) derived the implications of growth theory for business cycle fluctuations. To our surprise we found that, if total factor productivity (TFP) shocks are persistent and of the right magnitude,

> business cycle fluctuations are what growth theory predicts. Subsequently I (1986) found that these TFP shocks are highly persistent and of a magnitude that implies that they are the major contributor to business cycle fluctuations.

In Part II of the paper, Prescott went on to provide a list of, and a detailed survey of, the literature extant, on what he saw as open "Problems in Business Cycle Theory," (1998, 17):

> There is no shortage of important open problems in business cycle theory. What is in short supply are problems that are both important and analyzable using existing tools. My view is that whenever new tools are developed, it is a good time to search the set of important open problems for one that can be analyzed using these new tools. With this in mind I focus only on problems for which the needed tools have been recently developed or are being developed.

Prescott then listed what he saw as the main problems business cycle theory had to address. They included (1998, 17–23): the role of organizations, and the role of money in business cycles; the role of policy in determining labor-leisure time allocation; international business cycles; introducing contractual constraints using modern contract theory; introducing plant and irreversible investment; computing equilibrium when a distribution is part of the state variable; role of costly financial intermediation in the business cycle; and the role of varying number of shifts that plants operate. And, while he discussed the literature extant on these problems, many still remain open to this day.

Two years later, in their NBER Working Paper 7534 "Resuscitating Real Business Cycles," prepared for inclusion in Woodford and Taylor's *Handbook of Macroeconomics*, King and Rebelo wrote (2000, 3):

> Real business cycle analysis now occupies a major position in the core curriculum of nearly every graduate program.... The methods of the RBC research program are now commonly applied, being used in work in monetary economics, international economics, public finance, labor economics, asset pricing, and so on. In contrast to early RBC studies, many of these model economies involve substantial market failure, so that government intervention is desirable. In others, the business cycle is driven by shocks to the monetary sector or by exogenous shifts to beliefs. The dynamic stochastic general equilibrium model is firmly established as the laboratory in which modern macroeconomic analysis is conducted.

In a note to this, they wrote that (2000, 3 note 4): "One manifestation of the breadth of this intellectual impact is that Hall (1999) cites Berkeley's David Romer (1996) and Harvard's John Campbell (1994) for authoritative presentations of the basic RBC model."

Convergence and synthesis, 2002–2012

Taylor and McCallum: "convergence hypothesis," 2002

In the Spring 2002 issue of the NBER *Reporter*, McCallum published a survey piece which he called "Monetary Policy Analysis." In this, he talked about "the convergence of approaches used by academic and central bank economists." In July 2002, in answer to our queries, Taylor provided us with his retrospective assessment of developments in macroeconomics from 1976 onwards, comparing the evolution of what he called the "real business cycle school" to that of "monetary models with rational expectations and staggered price wage setting." He took the 1978 Kydland–Prescott NBER conference paper as a focal point. He wrote (personal communication, 7 July 2002):

> In the years prior to the 1978 conference where the Kydland–Prescott paper was presented, it was becoming clear that the "new classical" model was not able to provide an adequate empirical explanation of the role of money and monetary policy in the economy. Hence, those models ceased to be used or developed further empirically. This finding led to two important new research developments which have continued for the past last 25 years.
>
> One development was a real business cycle school, which simply abandoned the study of money and monetary policy—an essential purpose of the new classical models—and concentrated on other things, such as changes in productivity growth. The 1978 Kydland–Prescott paper is an early example of such work, so that the Kydland–Prescott paper was a precursor of later real business cycle models. However, I did not at that time, and do not now, see this paper as a transition from "new classical models" because the empirical and policy issues addressed by those models are so different from the new classical models. The economic issues that the real business cycle model are useful for addressing are similar to those addressed by neoclassical growth theory, as nicely illustrated by Edward Prescott's recent paper in the *American Economic Review* [Ely Lecture, "Prosperity and Depression, *AER* 92, May 2002, 1–15].
>
> The other development, *which had actually begun several years before 1978* [our emphasis], was to create monetary models with rational expectations and staggered price/wage setting that could be used to examine monetary policy and monetary policy rules in practice. *My 1979 Econometrica paper was an early example, but such models are now the work-horses of monetary policy research done at universities and central banks around the world* [our emphasis]. I think they have had a real impact on actual policymaking. Examples are the papers by Woodford, King, Weiland, McCallum, Levin, Williams and others in my recent edited NBER volume *Monetary Policy Rules* [1999] or the papers in the sessions "On Taylor Rules and Monetary Policy" or "Monetary Policy Rules in Practice" in the May 2002 *AER*. The models have three parts: a monetary policy rule, a

> price wage setting structure based on staggered price and wage setting (Taylor model or the Calvo variant), and a forward looking model of aggregate demand. These models are closer to the new classical models than the real business cycle models because they still focus on monetary policy.
>
> Is interesting to note, however, that there has been a convergence between the two developments in the last several years. This is not so evident in the May 2002 AER mentioned above, but is stressed by McCallum in the spring 2002 NBER *Reporter*.

In order to understand Taylor's assessment, we have to briefly look at the *development* of his own watershed 1979 *Econometrica* paper, entitled "Estimation and Control of a Macroeconomic model with Rational Expectations." It originated as a 1976 Columbia University Working Paper of the same title. The August 1976 version of this paper, with the title "Estimation and Stabilization with Rational Expectations Models," was presented by Taylor at the June 1977 Summer meeting of the Econometric Society in Ottawa, at the session on Macroeconomic Theory chaired by Fair, with Lucas as discussant (Program of June 1977 meeting, Econometrica, October 1977, 1744).

What may be called the McCallum–Taylor "convergence hypothesis," then, takes the following form. Starting from new classical and equilibrium business cycle headwaters, two research programs flowed: one characterized by the Kydland–Prescott and Long–Plosser approaches, from 1978–1983, which were not competing, but complementary models; the other, the Lucas-based monetary misperception equilibrium business cycle model, had only limited success in its attempt to explain the link between monetary shocks and real fluctuations, and was supplanted by the development of Taylor's model over the period 1976–1979. Indeed, while they address different issues, the RBC approach—change in productivity growth—and Taylor's model and the New Keynesian equilibrium business cycle approach—the role of money and monetary policy—converged, emerging as the "New Neoclassical Synthesis." It is to this that we now turn.

From "new neoclassical synthesis" to DSGE

In 1997, Goodfriend and King published "The New Neoclassical Synthesis and the Role of Monetary Policy." The main elements in the synthesis between the New Keynesian and RBC approaches—or, as they put it, "New Neoclassical Synthesis"—are: nominal and real rigidities; monopolistic competition; coordination failure; externalities; and multiple equilibrium models. Interestingly enough, as in the case of the RBC, Goodfriend has even extended the "New Neoclassical Synthesis" to the case of international adjustment (2007).

Now, there are a number of accounts of the evolution of the DSGE approach. For example, Fernández-Villaverde (2009, 6) asserts that it was the outcome of the augmentation of the elements listed above by "the stochastic neoclassical growth model of Kydland–Prescott," as manifest in Woodford (2003). In our view, however, the best account is that of Velupillai, in his 2011 paper "DSGE and beyond—computable and constructive challenges." There, he traces (2011, 3) the genesis and evolution of the DSGE approach from "its origins in the classic Arrow-Debreu General Equilibrium (ADGE), through Scarf's development of Computable General Equilibrium (CGE) theory, to DSGE via *Recursive Competitive Equilibrium* (RCE)" [our emphasis]—that is to say, the Prescott–Mehra approach, one of the building blocks of the RBC approach, as discussed in Chapter 1.

But let us leave the last word to the best example of the "convergence" between leading economist *and* central banker, in the form of Plosser's assessment of what he called the "rules of the game" of the New Keynesian DSGE framework. In a paper entitled "Macro Models and Monetary Policy Analysis" presented at the Bundesbank-Philadelphia Fed Spring 2012 Research Conference, Plosser wrote (2012, 2–3):

> New Keynesian DSGE models are the latest update to real business cycle, or RBC, theory. Given my own research in the area, it probably does not surprise many of you that I find the RBC paradigm a useful and valuable platform on which to build our macroeconomic models. One goal of real business cycle theory is to study the predictions of dynamic general equilibrium models, in which optimizing and forward-looking consumers, workers, employers, and investors are endowed with rational expectations. A shortcoming many see in the simple real business cycle model is its difficulty in internally generated persistent changes in output and employment from a transitory or temporary external shock to, say, productivity. The recognition of this problem has inspired variations on the simple model, of which the New Keynesian revival is an example.
>
> The approach taken in these models is to incorporate a structure of real and nominal frictions into the real business cycle framework. These frictions are placed in DSGE models, in part, to make real economic activity respond to anticipated and unanticipated changes in monetary policy, at least, in the short to medium run.... The rule of the game in these models is that interactions of these nominal frictions with real frictions give rise to persistent monetary nonneutralities over the business cycle. It is this monetary transmission mechanism that makes the new Keynesian DSGE models attractive to central banks.

Plosser concluded (2012, 8):

> The financial crises and recession have raised new challenges for policy makers and researchers. The degree to which policy actions, for better or worse, have become increasingly discretionary should give us pause as we try to evaluate policy choices in the context of the workhorse New Keynesian framework, especially given its assumption of credibly committed policymakers. Indeed, the Lucas critique would seem to take on new

> relevance in this post-crisis world. Central banks need to ask if discretionary policies can create incentives that fundamentally change the actions and expectations of consumers, workers, firms, and investors. Characterizing policy in this way also raises issues of whether the institutional design of central banks matters for evaluating monetary policy. I hope my comments today encourage you, as well as the wider community of economists, to pursue these research questions that are relevant to our efforts to improve our policy choices.

What started then, as the effort of a small group of economists—Kydland and Prescott, Long and Plosser, and some of their colleagues and students—in an attempt to explain business cycle fluctuations by linking them to economic growth, emerged as the new "core" of both modern macroeconomic theory and monetary policy-making.

RBC, DGE, and DSGE

In 1999, as cited above, Backus noted that the term "real business cycle" (RBC) was somewhat problematic, and suggested that a "poll" be taken amongst those who utilized its methodology regarding revising what it should be called. In April 2000, Zimmermann wrote (Economic Dynamics Newsletter volume 1, issue 2, April 2000):

> In 1983, Long and Plosser introduced the term "real business cycles" (RBC) just after Kydland and Prescott published their time-to-build paper. RBC stuck and has become the acronym for a methodology that is now applied to models that have nothing real and may not even be about real business cycles.
>
> In the first issue of the Economic Dynamics Newsletter, David Backus suggested that a vote should be taken to decide on a new and more appropriate acronym. Well, time has come to do exactly that. I have gathered some suggestions from prominent users of this theory and people that have helped shape it. Here they are, with some arguments to help you make a choice.

Zimmermann then turned to describe "the object of the vote":

> The acronym should represent the methodology whereby economic issues are addressed with dynamic general equilibrium models that are calibrated (or sometimes estimated) in order to obtain quantitative results and/or compute welfare measures. Feel free to differ on this definition.

He then listed "the choices": Applied Equilibrium Dynamics—AED; Dynamic General Equilibrium Model—DGE; Kydland–Prescott Model—KPM; Quantitative Equilibrium Dynamics—QED; Real Business Cycle Theory—RBC; Stochastic Calibrated Dynamic General Equilibrium—SCADGE.

Zimmerman then reported some of the responses he had received. He cited Prescott as saying:

> Long and Plosser introduced the term real business cycles to distinguish cycles induced by real factors from cycles induced by nominal factors and by financial crises. This I think is good language for this distinction. The term real business cycles has come to have a much broader meaning and I agree with David Backus that an acronym is needed for the development you describe in your email. The key concepts are quantitative or applied, dynamic, and general equilibrium. This suggests Quantitative Equilibrium Dynamics (QED) or Applied Economic Dynamics (AED).

He also provided Rotemberg's reply, which read:

> SCADGE (pronounced as a one syllable word) stands for Stochastic Calibrated Dynamic General Equilibrium and these are, to me, the key five words that describe these models. There are many varieties of dynamic general equilibrium models out there (including growth models, of course) and it seems important to distinguish these from the others. Calibration is not the only distinguishing feature, however, as this is done also in the fairly vast literature that calls itself CGE (or Computable General Equilibrium). What separates this from that is the explicit analysis of second moments, and that is why I put in the S.

According to Zimmerman, Wright, Backus, Tim Kehoe, Pat Kehoe, and Woodford all supported the term "DGE model." He reported that 75.9% of those polled supported "DGE."

Now, over the period *since* April 2000, the term "DSGE" has come to mean the utilization of RBC modeling methodology, rather than "DGE." This reflects both the plasticity and the metamorphosis of the Kydland–Prescott and Long–Plosser approaches, which evolved into a general methodological and modeling framework, utilized by academic researchers and central banks alike. In other words, it represents not only the *core* of quantitative macroeconomics, but the *consensus* of those who teach and conduct research using the approach developed by Kydland and Prescott, and Long and Plosser.

References

Adelman, I. and Adelman, F. (1959), "The Dynamic Properties of the Klein–Goldberger Model," *Econometrica* 27: 596–625.

Aftalion, A. (1913), *Periodic Crises of Overproduction.* Rivière: Paris.

Aftalion, A. (1927), *Monnaie, prix et change. Experiences recentes et theorie.* Recueil Sirey: Paris.

Aghion, P. and Howitt, P. (1998), *Endogenous Growth Theory.* MIT Press: Cambridge, MA.

Allais, M. (1962), "The Influence of the Capital-Output Ratio on Real National Income," *Econometrica* 30: 700–728.

Altug, S. (1983), "Gestation Lags and the Business Cycle: an Empirical Analysis," preliminary draft, Carnegie-Mellon University, revised, September.

Altug, S. (1986), "Time to Build and Aggregate Fluctuations: Some New Evidence," Working Paper 277, Federal Reserve Bank of Minneapolis, revised, August.

Altug, S. (1987), "Time to Build and Aggregate Fluctuations: Some New Evidence," revised, October.

Altug, S. (1989), "Time to Build and Aggregate Fluctuations: Some New Evidence," *International Economic Review* 30: 889–920.

Backus, D. (1999), "David Backus on International Business Cycles," *Economic Dynamics Newsletter*: 1, November.

Backus, D. and Kehoe, P. (1988), "International Evidence on the Historical Properties of Business Cycles," Manuscript. Federal Reserve Bank of Minneapolis, June.

Backus, D. and Kehoe, P. (1989), "International Evidence on the Historical Properties of Business Cycles," Working Paper 402, Federal Reserve Bank of Minneapolis.

Backus, D. and Kehoe, P. (1991), "International Evidence on the Historical Properties of Business Cycles," Staff Report 145, Federal Reserve Bank of Minneapolis.

Backus, D. and Kehoe, P. (1992), "International Evidence on the Historical Properties of Business Cycles," *American Economic Review* 82: 864–888.

Backus, D., Kehoe, P., and Kydland, F. (1991a), "International Real Business Cycles," Working Paper 426R, Federal Reserve Bank of Minneapolis, revised, October.

Backus, D., Kehoe, P., and Kydland, F. (1991b), "International Real Business Cycles" Staff Report 146, Federal Reserve Bank of Minneapolis, November.

Backus, D., Kehoe, P., and Kydland, F. (1992), "International Real Business Cycles" *Journal of Political Economy* 100: 745–775.

Backus, D., Kehoe, P., and Kydland, F. (1993a), "International Business Cycles: Theories vs. Evidence," Federal Reserve Bank of Minneapolis *Quarterly Review*, Fall: 14–29.

Backus, D., Kehoe, P., and Kydland, F. (1993b), "International Business Cycles: Theory and Evidence," NBER Working Paper 4493, October.

Backus, D., Kehoe, P., and Kydland, F. (1995), "International Business Cycles: Theory and Evidence," in Cooley, T. (ed.) *Frontiers of Business Cycle Research*, Princeton University Press: Princeton, NJ, 331–356.

Banks, F. (1977), "Review of Miller and Upton, *Macroeconomics: A Neoclassical Introduction* (1974)," *Kyklos* 30: 359–360.

Barro, R. (1979a), "A Capital Market in an Equilibrium Business Cycle Model," NBER Working Paper 326, March.

Barro, R. (1979b), "Developments in the Equilibrium Approach to Business Cycles," preliminary and incomplete, University of Rochester, July.

Barro, R. (1979c), "Developments in the Equilibrium Approach to Business Cycles," University of Rochester, revised, November.

Barro, R. (1980a), "The Equilibrium Approach to Business Cycles," University of Rochester, March.

Barro, R. (1980b), "Inter-temporal Substitution and the Business Cycle," NBER Working Paper 490, June.

Barro, R. (1980c), "A Capital Market in an Equilibrium Business Cycle Model," *Econometrica* 48: 1393–1417.

Barro, R. (1981a), "Inter-temporal Substitution and the Business Cycle," in *Carnegie Rochester Series on Public Policy* 14: 237–268.

Barro, R. (1981b), "The Equilibrium Approach to Business Cycles," in Barro, R. (ed.) *Money, Expectations and Business Cycles: Essays in Macroeconomics*. Academic Press: New York, 41–79.

Barro, R. (1984), *Macroeconomics* (1st edition), Wiley: New York.

Barro, R. (1987), *Macroeconomics* (2nd edition), Wiley: New York.

Barro, R. (1993), *Macroeconomics* (4th edition), Wiley: New York.

Barro, R. (2002a), personal communication, 18 January.

Barro, R. (2002b), personal communication, 18 January.

Barro, R. and King, R. (1982a), "Time Separable Preferences and Intertemporal Substitution Models of Business Cycles," University of Rochester, April.

Barro, R. and King, R. (1982b), "Time Separable Preferences and Intertemporal Substitution Models of Business Cycles," NBER Working Paper 888, May.

Barro, R. and King, R. (1984), "Time Separable Preferences and Intertemporal Substitution Models of Business Cycles," *Quarterly Journal of Economics* 99: 872–839.

Becker, G. (1980), letter to Ed Prescott, 24 November.

Black, F. (1978a), "General Equilibrium and Business Cycles," MIT Industrial Liaison Program, Sloan School Working Paper 5–44–78, April 1978.

Black, F. (1978b), "General Equilibrium and Business Cycles," Sloan School Working Paper 5–44–78, revised September 1978.

Black, F. (1979a), letter to Finn Kydland and Ed Prescott, and comments on Kydland and Prescott's NBER Conference Paper (1978d), 13 February.

Black, F. (1979b), "General Equilibrium and Business Cycles," Sloan School Working Paper, revised November 1979.

Black, F. (1981a), "Comments on 'Time to Build and the Persistence of Unemployment'," February. (Unpublished, sent to Kydland and Prescott).

Black, F. (1981b), letter to Ed Prescott, 9 March.

Black, F. (1981c), letter to Finn Kydland, 19 March.

Black, F. (1982), "General Equilibrium and Business Cycles," NBER Working Paper 950, August 1982.

Black, F. (1987), "General Equilibrium and Business Cycles," Chapter 13 in Black, F. *Business Cycles and Equilibrium*, Blackwell: Oxford and New York.

Blanchard, O. (2002), personal communication, 21 August.

Blinder, A. (2005), personal communication, 30 August.

Blinder, A. and Fischer, S. (1978), "Inventories, Rational Expectations, and the Business Cycle," Department of Economics Working Paper 220, Massachusetts Institute of Technology.

Brock, W. (1971), "Sensitivity of Optimal Growth Paths with Respect to a Change in Final Stocks," in Brockman, G. and Weber, W. (eds) *Contributions to the Von Neumann Growth Model*, Springer: New York, 73–89.

Brock, W. (1974), "Comments on Radner's paper 'Market Equilibrium and Uncertainty: Concepts and Problems'," in Intriligator, M. and Kendrick, D. *Frontiers of Quantitative Economics*, Volume 2, North Holland: Amsterdam, 91–92.

Brock, W. (1978a), "An Integration of Stochastic Growth Theory and the Theory of Finance," University of Chicago, 17 January.

Brock, W. (1978b), "An Integration of Stochastic Growth Theory and the Theory of Finance," University of Chicago, 9 February.

Brock, W. (1978c), "An Integration of Stochastic Growth Theory and the Theory of Finance—Part I: the Growth Model," Center for Mathematical Studies in Business and Economics, Report 7822, Department of Economics and Graduate School of Business, University of Chicago, April.

Brock, W. (1978d), "Asset Prices in a Production Economy," Report of Center for Mathematical Studies in Business and Economics, University of Chicago, April.

Brock, W. (1978e), "Asset Prices in a Production Economy," Social Science Working Paper 275, Division of Humanities and Social Sciences, California Institute of Technology, June.

Brock, W. (1979a), "An Integration of Stochastic Growth Theory and the Theory of Finance—Part I: the Growth Model," in Green, J. and Scheinkman, J. (eds) *General equilibrium, growth and trade: essays in honor of Lionel McKenzie*, Academic Press: New York, 165–192.

Brock, W. (1979b), "Asset Prices in a Production Economy," Social Science Working *Paper* 275, Division of Humanities and Social Sciences, California Institute of Technology, revised, July.

Brock, W. (1982), "Asset Prices in a Production Economy," in McCall, J. (ed.) *Economics of Information and Uncertainty*, Chicago: University of Chicago Press, 1–43.

Brock, W. and Majumdar, M. (1978), "Global asymptotic stability results for multisector models of optimal growth under uncertainty when future utilities are discounted," *Journal of Economic Theory* 18: 225–243.

Brock, W. and Mirman, L. (1972), "Optimal economic growth and uncertainty: the discounted case," *Journal of Economic Theory* 4: 479–513.

Brock, W. and Mirman, L. (1973), "Optimal economic growth and uncertainty: the no discounting case," *International Economic Review* 14: 560–573.

Brock, W. (1980), letter to J. Long, 5 December.

Brock, W. (2004), personal communication, 23 November.

Brunner, K. and Meltzer, A. (1977), "Introduction: Optimal Policies, Control Theory and Technology Exports," *Carnegie-Rochester Conference Series* 7: 1–6.

Brunner, K. and Meltzer, A. (1984), "Introduction: Essays on Macroeconomic Implications of Financial Labor Markets and Political Processes," *Carnegie-Rochester Conference Series* 21: 1–8.

Burns, A. (1947), "Keynesian Economics Once Again," *Review of Economic Statistics* 29: 252–267.

Burns. A. and Mitchell, W. (1946), *Measuring Business Cycles*. New York: National Bureau of Economic Research.

Cass, D. (1963), "Optimum Savings in an Aggregative Model of Capital Accumulation," Technical Report 5, Institute for Mathematical Studies in the Social Sciences, Stanford University, 27 November [draft of Chapter 1 of Cass (1965a), as cited by Koopmans (1965: 286)].

Cass, D. (1964a), "Studies in the Theory of Optimum Economic Growth," Technical Report, University of Chicago, Department of Economics Summer [draft of Chapters 1 and 3 of Cass (1965a)].

Cass, D. (1964b), "Optimum Growth in an Aggregative Model of Capital Accumulation: A Turnpike Theorem," Discussion Paper 178, Cowles Foundation, New Haven, CT.

Cass, D. (1965a), *Studies in the Theory of Optimum Economic Growth*. Unpublished PhD Dissertation, Stanford University.

Cass, D. (1965b), "Optimum growth in an aggregative model of capital accumulation," *Review of Economic Studies* 37: 233–240.

Cass, D. (1966), "Optimum growth in an aggregative model of capital accumulation: A Turnpike Theorem," *Econometrica* 34: 838–850.

Champernowne, D. (1945), "A Note on J. von Neumann's article on 'A Model of economic equilibrium'," *Review of Economic Studies* 13:10–18.

Chow, G. (1967), "Multiplier, accelerator, and liquidity preference in the determination of national income in the United States," *Review of Economic Statistics* 49: 1–15.

Chow, G. (2005), personal communication, 26 October.

Chow, G. and Athans, M. (1974), "Introduction to Selected Papers from the Second NBER Stochastic Control Conference," *Annals of Economic and Social Measurement* 3: 1–10.

Collard, D. (1996), "Pigou and Modern *Business Cycle* Theory," *Economic Journal* 106: 912–924.

Cooley, T. (1975), "A Comparison of Robust and Varying Parameter Estimates of a Macroeconometric Model," *The Annals of Economic and Social Measurement* 4: 373–388.

Cooley, T. (1976), "A State Space Approach to the Estimation of Price Expectations," *Proceedings of the IEEE Conference on Decision and Control* 15: 324–329.

Cooley, T. (1977), "Generalized Least Squares Applied to Time Varying Parameter Problems: A Comment," *Annals of Economic and Social Measurement* 6: 313–314.

Cooley, T. (ed.) (1995), *Frontiers of Business Cycle Research*. Princeton: Princeton University Press.

Cooley, T. (1997), "Calibrated Models," *Oxford Review of Economic Policy* 13: 55–69.

Cooley, T. (2006), personal communication, 18 December.

Cooley, T. (2013), personal communication, 23 May.

Cooley, T. and Hansen, G. (1989), "The Inflation Tax in a Real Business Cycle Model," *American Economic Review* 79: 733–748.

Cooley, T. and Hansen, G. (1991), "The Welfare Costs of Moderate Inflations," *Journal of Money, Credit and Banking* 23: 481–503.

Cooley, T. and Hansen, G. (1992), "Tax Distortions in a Neoclassical Monetary Economy," *Journal of Economic Theory* 58: 290–316.

Cooley, T. and Hansen, G. (1995), "Money and the Business Cycle," in Cooley, T. *Frontiers of Business Cycle Research*. Princeton: Princeton University Press, 175–216.

Cooley, T. and Hansen, G. (1997), "Unanticipated Money Shocks and the Business Cycle Reconsidered," *Journal of Money, Credit and Banking* 29: 624–648.

Cooley, T. and Hansen, G. (1998), "The Role of Monetary Shocks in Equilibrium Business Cycle Theory: Three Examples," *European Economic Review* 42: 605–617.

Cooley, T. and Prescott, E. (1973a), Tests of an Adaptive Regression Model," *Review of Economics and Statistics* 55: 248–256.

Cooley, T. and Prescott, E. (1973b), "An Adaptive Regression Model," *International Economic Review* 14: 364–371.

Cooley, T. and Prescott, E. (1973c), "Varying Parameter Regression: A Theory and Some Applications," *The Annals of Economic and Social Measurement* 2: 463–473.

Cooley, T. and Prescott, E. (1976), "Estimation in the presence of stochastic parameter variation," *Econometrica* 44: 167–184.

Cooley, T. and Prescott, E. (1995), "Economic Growth and Business Cycles," in Cooley, T. (ed.) *Frontiers of Business Cycle Research.* Princeton: Princeton University Press, 1–38.

Cooley, T., Hansen, G., and Prescott, E. (1994), "Equilibrium business cycles with idle resources and variable capacity utilization," Working Paper 94–22, Federal Reserve Bank of Philadelphia.

Cooley, T., Hansen, G., and Prescott, E. (1995), "Equilibrium Business Cycles with Idle Resources and Capacity Utilization," *Economic Theory* 6: 35–50.

Debreu, G. (1954), "Valuation Equilibrium and Pareto Optimality," *Proceedings of the National Academy of Science* 40: 588–592.

Desrousseaux, J. (1961), "Expansion stable et taux d'int´er^et optimal," *Annales des Mines*, November, 31–46.

Donaldson, J. and Mehra, R. (1983), "Stochastic Growth with Correlated Production Shocks," *Journal of Economic Theory* 29: 282–312.

Dorfman, R., Samuelson, P., and Solow, R. (1958), *Linear Programming and Economic Analysis.* New York: McGraw-Hill.

Dotsey, M. and King, R. (1988), "Rational Expectations Business Cycle Models: A Survey," *Federal Reserve Bank of Richmond Economic Review*, March/April: 3–15; reprinted from Newman, P., Eatwell, J., and Milgate, M. (eds) *The New Palgrave Dictionary of Economics* (1987), Macmillan: London and New York.

Edvardson, K. (2001), "Ragnar Frisch: an Annotated Bibliography," Report No. 4, Ragnar Frisch Center for Economic Research, Oslo, Norway.

Eisner, R. and Strotz, R. (1963), "The Determinants of Business Investment," in Suits, D. *et al.* , *Impacts of Monetary Policy*, Prentice Hall: Englewood Cliffs, NJ.

Feldstein, M. (1980), "Comment on Kydland and Prescott," in Fischer, S. (ed.) *Rational Expectations and Economic Policy*, NBER and University of Chicago Press: Chicago, 187–189.

Fernández-Villaverde, J. (2009), "The Econometrics of DSGE Models," NBER Working Paper 14677, National Bureau of Economic Research.

Fischer, S. (1977), "Long-Term Contracts, Rational Expectations, and the Optimal Money Supply Rule," *Journal of Political Economy* 85: 191–205.

Fischer, S. (1978), letter to Ed Prescott, 2 November.

Fischer, S. (1980), (ed.) *Rational Expectations and Economic Policy.* NBER and University of Chicago Press: Chicago.

Friedman, M. (1948), "A monetary and fiscal framework for economic stability," *American Economic Review* 38: 245–264.

Friedman, M. (1981), letter to W. Dewald, 25 August.

Friedman, M. (1997), "Computational experiments," *Journal of Economic Perspectives* 11: 209–212.

Frisch, R. (1927), "Sammenhengen mellem primærinvestering og reinvestering [The relationship between primary investment and reinvestmentt]," *Statsøkonomisk Tidsskrift* 41: 117–152.

Frisch, R. (1931), "Konjunkturbevegelsen som statistisk og som teoretisk problem [The business cycle as a statistical and a theoretical problem]," in *Förhandlingar vid Nordiska Nationalekonomiska Mötet i Stockholm 15–17 juni 1931*, Stockholm, Ivar Häggströms Boktrykkeri och Bokförlag AB, 127–147.

Frisch, R. (1933), "Propagation problems and impulse problems in dynamic economics," in *Economic Essays in Honour of Gustav Cassel*, London: George Allen and Unwin Ltd., 171–205.

Ghez, G. and Becker, G. (1975), *The Allocation of Time and Goods over the Life Cycle*. National Bureau of Economic Research: New York.

Goodfriend, M. (2007), "International Adjustment in the New Neoclassical Synthesis," Kiel Working Paper No. 1345, June.

Goodfriend, M. and King, R. (1997), "The New Neoclassical Synthesis and the Role of Monetary Policy," in Bernanke, B. and Rotemberg, J. (eds) *NBER Macroeconomics Annual 1997*, Volume 12, Cambridge MA: MIT Press.

Goodhart, C. and Presley, J. (1994), "Real business cycle theory: a restatement of Robertsonian economics?," *Economic Notes* 23: 275–291.

Gould, J. (1968), "Adjustment Costs in the Theory of Investment of the Firm," *Review of Economic Studies* 35: 47–56.

Haavelmo, T. (1960). *A Study in the Theory of Investment*. Chicago: The University of Chicago Press.

Haberler, G. (1937), *Prosperity and Depression: A Theoretical Analysis of Cyclical Movements*. Geneva: League of Nations.

Hall, R. (1977), "Investment, Interest Rates, and the Effects of Stabilization Policies," *Brookings Papers on Economic Activity* 1: 61–121.

Hall, R. (1980), "Comment on Kydland and Prescott," in Fischer, S. (ed.) *Rational Expectations and Economic Policy*. NBER and University of Chicago Press: Chicago, 191–192.

Hall, R. (2002), personal communication, 2 July.

Hall, R. and Jorgenson, D. (1967), "Tax policy and investment behavior," *American Economic Review* 57: 391–414.

Hansen, A. (1947), *Economic Policy and Full Employment*. New York: McGraw-Hill Book Co.

Hansen, G. (1984), "Indivisible Labor and the Business Cycle," (Chapter 1, doctoral dissertation), University of California Santa Barbara, November.

Hansen, G. (1985a), "Indivisible Labor and the Business Cycle," (Chapter 1, doctoral dissertation), University of California Santa Barbara, revised, June.

Hansen, G. (1985b), "Indivisible Labor and the Business Cycle," *Journal of Monetary Economics* 16: 309–327.

Hansen, G. (1986a), *Three Essays on Labor Indivisibility and the Business Cycle*. University of Minnesota, PhD thesis.

Hansen, G. (1986b), "Growth and Fluctuations," seminar handout, Federal Reserve Bank of Minneapolis, 17 March.

Hansen, G. (1986c), "Growth and Fluctuations," (Chapter 2, doctoral dissertation), University of California, Santa Barbara, November.

Hansen, G. (1986d), "Fluctuations in Total Hours Worked: a Study Using Efficiency Units," (Chapter 3, doctoral dissertation), University of California, Los Angeles, December.

Hansen, G. (1989), "Technical Progress and Aggregate Fluctuations," UCLA Economics Working Paper 546, UCLA Department of Economics.

Hansen, G. (1991), "The Cyclical and Secular Behavior of the Labor Input: Comparing Efficiency Units and Hours Worked," Working Paper 36, California Los Angeles—Applied Econometrics.

Hansen, G. (1993), "The Cyclical and Secular Behavior of the Labor Input: Comparing Efficiency Units and Hours Worked," *Journal of Applied Econometrics* 8: 71–80.

Hansen, G. (1997), "Technical progress and aggregate fluctuations," *Journal of Economic Dynamics and Control* 21: 1005–1023.

Hansen, G. (2006), personal communication, 27 November.

Hansen, G. and Prescott, E. (1992), "Recursive Methods for Computing Equilibria of Business Cycle Models," Discussion Paper 36, Institute for Empirical Macroeconomics, Federal Reserve Bank of Minneapolis.

Hansen, G. and Wright, R. (1992), "The Labor Market in Real Business Cycle Theory," *Quarterly Review*, Federal Reserve Bank of Minneapolis, Spring, 2–12.

Hansen, L. and Heckman, J. (1996), "The empirical foundations of calibration," *Journal of Economic Perspectives* 10: 87–104.

Harris, M. (1978), "Notes Sets for Dynamic Competitive Analysis," unpublished manuscript, Carnegie-Mellon University.

Harris, M. (1987), *Dynamic Economic Analysis*, New York: Oxford University Press.

Heckman, J. (1984), "Comments on the Ashenfelter and Kydland Papers," Carnegie-Rochester *Conference Series on Public Policy* 21: 209–224.

Hicks, J. (1973), "Recollections and documents," *Econometrica* (n.s.) 40: 2–11.

Hodrick, R. (2005a), personal communication, 24 December.

Hodrick, R. (2005b), personal communication, 25 December.

Hodrick, R. and Prescott, E. (1978), "Post-war U.S. business cycles: a descriptive empirical investigation," Carnegie-Mellon Working Paper 4–78–79, August 1978.

Hodrick, R. and Prescott, E. (1980), "Post-war U.S. business cycles: an empirical investigation," Discussion paper No. 451, revised November 1980.

Howitt, P. (2005), personal communication, 5 September.

Hurwicz, L. (1947), "Review of Measuring Business Cycles," *Journal of the American Statistical Association* 42: 461–467.

Intriligator, M. and Kendrick, D. (1974), (eds) *Frontiers of Quantitative Economics, Vol. 2*. Amsterdam: North Holland Publishing Company.

Joines, D. (2006), "How Ricardian is the Life-Cycle Model?," Working Paper, Department of Finance and Business Economics, Marshall School of Business, University of Southern California, September.

Jorgenson, D. (1963), "Capital Theory and Investment Behavior," *American Economic Review* 53:247–259.

Kehoe, T. and Prescott, E. (1995), "The Discipline of Applied General Equilibrium," *Economic Theory* 6: 1–12.

Kendrick, D. (2005a), "Stochastic control for economic models: past, present and the paths ahead," *Journal of Economic Dynamics and Control* 29: 3–30.

Kendrick, D. (2005b), personal communication, 26 October.

King, R. (1980), "Money, Wages and the Business cycle," unpublished, University of Rochester, October.

King, R. (1982), "Investment, Imperfect Information and Equilibrium Business Cycle Theory," unpublished, University of Rochester, February.

King, R. (2007a), personal communication, 28 June.

King, R. (2007b), interview, 29 June, Boston University.

King, R. and Plosser, C. (1981a), "The Behavior of Money, Credit and Prices in a Real Business Cycle," Working Paper *GPB* [Center for Research in Government Policy and Business] *81–8*, University of Rochester.

King, R. and Plosser, C.. (1981b), "The Behavior of Money, Credit and Prices in a Real Business Cycle," presented at the University of Konstanz, June.

King, R. and Plosser, C. (1981c), "The Behavior of Money, Credit and Prices in a Real Business Cycle," presented at the October 1981 NBER Economic Fluctuations Group Meeting, University of Chicago, 9–10 October.

King, R. and Plosser, C. (1982), "The behavior of money, credit and prices in a real business cycle," NBER Working Paper No. 853, February.

King, R. and Plosser, C. (1984a), "Money, credit and prices in a real business cycle," *American Economic Review* 74: 363–380.

King, R. and Plosser, C. (1984b), "Production, Growth and Business Cycles," unpublished manuscript, University of Rochester.

King, R. and Plosser, C. (1986), "Nominal Surprises, Real Factors and Propagation Mechanisms," Rochester Center for Economic Research Working Paper 50, July.

King, R. and Plosser, C. (1988), "Real business cycles: introduction," *Journal of Monetary Economics* 21: 191–193.

King, R. and Rebelo, S. (2000), "Resuscitating Real Business Cycles," NBER Working Paper 7534.

King, R., Plosser, C., and Rebelo, S. (1988a), "Production, Growth and Business Cycles, I: The Basic Neo-classical Model," *Journal of Monetary Economics* 21: 195–232.

King, R., Plosser, C., and Rebelo, S. (1988b), "Production, Growth and Business Cycles, II: New Directions," *Journal of Monetary Economics* 21: 309–343.

King, R., Plosser, C., and Rebelo, S. (2001), "Production, Growth and Business Cycles: Technical Appendix," June.

King, R., Plosser, C., and Rebelo, S. (2002), "Production, Growth and Business Cycles: Technical Appendix," *Computational Economics*, 20: 87–116.

Koopmans. T. (1947), "Measurement Without Theory," *Review of Economics and Statistics* 29: 61–172.

Koopmans. T. (1963), "Economic Growth at a Maximal Rate," paper presented at July 1963 meeting of Econometric Society, Copenhagen.

Koopmans. T. (1964), "Economic Growth at a Maximal Rate," *The Quarterly Journal of Economics* 78: 355–394.

Koopmans. T. (1965), "On the Concept of Optimal Economic Growth," paper presented at the Vatican Study Week on the *Econometric Approach to Development Planning*, Rome, Pontifical Academy of Science, 7–13 October.

Kydland, F. (1973), *Decentralized macroeconomic planning.* Unpublished PhD thesis, Carnegie-Mellon University.

Kydland, F. (1975), "Noncooperative and dominant player solutions in discrete dynamic games," *International Economic Review* 16: 321–335.

Kydland, F. (1976), "Decentralized stabilization policies: optimization and the assignment problem," *Annals of Economic and Social Measurement* 5: 249–261.

Kydland, F. (1977), "Equilibrium solutions in dynamic dominant-player models," *Journal of Economic Theory* 15: 307–324.

Kydland, F. (1980), "Analysis and policy in competitive models of economic fluctuation," unpublished manuscript, Carnegie-Mellon University, May 1980.

Kydland, F. (1981), "Analysis and policy in competitive models of business fluctuation," Carnegie-Mellon Working Paper No. 74–79–90, revised April 1981.

Kydland, F. (1983a), "Non-separable utility and labor supply," Working Paper E-83–10, Hoover Institution, May.

Kydland, F. (1983b), "Non-separable utility and labor supply," Working Paper E-83–10, Hoover Institution, revised, August.

Kydland, F. (1984a), "Labor Force Heterogeneity and the Business Cycle," *Carnegie-Rochester Conference Series on Public Policy* 21: 173–208.

Kydland, F. (1984b), "A Clarification: Using the Growth Model to Account for Fluctuations—Reply to James Heckman," *Carnegie-Rochester Conference Series on Public Policy* 21: 225–230.

Kydland, F. (1987), "The role of money in a business cycle model," Carnegie-Mellon University, revised December 1987.

Kydland, F. (1989a), "Monetary policy in models with capital," in van der Ploeg, F. and de Zeeuw, A. (eds) *Dynamic policy games in economies*. Amsterdam: North Holland.267–288.

Kydland, F. (1989b), "The role of money in a business cycle model," Discussion paper No. 23, Institute for Empirical Macroeconomics, Federal Reserve Bank of Minneapolis and University of Minnesota, December 1989.

Kydland, F. (1993), "Business cycles and aggregate labor-market fluctuations," Working Paper 9312, Federal Reserve Bank of Cleveland.

Kydland, F. (2004), "Traditional/Recent Business Cycle Theory," *Praktisk økonomi og finans* 4, 1–12.

Kydland, F. (2005a), Nobel autobiography, from Frangsmyr, T. (ed.) *Les Prix Nobel, The Nobel Prizes 2004*, Nobel Foundation, Stockholm, 2005.

Kydland, F. (2005b, interview), 10 October.

Kydland, F. (2005c), personal communication, 24 October.

Kydland, F. (2006), personal communication, 30 August.

Kydland, F. and Prescott, E. (1973), "Optimal stabilization policy: a new formulation," presented at the NBER-NSF Conference on Stochastic Control and Economic Systems, Chicago, June 1973.

Kydland, F. and Prescott, E. (1974), "Optimal stabilization: a new approach," in Vogt, W. and Mickle, M. (eds) *Modeling and Simulation*, vol. 5, Proceedings of 5th Annual Conference on Modeling and Simulation, Pittsburgh, May 1974; 217–222.

Kydland, F. and Prescott, E. (1975a), "The Inconsistency of Optimal Policy," Discussion Paper 06/75, Norwegian School of Economics and Business Administration, Bergen, June.

Kydland, F. and Prescott, E. (1975b), "Rules Rather than Discretion: The Inconsistency of Optimal Plans," Working Paper 27–75–76, Carnegie-Mellon University, June.

Kydland, F. and Prescott, E. (1975c), "Rules Rather than Discretion: The Inconsistency of Optimal Plans," Working Paper 27–75–76, Carnegie-Mellon University, October.

Kydland, F. and Prescott, E. (1977a), "Rules rather than discretion: the inconsistency of optimal plans," *Journal of Political Economy* 85: 473–492.

Kydland, F. and Prescott, E. (1977b), "Rational expectations, dynamic optimal taxation, and the inapplicability of optimal control," GSIA Working Paper, Carnegie-Mellon University, November 1977, revised May 1978.

Kydland, F. and Prescott, E. (1978a), "Persistence of unemployment in equilibrium," unpublished, background material for GSIA seminar, 19 April 1978.

Kydland, F. and Prescott, E. (1978b), "On the possibility and desirability of stabilization policy," September 1978; preliminary version, prepared for NBER conference, 13–14 October 1978.

Kydland, F. and Prescott, E. (1978c), "On the possibility and desirability of stabilization policy," September 1978; prepared for NBER conference, 13–14 October 1978.

Kydland, F. and Prescott, E. (1978d), "A competitive theory of fluctuations and the feasibility and desirability of stabilization policy," NBER conference paper, October 1978; revised, December 1978.

Kydland, F. and Prescott, E. (1979), "Time to build and equilibrium persistence of unemployment," unpublished draft manuscript, revised, October 1979.

Kydland, F. and Prescott, E. (1980a), "A competitive theory of fluctuations and the feasibility and desirability of stabilization policy," in Fischer, S. (ed.) (1980), *Rational Expectations and Economic Policy.* NBER and University of Chicago Press: Chicago, 169–187.

Kydland, F. and Prescott, E. (1980b), "Time to build and the persistence of unemployment," Working Paper No. 28–80–81, Carnegie-Mellon University, September.

Kydland, F. and Prescott, E. (1980c), "Time to build and the persistence of unemployment," Working Paper No. 28–80–81, Carnegie-Mellon University, December.

Kydland, F. and Prescott, E. (1980d), "Dynamic optimal taxation, rational expectations and optimal control," *Journal of Economic Dynamics and Control* 2: 79–81.

Kydland, F. and Prescott, E. (1981a), "Time to build and aggregate fluctuations," Working Paper *No. 28–80–81*, Carnegie-Mellon University, revised, September 1981.

Kydland, F. and Prescott, E. (1981b), "Time to build and aggregate fluctuations," Working Paper No. 28–80–81, Carnegie-Mellon -University, revised, December 1981.

Kydland, F. and Prescott, E. (1982), "Time to build and aggregate fluctuations," *Econometrica* 50: 1345–1370.

Kydland, F. and Prescott, E. (1986a), "The Workweek of Capital and its Cyclical Implications," unpublished manuscript.

Kydland, F. and Prescott, E. (1986b), "The Workweek of Capital and its Cyclical Implications," unpublished manuscript, revised, October.

Kydland, F. and Prescott, E. (1987), "The Workweek of Capital and its Cyclical Implications," Working Paper 267, Federal Reserve Bank of Minneapolis, August.

Kydland, F. and Prescott, E. (1988), "The Workweek of Capital and its Cyclical Implications," *Journal of Monetary Economics* 21: 343–360.

Kydland, F. and Prescott, E. (1989), "Hours and Employment Variation in Business Cycle Theory," Discussion Paper 17, Institute for Empirical Macroeconomics, Federal Reserve Bank of Minneapolis, August.

Kydland, F. and Prescott, E. (1990), "Business Cycles: Real Facts and a Monetary Myth," Federal Reserve Bank of Minneapolis *Quarterly Review*, Spring, 3–18.

Kydland, F. and Prescott, E. (1991a), "The Econometrics of the General Equilibrium Approach to Business Cycles," *Scandinavian Journal of Economics* 93: 161–178.

Kydland, F. and Prescott, E. (1991b), "Hours and Employment Variation in Business Cycle Theory," *Economic Theory* 1: 63–81.

Kydland, F. and Prescott, E. (1993), "Cyclical Movements of the Labor Input and its Implicit Real Wage," Federal Reserve Bank of Cleveland *Economic Review* 29: 12–23.

Kydland, F. and Prescott, E. (1994), "The Computational Experiment: an Econometric Tool," Staff Report 178, Federal Reserve Bank of Minneapolis.

Kydland, F. and Prescott, E. (1996), "The Computational Experiment: an Econometric Tool," *Journal of Economic Perspectives* 10: 69–85.
Kydland, F. to Prescott, E. (1975, 11 June), letter.
Kydland, F. to Prescott, E. (1975, 13 June), letter.
Kydland, F. to Prescott, E. (1975, 4 September), letter.
Kydland, F. to Prescott, E. (1975, 12 September), letter.
Kydland, F. to Prescott, E. (1975, 25 September), letter.
Kydland, F. to Prescott, E. (1975, 6 October), letter.
Kydland, F. to Prescott, E. (1975, 10 October), letter.
Kydland, F. to Prescott, E. (1975, 4 November), letter.
Kydland, F. to Prescott, E. (1976, 22 June), letter.
Kydland, F. to Prescott, E. (1976, 2 July), letter.
Kydland, F., Hutz, J., and Sedlacek, G. (1982), "Inter-temporal substitution and labor supply," Carnegie-Mellon Working Paper, revised 1982.
Kydland, F., Hutz, J., and Sedlacek, G. (1988), "Inter-temporal preferences and labor supply," *Econometrica* 56: 335–360.
Long, J. and Plosser, C. (1980), "Real business cycles," Working Paper, University of Rochester, November.
Long, J. and Plosser, C. (1982a), letter to Sam Peltzman, 9 April.
Long, J. and Plosser, C. (1982b), letter to Sam Peltzman, 15 June.
Long, J. and Plosser, C. (1983), "Real business cycles," *Journal of Political Economy* 91: 36–69.
Long, J. and Plosser, C. (1987), "Sectoral vs. Aggregate Shocks in the Business Cycle," *American Economic Review* 77: 333–336.
Lovell, M. (2005a), personal communication, 8 November.
Lovell, M. (2005b), personal communication, 17 November.
Lovell, M. and Prescott, E. (1968), "Money, multiplier accelerator interaction, and the business cycle," *Southern Economic Journal* 35: 60–72.
Lovell, M. and Prescott, E. (1970), "Multiple regression with inequality constraints: pre-testing bias, hypothesis testing and efficiency," *Journal of the American Statistical Association* 65: 913–925.
Lucas, R. (1967a), "Optimal Investment Policy and Flexible Accelerator," *International Economic Review* 8: 78–85.
Lucas, R. (1967b), "Adjustment Costs in the Theory of Supply," *Journal of Political Economy* 75: 321–334.
Lucas, R. (1972), "Expectations and the neutrality of money," *Journal of Economic Theory* 4: 103–123.
Lucas, R. (1973a), "Econometric policy evaluation: a critique," draft prepared for the Phillips curve conference, University of Rochester, 20–21 April 1973.
Lucas, R. (1973b), "Econometric policy evaluation: a critique," revised May 1973.
Lucas, R. (1975), "An equilibrium model of the business cycle," *Journal of Political Economy* 83: 1113–1144.
Lucas, R. (1976a), "Econometric policy evaluation: a critique," *Carnegie-Rochester Conference Series on Public Policy* 1: 19–46.
Lucas, R. (1976b), "Understanding business cycles," paper prepared for the Kiel Conference on Growth without Inflation, June 22–23.
Lucas, R. (1977), "Understanding business cycles," *Carnegie-Rochester Conference Series on Public Policy* 5: 7–29.

Lucas, R. (1978), "Asset Prices in an Exchange Economy," *Econometrica* 46: 1429–1445.

Lucas, R. (1980), "Methods and Problems in Business Cycle Theory," *Journal of Money, Credit and Banking* 12: 696–715.

Lucas, R. (1981), letter to Chris Sims, 23 January.

Lucas, R. (1987), *Models of Business Cycles.* Oxford: Basil Blackwell.

Lucas, R. (2001), "Professional memoir," 5 April 2001.

Lucas, R. (2005), "Present at the creation: reflections on the 2004 Nobel Prize to Finn Kydland and Edward Prescott," *Review of Economic Dynamics* 8: 777–779.

Lucas, R. (2006), personal communication, 13 August.

Lucas, R. and Prescott, E. (1971), "Investment under Uncertainty," *Econometrica* 39: 659–681.

Lucas, R. and Prescott, E. (1973), "Equilibrium Search and Unemployment," unpublished manuscript, revised, March.

Lucas, R. and Prescott, E. (1974), "Equilibrium Search and Unemployment," *Journal of Economic Theory* 7: 188–209.

Lucas, R. and Rapping, L. (1969), "Real Wages, Employment, and Inflation," Journal of Political Economy 77: 721–754.

Lundquist, L. and Sargent, T. (2000), *Recursive Macroeconomic Theory* (1st edition), Cambridge MA: MIT Press.

Lundquist, L. and Sargent, T. (2004), *Recursive Macroeconomic Theory* (2nd edition), Cambridge MA: MIT Press.

Malinvaud, E. (1965), "Croissances Optimales dans un Modele Macroecononomique," in *Study Week on the Econometric Approach to Development Planning 7–13 October.* Rome: Pontifical Academy of Science.

Mankiw, G. (1989), "Real Business Cycles: A New Keynesian Perspective," *Journal of Economic Perspectives* 3: 79–90.

Mansur, A. and Whalley, J. (1984), "Numerical Specification of Applied General Equilibrium Models: Estimation, Calibration and Data," in Scarf, H. and Shoven, J. (eds) Applied General Equilibrium Analysis. Cambridge University Press, New York, 69–127.

McCallum, B. (1980), "Rational Expectations and Macroeconomic Stabilization policy: an overview," *Journal of Money, Credit and Banking* 12: 716–746.

McCallum, B. (1982), "Macroeconomics After a Decade of Rational Expectations: Some Critical Issues," Federal Reserve Bank of Richmond *Economic Review* 68: 3–12.

McCallum, B. (1986), "On 'Real' and 'Sticky Price' Theories of the Business Cycle," *Journal of Money, Credit and Banking* 18: 397–414.

McCallum, B. (1987), "Real Business Cycles," unpublished manuscript, Carnegie-Mellon University.

McCallum, B. (1988), "Real Business Cycle Models," Working Paper No. 2480, National Bureau of Economic Research, January.

McCallum, B. (1989), "Real Business Cycle Models," in Barro, R. J. (ed.) *Modern Business Cycle Theory.* Blackwell, Oxford, 17–50.

McCallum, B. (2002), "Monetary Policy Analysis," *NBER Reporter*, Spring.

McCallum, B. and Nelson, E. (2000), "An Optimizing IS-LM Specification for Monetary Policy and Business Cycle Analysis," Working Paper 5875, National Bureau of Economic Research.

McGrattan, E. (2006), "Real Business Cycles," Federal Reserve Bank of Minneapolis Staff Report 370, February [prepared for *New Palgrave Dictionary of Economics,* 2nd edition].

Meade, J. (1936), *An Introduction to Economic Analysis and Policy*. London: Oxford University Press.

Meade, J. (1961), *A Neo-Classical Theory of Economic Growth*. London: Allen and Unwin.

Mehra, R. (1977), *Essays in Financial Economics*. PhD thesis, GSIA, Carnegie-Mellon University.

Mehra, R. (2005a), personal communication, 6 September.

Mehra, R. (2005b), personal communication, 7 September.

Mehra, R. (2005c), additional personal communication, 7 September.

Miller, M. and Upton, C. (1974), *Macroeconomics: A Neoclassical Introduction*. Homewood, Illinois: Richard D. Irwin.

Mirman, L. (1970a), *Two Essays on Uncertainty and Economics*. PhD thesis, University of Rochester, 1970.

Mirman, L. (1970b), "The Steady State Behavior of the Class of One Sector Growth Models with Uncertain Technology," unpublished, 1970.

Mirman, L. (1971), "Uncertainty and Optimal Consumption Decisions," *Econometrica* 39: 179–185.

Mirman, L. (1972), "On the Existence of Steady State Measures for One Sector Growth Models with Uncertain Technology," *International Economic Review* 13: 271–286.

Mirman, L. (1973), "The Steady State Behavior of the Class of One Sector Growth Models with Uncertain Technology," *Journal of Economic Theory* 6: 219–242.

Mirman, L. (2007), personal communication, 8 February.

Mirman, L. and Zilcha, I. (1975), "On Optimal Growth Under Uncertainty," *Journal of Economic Theory* 11: 329–339.

Mirman, L. and Zilcha, I. (1977), "Characterizing Optimal Policies in a One-Sector Model of Economic Growth Under Uncertainty," *Journal of Economic Theory* 14: 389–401.

Mirrlees, J. (1967), "Optimum Growth When Technology is Changing," *Review of Economic Studies* 34: 95–124.

Mitchell, W. (1913), *Business Cycles*. Berkeley: University of California Press.

Mitchell, W. (1916), "Review of Roberson's *Industrial Fluctuations* (1915)," *American Economic Review* 6: 638–639.

Mitchell, W. (1923), "Business Cycles," in *Business Cycles and Unemployment*, Committee of the President's Conference on Unemployment, and a Special Staff of the National Bureau, New York: NBER, 7–20.

Mitchell, W. (1927), *Business Cycles: the problem and its setting*. New York: National Bureau of Economic Research.

Modigliani, F. (1977), "Should control theory be used for economic stabilization?: A comment," *Carnegie-Rochester Conference Series on Public Policy*, 7: 85–91.

NBER (1974), *Conference Report*, March.

NBER (1981), *Report of Chicago meeting*, October.

NBER (1986), *Reporter*, Fall.

NBER (2002), *Reporter*, Spring.

Nelson, C. (1980), letter to Robert Hodrick, 10 June.

Nelson, C. (2002), personal communication, 3 October.

Nelson, C. and Plosser, C. (1980), "Trends and random walks in macroeconomic time series," University of Washington Discussion paper 80–13, August 1980.

Nelson, C. and Plosser, C. (1981), "Trends and random walks in macroeconomic time series: some evidence and implications," Working Paper Series No. GPB 80–11, University of Rochester, revised December 1981.

Nelson, C. and Plosser, C. (1982), "Trends and random walks in macroeconomic time series: some evidence and implications," *Journal of Monetary Economics* 10: 139–162.

Nelson, E. (2004), "Money and the Transmission Mechanism in the Optimizing IS-LM Specification," *History of Political Economy* 36: 271–304, Supplement.

Obstfeld, M. and Rogoff, K. (2001), "The Six Major Puzzles in International Macroeconomics: Is There a Common Cause?," in NBER *Macroeconomics Annual* 2000, Volume 15, National Bureau of Economic Research: New York, 339–412.

Parkin, M. (2002), personal communication, 21 August.

Peltzman, S. (1982), letter to John Long and Charles Plosser, 1 April.

Phelps, E. (1961), "The Golden Rule of Accumulation," *American Economic Review* 51: 638–643.

Phelps, E. and Taylor, J. (1975), "Stabilizing Properties of Monetary Policies under Rational Price Expectations," Columbia University Department of Economics Working Paper 75–7607, July.

Phelps, E. and Taylor, J. (1977), "Stabilizing Powers of Monetary Policy under Rational Expectations," *Journal of Political Economy* 85: 163–190.

Pigou, A. (1920), *The Economics of Welfare.* London: Macmillan.

Pigou, A. (1927), *Industrial Fluctuations.* London: Macmillan.

Plosser, C. (1989a), "Understanding Real Business Cycles," *Journal of Economic Perspectives* 3: 51–77.

Plosser, C. (1989b), "Money and Business Cycles: A Real Business Cycle Interpretation," September. Unpublished Working Paper, University of Rochester.

Plosser, C. (1989c), "Money and Business Cycles: A Real Business Cycle Interpretation," presented at the Federal Reserve Bank of St. Louis, October.

Plosser, C. (1989d), "Money and Business Cycles: A Real Business Cycle Interpretation," Rochester Center for Economic Research Working Paper 210, December.

Plosser, C. (1990), "Money and Business Cycles: A Real Business Cycle Interpretation," Working Paper 3221, National Bureau of Economic Research.

Plosser, C. (2012), "Macro Models and Monetary Policy Analysis," paper presented at the Bundesbank Federal Reserve Bank of Philadelphia, Spring 2012 Research Conference, Eltville, Germany, 25 May.

Prescott, E. (1967), *Adaptive decision rules for macroeconomic planning.* Unpublished PhD thesis, Carnegie Institute of Technology.

Prescott, E. (1971), "Adaptive decision rules for macroeconomic planning," *Western Economic Journal* 9: 369–378.

Prescott, E. (1972), "The multi-period control problem under uncertainty," *Econometrica* 40: 1043–1058.

Prescott, E. (1973), "A general equilibrium approach to macroeconomic policy evaluation," plan of research for application for a Guggenheim Fellowship.

Prescott, E. (1973, 3 July), letter to Neil Wallace.

Prescott, E. (1973, 12 October), letter to Finn Kydland.

Prescott, E. (1974), "Money, expectations and the business cycle," Discussion paper, 4 April.

Prescott, E. (1974, 2 January), letter to Finn Kydland.

Prescott, E. (1974, 26 April), letter to Finn Kydland.

Prescott, E. (1974, 18 July), letter to Finn Kydland.

Prescott, E. (1975, 2 June), letter to Finn Kydland.

Prescott, E. (1975, 3 July), letter to Finn Kydland.

Prescott, E. (1975, 22 August), letter to Finn Kydland.

Prescott, E. (1975, 18 September), letter to Finn Kydland.

Prescott, E. (1975, 2 October), letter to Finn Kydland.

Prescott, E. (1975, 23 October), letter to Finn Kydland.

Prescott, E. (1975, 29 December), letter to Finn Kydland.

Prescott, E. (1976, 21 May), letter to Finn Kydland.

Prescott, E. (1976, 11 August), letter to Finn Kydland.

Prescott, E. (1976, 19 October), letter to Finn Kydland

Prescott, E. (1977a), "Should control theory be used for economic stabilization?," *Carnegie-Rochester Conference Series on Public Policy* 7: 13–38.

Prescott, E. (1977b), "Should control theory be used for economic stabilization?: a rejoinder," *Carnegie-Rochester Conference Series on Public Policy* 7: 101–102.

Prescott, E. (1979, 26 February), letter to Fischer Black.

Prescott, E. (1979, 4 June), letter to Etyan Sheshinski.

Prescott, E. (1980a), "Comments on the current state of the theory of aggregate investment behavior," *Carnegie-Rochester Conference Series on Public Policy* 12: 93–101.

Prescott, E. (1980b), letter to Nelson, 5 November, 1980.

Prescott, E. (1981a), letter to Fischer Black, 25 February.

Prescott, E. (1981b), letter to Charles Plosser, 24 March.

Prescott, E. (1981c), letter to Fischer Black, 26 March.

Prescott, E. (1981d), letter to Fischer Black, 28 March.

Prescott, E. (1981, 6 October), letter to Milton Friedman.

Prescott, E. (1983), "'Can the cycle be reconciled with a consistent theory of expectations'—or a progress report on business cycle theory," Working Paper 239, Federal Reserve Bank of Minneapolis.

Prescott, E. (1986a), "Theory ahead of business-cycle measurement," *Carnegie-Rochester Conference Series on Public Policy* 25: 11–44.

Prescott, E. (1986b), "Theory ahead of business cycle measurement," *Quarterly Review*, Federal Reserve Bank of Minneapolis, Fall, 9–22.

Prescott, E. (1987), "A response to Bennett T. McCallum's attack on Applied Real Business Cycle Theory," unpublished manuscript, March.

Prescott, E. (1998), "Business cycle research: methods and problems," Federal Reserve Bank of Minneapolis, Working Paper 590, revised October 1998.

Prescott, E. (2001), personal communication, 29 December.

Prescott, E. (2002), personal communication, 24 July.

Prescott, E. (2004), "The transformation of macroeconomic policy and research," Nobel Prize lecture, 8 December, 2004 (on Nobel website).

Prescott, E. (2005a), personal communication, 7 November.

Prescott, E. (2005b), personal communication, 16 November.

Prescott, E. (2005c), personal communication, 20 November.

Prescott, E. (2005d), additional personal communication, 20 November.

Prescott, E. (2005e), additional personal communication, 20 November.

Prescott, E. (2006a), personal communication, 8 August.

Prescott, E. (2006b), additional personal communication, 8 August.

Prescott, E. (2006c), personal communication, 15 August.

Prescott, E. (2006d), personal communication, 17 August.

Prescott, E. (2006e), "The transformation of macroeconomic policy and research," *Journal of Political Economy* 114: 203–235.

Prescott, E. (2007), personal communication, 2 January.

Prescott, E. (2008), personal communication, 13 February.

Prescott, E. and Mehra, R. (1977), "Recursive competitive equilibria and capital asset pricing," Discussion paper, December 1977.

Prescott, E. and Mehra, R. (1978), "Recursive competitive equilibria: the case of homogenous households," Columbia University Graduate School of Business Working Paper.

Prescott, E. and Mehra, R. (1980), "Recursive competitive equilibria: the case of homogenous households," *Econometrica* 48: 1365–1379.

Program of Econometric Society Fall 1978 North America Meeting, *Econometrica* 47: 235–251.

Program (1982), ASSA/AER.

Radner, R. (1960), "Paths of economic growth that are optimal with regard only to final states: two 'turnpike theorems'," Working Paper 7, Bureau of Business and Economic Research, University of California, Berkeley.

Radner, R. (1961), "Paths of economic growth that are optimal with regard only to final states: a turnpike theorem," *Review of Economic Studies* 76: 98–104.

Radner, R. (1968), "Competitive equilibrium under uncertainty," *Econometrica* 36: 31–58.

Radner, R. (1970), "Problems in the theory of markets under uncertainty," *American Economic Review* 60: 454–460.

Radner, R. (1971), "Balanced stochastic growth at a maximum rate," in Brockman, G. and Weber, W. (eds) *Recent contributions to the Von Neumann growth model* Berlin: Springer.

Radner, R. (1974), "Market Equilibrium and Uncertainty: Concepts and Problems," in Intriligator, M. and Kendrick, D. (eds) *Frontiers of Quantitative Economics*, Volume 2, Amsterdam: North-Holland, 43–105.

Ramsey, F. (1928), "A Mathematical Theory of Saving," *Economic Journal* 38: 543–559.

Referee's report (1979), on Prescott and Mehra (1979).

Report of Econometric Society meeting 1933, *Econometrica* 1934.

Report of Econometric Society meeting 1936, *Econometrica* 1937.

Robertson, D. (1915), *A Study of Industrial Fluctuation: An Enquiry into the Character and Causes of the So-called Cyclical Movements of Trade*, London: P.S. King.

Robinson. J. (1962), "A Neo-classical Theorem," *Review of Economic Studies* 29: 219–226.

Rogerson, R. (1988), "Indivisible labor, lotteries and equilibrium," *Journal of Monetary Economics* 21: 3–16.

Rogoff. K. (1986), "Theory ahead of business cycle measurement: A comment on Prescott," *Carnegie-Rochester Conference Series on Public Policy*, 25: 45–47.

Royal Swedish Academy of Sciences (2004), "Finn Kydland and Edward Prescott's contribution to dynamic macroeconomics: the time consistency of economic policy and the driving forces behind business cycles," Advanced information on the Bank of Sweden Prize in Economic Science in Memory of Alfred Nobel, 11 October 2004.

Sargent, T. (1973), "Rational Expectations, the Real Rate of Interest, and the Natural Rate of Unemployment," Brookings *Papers on Economic Activity* 2: 429–480.

Sargent, T. (1978), "Estimation of dynamic labor demand schedules under rational expectations," *Journal of Political Economy* 86: 1009–1044.

Sargent, T. and Wallace, N. (1976), "Rational expectations and the theory of economic policy," *Journal of Monetary Economics*, 2: 169–183.

Scarf, H. (1967). "On the Computation of Equilibrium Prices," Cowles Foundation Discussion Papers 232, Cowles Foundation for Research in Economics, Yale University, published as "On the computation of equilibrium prices" in Feller, W. (ed.) *Ten economic studies in the tradition of Irving Fischer.* New York: Wiley, 207–230.

Shaw, E. (1947), "*Burns and Mitchell* on Business Cycles; a review of 'Measuring Business Cycles'," *Journal of Political Economy*, 55: 281–298.

Shell, K. (1967), "A Model of Inventive Activity and Capital Accumulation," in Shell, K. (ed.) *Essays on the Theory of Optimal Economic Growth*, Cambridge, MA: MIT Press, 67–85.

Sheshinski, E. (1979), letter to Prescott, 5 March.

Shinkai, Y (1960), "On Equilibrium Growth of Capital and Labour," *International Economic Review* 1: 107–111.

Shoven, J, and Whalley, J. (1972), "A general equilibrium calculation of the effects of differential taxation of income from capital in the U.S.," *Journal of Public Economics* 1: 281–322.

Shoven, J, and Whalley, J. (1973), "General Equilibrium with Taxes: A Computational Procedure and an Existence Proof," *Review of Economic Studies* 60: 475–490.

Shoven, J, and Whalley, J. (1975), "Equal Yield Tax Alternatives: General Equilibrium Computational Techniques," *Technical Report* No. 150 (R), Institute for Mathematical Studies in the Social Sciences, Stanford University, August.

Shoven, J, and Whalley, J. (1977), "Equal yield tax alternatives: General equilibrium computational techniques," *Journal of Public Economics*, 8: 211–224.

Sims, C. (1981), letter to Prescott, 26 June.

Slutzky, E. (1937), "The summation of random causes as the source of cyclical processes," *Econometrica* 5: 105–146.

Smith, C. (1975), "Review of *Macroeconomics: A Neoclassical Introduction*, by Miller and Upton," *Journal of Finance* 30: 1182–1184.

Solow, R. (1956), "A contribution to the theory of economic growth," *Quarterly Journal of Economics* 70: 65–94.

Solow, R. (1957), "Technical change and the aggregate production function," *Review of Economics and Statistics* 39: 312–320.

Spear, S. and Wright, R (1998), "Interview with David Cass," *Macroeconomic Dynamics* 2: 533–558.

Spear, S. and Young, W. (2013a), "Optimum savings and optimal growth: the Cass-Malinvaud-Koopmans nexus," *Macroeconomic Dynamics* (forthcoming).

Spear, S. and Young, W. (2013b), "Two sector growth, optimal growth and the turnpike: amalgamation and metamorphosis," *Macroeconomic Dynamics* (forthcoming).

Srinivasan, T. (1962), "On a Two-Sector Model of Growth," Discussion paper 139 (revised), Cowles Foundation, New Haven, CT.

Stokey, N., Lucas, R., and Prescott, E. (1989), *Recursive methods in economic dynamics* Cambridge, MA: Harvard University Press.

Summers, L. (1986), "Some skeptical observations on real business cycle theory," *Quarterly Review*, Federal Reserve Bank of Minneapolis, Fall, 23–27.

Swan, T. (1956), "Economic Growth and Capital Accumulation," *Economic Record* 32: 334–361.

Swan, T. (1963), "Longer-Run Problems of the Balance of Payments," in Arndt, H. and Corden, M. (eds) *The Australian Economy*. Sydney: Cheshire, 384–395.

Taylor, J. (1975), "Monetary Policy during a Transition to Rational Expectations," *Journal of Political Economy* 83: 1009–1022.

Taylor, J. (1976), "Estimation and Control of a Macroeconomic model with Rational Expectations," Working Paper, Columbia University.

Taylor, J. (1977), "Control Theory and Economic Stabilization: A Comment," *Carnegie-Rochester Conference Series on Public Policy* 7: 93–98.

Taylor, J. (1979), "Estimation and Control of a Macroeconomic Model with Rational Expectations," *Econometrica* 47: 1267–1286.

Taylor, J. (1980), "Comment on Kydland and Prescott," in Fischer, S. (ed.) *Rational Expectations and Economic Policy*. NBER and University of Chicago Press: Chicago, 191–194.

Taylor, J. (1981), "Report on Kydland and Prescott's 'Time to build and the persistence of unemployment'," unpublished referee's report.

Taylor, J. (2002), personal communication, 7 July.

Taylor, J. (2006), personal communication, 21 October.

Tinbergen, J. (1933), "The notion of horizon and expectancy in dynamic economics," *Econometrica* 1: 247–264.

Tinbergen, J. (1935), "Annual Survey: Suggestions on quantitative business cycle theory," *Econometrica* 3: 241–308.

Tinbergen, J. (1938), "On the theory of business cycle control," *Econometrica* 6: 22–39.

Tinbergen, J. (1939), *Statistical Testing of Business Cycle Theories: Vol. I: A Method and its Application to Investment Activity; Vol II: Business Cycles in the United States of America, 1919–1932*. Geneva: League of Nations.

Tinbergen, J. (1942), "Critical remarks on some business-cycle theories," *Econometrica* 10: 129–146.

Tobin, J. (1955), "A Dynamic Aggregative Model," *Journal of Political Economy* 63: 103–115.

Tobin, J. (1963), "Commercial Banks as Creators of 'Money'," Cowles Foundation Discussion Papers 159, Cowles Foundation for Research in Economics, Yale University.

Tobin, J. (1970), "Money and Income: Post Hoc Ergo Propter Hoc?," *Quarterly Journal of Economics* 84: 301–317.

Treadway, A (1969), "On rational entrepreneurial behavior and the demand for investment," *Review of Economic Studies* 36: 227–239.

Turnovsky, S. and Brock, W. (1980), "Time consistency and optimal government policies in perfect foresight equilibrium," *Journal of Public Economics* 13: 183–212.

Turnovsky, S. and Brock, W. (1981), "The analysis of macroeconomic policies in perfect foresight equilibrium," *International Economic Review* 22: 179–209.

Upton, C. (2006), personal communication,15 November.

Upton, C. (2007), personal communication, 2 January.

Upton, C. (2013, 18 February), personal communication.

Upton, C. (2013, 19 February), personal communication.

Uzawa, H. (1961), "On a Two-Sector Model of Economic Growth" *Review of Economic Studies*, 29: 40–47.

Uzawa, H. (1965), Optimum Technical Change in An Aggregative Model of Economic Growth Author(s): *International Economic Review*, 6:. 18–31.

Velupillai, K. (2011), "DSGE and beyond—computable and constructive challenges," Discussion Paper 10, ASSRU, Department of Economics, University of Trento.

Von Neumann, J. (1945), "A Model of General Economic Equilibrium," *Review of Economic Studies* 13: 1–9.

Von Weizsäcker, C. (1962), *Wachstum, Zins und Optimale Investifionsquote*. Basel: Kyklos-Verlag.

Whalley, J. (2004), personal communication, 24 December.

Whalley, J. (2007, 26 February), personal communication.

Whalley, J. (2007, 27 February), personal communication.

Woodford, M. (2000), "Interview with William A. Brock," *Macroeconomic Dynamics* 4: 108–138.

Woodford, M. (2003), *Interest and Prices: Foundations of a Theory of Monetary Policy.* Princeton: Princeton University.

Young, W. (1987), *Interpreting Mr. Keynes: the IS-LM Enigma.* Oxford: Blackwell-Polity.

Young, W. (1989), *Harrod and his Trade Cycle Group.* Basingstoke: Macmillan.

Young, W. (2004), personal correspondence to J. Whalley, 15 December.

Young, W. and Darity, W. (2001), "The early history of rational and implicit expectations," *History of Political Economy* 33: 773–813.

Young, W., Darity, W., and Leeson, R. (2004), *Economics, Economists and Expectations.* London: Routledge.

Zimmerman, C. (2000), "Real Business Cycle: results of a poll," *Economic Dynamics Newsletter* 1, April.

Index

Made in the USA
Las Vegas, NV
04 November 2024

2d9e54fc-5e00-448f-96c7-9daf2e51c396R01